DATA-BASE

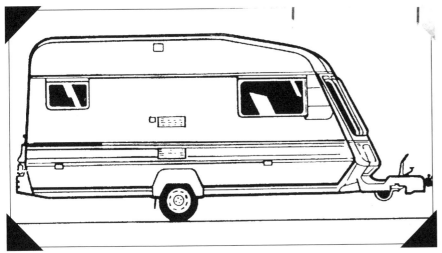

This page enables you to compile a list of useful data on your caravan, so that whether you're ordering spares or just checking the tyre pressures, all the key information - the information that is personal to your caravan - is easily within reach

Make ....

Model ....

Body colour/s ....

Paint code no./s (if known) ....

Year of manufacture...

CRIS number (if applicable)...................................

Chassis number..

Caravan number ....

Ex-works weight...

Maximum laden weight...

Load margin...

Body length...

Overall length..

Overall width...

Tyre pressures ....

Fridge type ....

Heater type ....

Oven model ....

Door key number...

Security lock number (if applicable).......................

Dealership caravan purchased from:

....

....

Modifications:

Information that might be useful when you need to purchase parts: ....

....

....

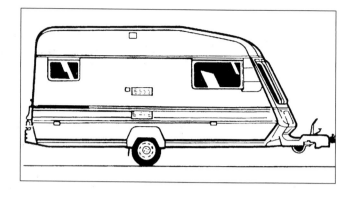

A PORTER PUBLISHING Book

First published 1995

© Porter Publishing Ltd 1995

Published and Produced by
Porter Publishing Ltd
The Storehouse
Little Hereford Street
Bromyard
Hereford
England HR7 4DE

British Library Cataloguing in Publication Data
Porter, Lindsay and Waller, Ian
Caravan Step-by-Step Owner's Manual & Service Guide

ISBN 1-899238-04-2

Authors: Lindsay Porter and Ian Waller
Series Editor: Lindsay Porter
Design: Lyndsay Berryman, Pineapple Publishing
Printed in England by The Trinity Press, Worcester

Other Titles in the Series
MGB (all models including MGC, V8 and RV8) Service Guide
Land Rover Series I, II, III Service Guide
Land Rover Defender, 90, 110 Service Guide
Mini (all models 1959-on) Service Guide
VW Beetle (all models to 1980) Service Guide
Absolute Beginners Service Guide
Diesel Car Engine Service Guide
MG Midget and Austin Healey Sprite Service Guide
Classic 'Bike Service Guide

- *with more titles in production* -

Caravan

Step-by-Step Owner's Manual & Service Guide

by Lindsay Porter and Ian Waller

FOREWORD

There's no doubt that caravanning is big business. Of the 42.7 million holiday trips made in England each year, 7.7 million (18%) were caravan holidays and it is probable that there are something like 500,000 touring caravans in use in the UK today.

With those figures in mind, it makes it all the more surprising that, unlike the solo car driver where reference manuals abound, there really are very few books published on the subject of caravanning as a whole, let alone how to service an outfit.

It's easy to forget that a caravan is a road vehicle and therefore requires regular servicing and maintenance, in particular the braking system, wheels, tyres and road lighting. The need for safety on the roads over-rides all other considerations.

The Caravan Club welcomes Porter Publishing's "The Caravan Owner's Manual & Service Guide", and is heartened to see a new publication giving advice to existing and potential caravanners on all aspects of towing, particularly the emphasis on the 85% weight ratio and correct loading. The caravan needs to be viewed as a road vehicle which requires careful servicing and maintenance, leading to greater safety and hence enjoyment for everyone concerned.

After all, that is the every essence of caravanning - your journey out on the road is purely a means to an ends - whether that be enjoying the beautiful British countryside, using your caravan as an accommodation base while you spend time on your favourite hobby, or, for the more adventurous, trips to Europe and beyond.

However you use your caravan, I'm sure that by heeding the tips and advice given in this new book you'll be able to enjoy the freedom and independence that all caravanners come to appreciate.

Ted Holt
Chairman, Technical Committee
The Caravan Club

Ted Holt
Chairman, Technical Committee
The Caravan Club

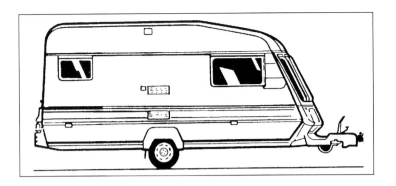

CONTENTS

Acknowledgements

As with all of the books in the Series, the compilation of this one has been a real team effort. In fact, one of the great things about it has been the large number of kind and helpful people that one has come across. It speaks volumes for the wonderful world of caravanning that so much support and assistance was so freely made available, often at incredibly short notice. In no particular order, I would like to thank Marsha Williams of The Caravan Club for pointing me in several (useful!) directions at once and to John Parsons, the Club's Technical Officer, whose advice was invaluable, and similar thanks are given to Bob Stanton, Public Relations Officer of The Camping and Caravanning Club for his kind advice. From the manufacturers, Ian Stanford of AL-KO Kober, Brian Smart of AP Lockheed, Chris Powdrill of Peak Trailers and Richard Toon of BPW and Knott UK were all sources of excellent assistance and advice. Glen Williams proprietor of Dinmore Caravans and Sales Manager, Brian Giles kindly assisted with last minute photo sessions, while my father-in-law Ken Maynard - a man who was actually towing his caravan on his way to a holiday in Spain the first time I met him - in May 1966 - has provided several pearls of wisdom. Grateful thanks - and happy caravanning - to them all!

Lindsay Porter, Bromyard

Compiling this user guide has been a thoroughly worthwhile and educational experience. It has also only been possible due to the help, expertise, time and patience of a number of people, both within the caravan industry and outside.

Special thanks must straight away go to Caravan Plus and Caravan Life magazines and particularly Paul Elmer and Dave Lilley for allowing me invaluable access to their records and data, without which compiling this guide would have taken an awful lot more time and effort. Similarly, photographer Peter Greenhalf's help and assistance has been invaluable.

From an industry point of view, the expertise of the people at AL-KO Kober, Carver, Whale, Thetford, W4, ABI, Bailey, Chichester Caravans of Redhill and Pickwick Caravans of Wiltshire must also get special mention for their generosity of help and patience with putting up with endless pestering telephone calls confirming all manner of technical details. Of these individual votes of thanks must be extended to Vernon Anderson, John Clark, Iain Stanford and Tim Carver.

A special mention must also be made to the many grass roots caravanners who offered advise and help as to what the content of this guide should include. To these I would particularly like to mention Barbara and Bryan Waller for supplying a critical users eye-view.

Thanks also to Nic for simply putting up with almost constant caravan talk for the months that this guide was actually being put into words.

Many thanks to everyone listed here as well as to anyone else whom I might inadvertently have missed.

Ian Waller

Introduction to Caravanning

Welcome to caravanning. With around 600,000 caravans estimated to be in use in Britain, it is no surprise that caravanning is one of the most popular leisure pursuits on offer to a whole variety of people. Todays modern caravan offers many of the comforts of home in a compact, easy to transport design with a range of makes and models to suit most tastes.

For many of us, our first taste of caravanning was as a child on a family holiday by the sea. Caravanning back then, however, often used to be little more than staying in a leaky box on wheels in the corner of some remote field by the sea. Fortunately, things have changed.

Now available with mains electric hook-ups, hot and cold running water, domestic style kitchens, showers, toilets, double glazing and winter insulation, todays modern caravans offer everything you will require for all year round holidays. Combine that with a huge variety of sites, at home and abroad, and it's no surprise that caravanning is such a popular pastime.

The main attraction of caravanning for many enthusiasts is its ease of use and relative lack of planning. There's none of the waiting around for your flight, none of the uncertainty of what you'll be getting from hotel rooms and little of the planning that is required from most other types of holidaying.

With a caravan, you can pretty well hitch up and go whenever and wherever you want. Apart from peak holiday times, getting a space, or pitch as they are known, on most caravan sites requires little or no booking in advance. And once you are on site, no matter where you are staying, you always know what to expect when you return to your own little home on wheels after a day out.

Caravanning overseas has now also become more popular and straightforward. Most European countries offer an excellent range of sites while ferry travel has never been easier. There are even now companies such as Eurocamp who will carry out all the planning for your overseas caravanning holiday for you, leaving you to simply catch the ferry and turn up at your site.

For newcomers to caravanning, one of the best ways to be sure of expert help is to join one of the clubs available for caravanners. The two largest clubs are The Caravan Club and The Camping and Caravanning Club. Both are national organisations with hundreds of thousands of members able to call on extensive and well organised resources to provide a host of services for the caravanning public.

These services include each club's own national network of sites, ranging from basic farm sites with little more in the way of facilities than a tap and a drain, to large, multi-pitch affairs offering a comprehensive range of services.

Both clubs also offer such benefits as insurance coverage, towing tuition, overseas holiday packages and advice and information services.

Many individual makes of caravan also have their own owner's clubs which organise their own rallies and get-togethers over weekends throughout the year. Similarly, many work's social clubs have individual caravan groups. There are even specialist owner's clubs for retired, single and deaf caravanners, as well as a host of other specialist-interest related groups.

These owner's clubs make excellent opportunities for caravanners to meet like-minded enthusiasts and get away for low-cost holidays across the country. To contact an owner's club, simply give the relevant caravan manufacturer a telephone call and they will be able to put you in touch with the club secretary. Alternatively, call one of the specialist caravan magazines that are available at most large newsagents.

Ian Waller

CHAPTER 1 - SAFETY FIRST!

Although the modern caravan is mechanically relatively simple when compared with the modern motor car, it is still extremely important to bear in mind a number of essential safety considerations before any work is carried out.

By carrying out your own servicing and maintenance work on your caravan you are taking on the responsibility for both your own safety and the safety of those working with you. It is therefore strongly advisable that any work is carefully planned in advance with particular care being taken for safety.

It is also advisable to take as much time as is necessary with any work that is carried out. Remember that many accidents are caused by rushing to get work done.

BEFORE using any specialist tools or materials, be sure to consult the necessary safety and operational instructions from the manufacturers and suppliers.

ALWAYS disconnect both the caravan's 12V DC and 240V AC electrical supplies before starting any work.

ALWAYS disconnect the gas supply at the source and check that all the pilot lights are out before starting any work in a caravan.

WHENEVER carrying out any work on the running gear or chassis of a caravan make sure that the wheels are firmly chocked.

WHEN using a jack on the caravan, make sure that you locate and use the correct jacking points. Before working under the caravan make sure that you use axle stands and wind the caravan's corner steadies down placing secure blocks beneath the steadies if they no longer reach the ground.

WIPE UP any spilt oil, grease or water off the floor immediately, before there is an accident.

MAKE SURE that the correct tools are used for the job.

NEVER take any risky short cuts or rush to finish a job. Plan ahead and allow plenty of time.

BE meticulous and keep the work area tidy - you will avoid frustration, work better and lose less.

KEEP children and animals right away from the work area and from unattended caravans.

ALWAYS wear eye protection when working under a caravan and when using any power tools.

BEFORE undertaking any dirty jobs, use a barrier cream on your hands as a protection against infection. Preferably, wear thin gloves, available from DIY outlets.

REMOVE your wrist watch, rings and other jewellery before doing any work on the caravan - and especially when working on the electrical system.

ALWAYS tell someone what you are doing and have them regularly check that all is well, especially when working alone or under the vehicle.

ALWAYS seek specialist advice if you are in doubt about any job. The safety of your caravan affects you, your family and other road users.

ALWAYS use genuine original equipment spares built to the correct safety standards.

Mains Electricity

Always disconnect the caravan's mains electricity supply before commencing any work.

Never bypass the caravans RCD (Residual Current Device) circuit breakers for any reason at all.

Whenever you have carried out any work on a caravan's mains electricity system, have it checked by an approved electrician before using it.

When working with power tools, use rechargeable tools and a DC inspection lamp, powered from a remote 12V battery - both are much safer. However, if you do use a mains powered inspection lamp, power tool etc, ensure that the appliance is wired correctly to its plug, that wherever necessary it is properly earthed (grounded) and that the fuse is

1. Always have a fire extinguisher close to hand when working on your caravan. You should also have a suitable fire extinguisher permanently mounted inside the 'van. Have it checked every year.

SAFETY FIRST!

of the correct rating for the appliance concerned. Do not use any mains powered equipment in damp conditions or in the vicinity of fuel, fuel vapour or the caravan battery.

Before using any mains powered electrical equipment, take one more simple precaution - use an RCD (Residual Circuit Device) circuit breaker. Then, if there is a problem, the RCD circuit breaker reduces the risk of electrocution by instantly cutting the power supply.

The Battery

Always disconnect the battery before commencing any work on the 12V electrical system.

Don't smoke or allow a naked flame, or cause a spark near the caravan's battery, even in a well ventilated area. A certain amount of highly explosive hydrogen gas will be given off as part of the normal charging process.

When charging the battery from an external source, disconnect both battery leads before commencing the charging. If the battery is not of the 'sealed for life' type, loosen the filler plugs or remove the cover before charging. For best results the battery should be given a low rate 'trickle' charge overnight. Do not charge at an excessive rate or the battery may burst.

Always wear gloves and goggles when carrying or topping up the battery. Even in diluted form (as in the battery) the acid electrolyte is extremely corrosive and must not be allowed to contact the eyes, skin or clothes.

Gas System

Recent changes in the law now make it an offence for anyone other than trained engineers to carry out any work on gas appliances. Any person that is qualified to carry out work on the gas system should be registered with CORGI - The Council For Registered Gas Installers. Check their credentials before allowing them to work on your caravan - your life could depend on it!

Brakes and Asbestos

Whenever you work on the braking system mechanical components, or remove front or rear brake pads or shoes:

i) wear an efficient particle mask,

ii) wipe off all brake dust from the work area (never blow it off with compressed air),

iii) dispose of brake dust and discarded shoes or pads in a sealed plastic bag,

iv) wash hands thoroughly after you have finished working on the brakes and certainly before you eat or smoke,

v) replace shoes and pads only with asbestos-free shoes or pads. Note that asbestos brake dust can cause cancer if inhaled.

Obviously, a caravan's brakes are among its most important safety related items. Do not dismantle your caravan's brakes unless you are fully competent to do so. If you have not been trained in this work, but wish to carry out the jobs described in this book, it is strongly recommended that you have a garage or qualified mechanic check your work before using the caravan.

Jack and Axle Stands

Whenever you are planning to jack a caravan, it is essential that you use only the correct sort of jack. It is also very important to locate the correct jacking points. If your caravan is not equipped with a specific jacking point, only jack the caravan up from under the axle and as close to the chassis as possible.

Special care must be taken when any type of lifting equipment is used. Jacks

2

2. Unlike car wheelnuts, caravan wheelnuts are notorious for coming loose, especially on the left-hand side - the direction of rotation of the wheel unscrews the nuts. Check regularly with a torque wrench.

are made for lifting the caravan only, not for supporting it. Never work under a caravan using only a jack to support the weight. Jacks must be supplemented by adequate additional means of support, such as axle stands, positioned under secure, load-bearing parts of the chassis or axle.

When replacing a wheel always use the correct torque settings and the correct North, South, East, West sequence of tightening.

Never overtighten the wheelnuts as this can misshapen the wheel rim but always check wheelnut tightness with a torque wrench at regular intervals.

Chassis

Never drill a galvanised chassis as it could weaken the structure. Never weld any galvanised material as it could create toxic fumes.

WORKSHOP SAFETY - GENERAL

1. Always have a fire extinguisher of the correct type at arm's length when working on your caravan.

If you do have a fire, DON'T PANIC! Use the extinguisher effectively by directing it at the base of the fire.

2. NEVER use a naked flame near petrol or anywhere in the workplace.

3. KEEP your inspection lamp well away from any source of petrol (gasoline) and bottled gas.

4. NEVER use petrol (gasoline) to clean parts. Use paraffin (kerosene) or white spirits.

5. NO SMOKING! There's a risk of fire or transferring dangerous substances to your mouth and, in any case, ash falling into mechanical components is to be avoided!

6. BE METHODICAL in everything you do, use common sense, and think of safety at all times.

CHAPTER 2 - BUYING GUIDE

Where To Buy?

The Caravan Club reminds members that in general, it's best to buy from a local dealer. This is because caravans, like most other consumer goods, can need care and attention, and this is often required during the warranty period. If you were to live in, say, Birmingham but see a caravan for sale while you're on holiday in Cornwall, just imagine how many miles you would have to clock-up if you had to return the caravan for attention, then go back to collect it only to find that a further trip is necessary because the work is not complete or has not been done to your satisfaction. You could also find that a local dealer may treat you with a little more consideration simply because you live close enough to come back and make a fuss if anything you were promised turns out not to be the case!

Also avoid impulse buying of a foreign caravan unless it is imported by a well established UK subsidiary. Foreign makes often come and go and so you may be left with a caravan for which it is extremely difficult to obtain spares. You may also be amazed to find that foreign caravans, like foreign cars, may be more expensive to insure - in fact this would be because spares may be expensive or difficult to obtain if they're needed. Also make absolutely sure that any imported 'van conforms with UK Construction and Use Regulations and to UK Legal Requirements with regard to the electricity supply and the gas supply. You may also find that any mains sockets are not compatible with any of your plugs! A further point worth bearing in mind is that some continental 'vans are not as well equipped as British ones, so make sure that an apparent bargain is all that it seems.

Dealing With The Dealers

Most salesmen and women receive a commission for every sale they make, so they will know all the tricks in the book to encourage you to "close" a deal on the spot, whether it's in your best interests or not. Make a BIG POINT whenever going to look at a caravan, of never saying you will buy it there and then. Make a pact between yourself and your partner that you will "go away and think about it", no matter what the salesman or woman says. He or she is likely to tell all sorts of porkies, such as that someone else has shown an interest, or that caravans of this type/in this condition/at this time of year (delete according to choice) are difficult to come by, but this is virtually never true, so don't be swayed. In fact, if you've never owned a caravan before, you should regard the process of deciding which type of caravan to buy as part of the fun and spend weeks or months reading the caravan magazines and visiting as many sales sites as possible so that you can have an excellent all-round view of the field.

*INSIDE INFORMATION: When you **think** you have identified the right type of caravan for you, try hiring one for at least a few days to see if you have made the right decision.*

With so many manufacturers to choose from and more than 200 dealerships to visit in the UK, there is a wide variety of caravans on offer. And when the used market, including both private and dealer sales, is also taken into consideration, the choice is further increased.

As with the car market, dealers vary from those selling one make of caravan to large outlets selling a wide range of manufacturers' caravans. Obviously the larger dealers offer a greater variety of models.

However, it is still advisable to shop around, visiting as many different dealerships as possible. Buying a caravan is generally a major purchase and only by taking your time and by seeing as many different makes and models as possible can you be sure of picking the right one for you.

As with any purchase, the price of an individual caravan is determined by its age, condition, quality and the amount of extras that you get with it. If you're looking to part exchange your present caravan for a newer or better equipped alternative, most dealers are only too happy to oblige. However, with part exchanges it is certainly worth shopping around.

Buying A New Caravan

When buying a new caravan prices differ quite substantially from dealer to dealer due to the variety of sales and special offers available across the country. However, it is always particularly worthwhile looking out for special offers around the months of September to December when dealers are particularly keen to clear remaining stock to make room for models for the new year.

It's also a good idea to get along to some of the increasing number of major caravan shows held each year across the country. The biggest of these are at Earls Court in London, The National Exhibition Centre in Birmingham and G-Mex in Manchester. These are excellent opportunities to see a wide range of caravans under one roof. They are often a great place to get a better than usual deal on a new caravan.

All new models should come with at least a year's warranty. Do remember though, that with most caravan dealers and manufacturers the warranty only applies to the dealership where you bought the caravan. So if you decide to buy a caravan from a dealer some miles away, be prepared to have to take it back to that same dealer if any future work is required. This is particularly relevant if you buy a caravan at a show where dealers may, for instance come from Sheffield to exhibit in London.

Buying A Used Caravan

As for buying a used caravan, either privately or through a dealer, it is still advisable to shop around. However, if you are after a specific model you should remember that availability may not be as wide as with a new caravan. In such a case you should be prepared to pay slightly above the odds.

When buying a relatively new used caravan from a dealer it is worth finding out if a warranty is available, either for free or at extra cost. Spending a few extra pounds on a warranty when you buy the caravan might save you a good deal more if a serious problem arises within the following few months.

It is extremely doubtful that any sort of warranty will be offered either on very old caravans from a dealership or on any caravans from a private sale.

Perhaps the most important thing to look out for when buying a used caravan is damp, also known as water ingress. Damp can get into a caravan through badly sealed seams and damaged bodywork, and may cause extensive damage to the main structure of a caravan.

BUYING GUIDE

To check for damp look out for cases of water staining and mould. Use your nose and have a good sniff around for damp smells. It's also a good idea to invest in a damp detector to check all internal seams. If any sign of damp is found, make sure that the dealer agrees to deal with it before buying the caravan. And remember, damp cannot be cured by leaving the caravan out in warm weather to let it dry.

When buying a used caravan, also be sure to look out for the following:

1A. Check that the information on the manufacturer's name plate matches the information given by the vendor

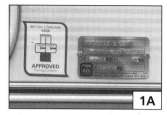
1A

1B. Check the chassis for distortion and check the corner steadies for damage. Modern caravans have a galvanised steel chassis which are generally trouble free. However, for older caravans with painted steel chassis carefully check for any signs of rust or damage. Ask the dealer if the caravan can be raised on a ramp.

1B

1C. Check the hitch coupling for wear (it should not be too easy to move the shaft forwards and backwards and there should be no up and down play).

1C

1D. Check the tyres for cracks, wear and the depth of tread. Like cars, the tread depth on caravan tyres should be at least 1.6mm.

Check the bodywork for damage.

Check the sealant in joints and around windows and doors for drying and cracking.

1D

1E. Check the car to caravan cable and mains electricity connections for signs of damage or wear.

1E

1F. Check for signs of amateurish DIY jobs and alterations, in particular with the gas and electricity appliances.

One additional point to consider when buying a used caravan is that models built before 1988 are generally unsuitable for having a standard cassette toilet fitted. This therefore often decreases both their value and their potential for being upgraded.

1F

Auctions

2. Caravan auctions are becoming increasingly popular across the country and offer a way of buying a caravan often at a price well below its book value. However, there are risks when buying at an auction. Often caravans for sale at an auction are sub-standard models that dealers or private individuals may have otherwise failed to sell. As it is exceptionally rare for any sort of warranty to be offered with a caravan bought at an auction, extra care should be taken in checking them for damage and damp. (Illustration, courtesy AP Lockheed)

2

What Will My Car Tow?

This is the area that seem to cause most concern to caravanners and potential caravanners alike. The Caravan Club and The Camping and Caravan Club both recommend the "85% Rule": an outfit in which the loaded caravan weighs more than 85% of the unladen weight of the car is more likely to be unstable and to cause snaking. Of course, there's more to it than that, including the way in which the caravan is loaded and the use of correct tyre pressures among others (see *Chapter 3, Using Your Caravan*) but the "85% Rule" is a good starting point.

You should also check the maximum allowable towing limit for the car. With some cars this is actually lower than 85% of its kerbweight. Whatever the maximum towing limit, if it is exceeded there is a good chance that the car's warranty with be invalidated and you will also be breaking the law.

Most caravans will have their unladen and laden weights recorded in one of two places. Firstly, check the caravan's owner's manual which should be kept in the caravan at all times. The second place to check is the caravan's maker's plate. This can generally be found either by the caravan's entrance door or at the front on the A-frame.

If you can't locate the maker's plate then check with your local dealer or give the manufacturer a telephone call. Finding out the weights of your caravan is vital in ensuring that not only is the outfit safe but also within legal limitations. Towing an overloaded outfit could be seen as dangerous driving and therefore lead to a criminal prosecution.

3A. Use this graph to make sure that your caravan is a suitable match for your towcar. Simply find the kerbside weight of your car on the horizontal axis and the caravan's maximum laden weight along the vertical axis. Then check where the two points meet in the middle of the graph. If that point is in the 'NO PROBLEM' area, then your outfit is well matched. If it's in the shaded area, then only proceed if you're an experienced caravanner. If, however, it's in the 'NO GO AREA', unfortunately the outfit is an unsuitable match. (Illustration, courtesy Caravan Plus Magazine.)

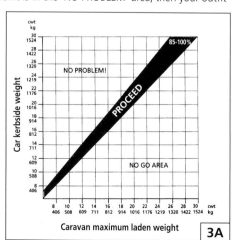
3A

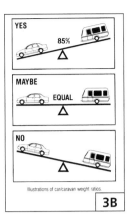

Illustrations of car/caravan weight ratios.

3B

3B. Please note that the "85% Rule" is not a legal weight ratio requirement (and in fact there is no such legal requirement) but the law does require that caravans, the vehicles towing them and the loads carried must be in such condition that no nuisance or danger is caused to other road users. (And of course, if the condition of your outfit does not comply, it will also be a nuisance and danger to you!) In summary, The Caravan Club suggests that the following guidelines are borne in mind:

i) The lower the laden weight of a trailer caravan when towed on the public highway, the safer the outfit.

ii) In any case, the laden weight of the caravan should never exceed the kerbside weight of the towing vehicle.

iii) The nearer the caravan laden weight approaches the one to one ratio, the more careful the driver must be.

Chapter 3, Using Your Caravan looks closely at what is meant by the 'nose weight' of the caravan. Most car manufacturers state a maximum permitted weight to be borne by the car's towball (the nose weight of the caravan) and caravan manufacturers may sometimes quote an ex-works nose weight - which is about as much use to you as a weather forecast for Alaska. Once the caravan is laden, the nose weight will change dramatically, but as a guide, the optimum nose weight of the caravan is generally 7% of its laden weight. You can use this information by checking the maximum laden weight of a caravan before purchasing it so that you can ensure that this figure is not in excess of your car's limit. (See your car's handbook or telephone your car's manufacturer's Customer Services Department.)

Even though your caravan may not exceed the recommended nose weight limit of your car, the rear end of the car may still sag and cause some outfit instability and require re-setting of headlamps if you are to be driving at night. This can be an all round nuisance and gives you another reason why you should test-drive a caravan for an extended period before purchase. Cars which have variable or self-levelling suspension don't tend to suffer from this problem and some estate cars also have stiffer rear springing than their saloon counterparts. It is often possible to beef up the rear suspension or fit suspension aids and The Caravan Club can supply members with a leaflet on the subject, or consult your local caravan dealership or your car main dealership.

Which Caravan Suits You

There are many different types, prices and models of caravan and it is vital that you pick the one that suits your requirements. Obviously price is a major consideration, although even if you cannot afford a caravan right away, some larger dealerships may offer their own credit schemes.

Consider how many people will be using the caravan at one time. One way that caravans are classified is by the number of 'berths' that they have e.g. two, four or five berth. In some circumstances, however, this should not be taken too literally. Some couples prefer having a four berth so that perhaps they have extra sleeping room should they wish to take friends or grandchildren away with them occasionally.

Bear in mind that, while larger caravans undoubtedly possess more home comforts than smaller ones, each extra foot of body length equals approximately 50 kilogrammes (just under one cwt) of extra weight. As a rule, you're best off towing the shortest and lightest caravan that suits you - and you'll be saving money too! Also bear in mind that a good quality awning will give you extra sleeping accommodation as well as somewhere to put wet weather gear and wellies and, when the sun beats down, it will provide you with a shady spot in which to take your meals.

Also bear in mind that, not only will a longer and therefore heavier caravan be more difficult to tow, it will also be more difficult to manoeuvre and harder work to man-handle on site and in your parking space at home. The maximum length of caravan that may be towed on British roads by vehicles up to the size of a Range Rover, for instance, is 7 metres (22 ft. 11.5 in.) and the maximum width is 2.3 metres (7 ft. 6.5 in.). When you also consider the extra ferry charges incurred by owners of long caravans you start to realise that, unless you're really determined, the extra length may not be worthwhile after all.

If you're determined to go down the long caravan route, you may consider one with twin axles (and four wheels and tyres, of course). Such caravans undoubtedly tend to tow with greater stability but, unless you are a real ace at manoeuvring your caravan into precisely the right spot with your tow car, you'll find a twin-axle caravan devilishly hard work to manoeuvre on site by hand. Some models are seeking to overcome this problem, however, by fitting a rear axle that can be hydraulically lifted clear of the ground, but the complexity and the weight penalty just keeps on growing!

Which Layout?

4

4. This is almost like asking how long is a piece of string but there are certain points that you should consider in order of priority. The first one is to establish how many berths you will need, remembering that adults as well as children can sleep in the awning. On the other hand, not everyone wants to sleep in the awning if the weather is particularly cold outside!

Don't take manufacturer's claims at face value and always use a tape measure to be certain that each berth is long enough. Five or six berth caravans may only have two berths long enough for adults! Also bear in mind that the comfort of a bed can make or break your enjoyment of a holiday, especially if you suffer from back problems. Compare cushion depths between caravans and also look at the way the small pieces fit together: you'll be surprised how a knee or an elbow can find its way between the cracks in the middle of the night and wake you up with a jolt! All of this is yet another good reason for testing out a caravan in real life before committing your hard earned cash.

If you have children, it can be useful to have two dining areas because one of them, screened off, can become the children's bedroom at night, leaving you to read or watch TV in peace. This layout also results in a centre kitchen which is the ideal layout as far as caravan balance on the road is concerned. Most of the weight you carry in your caravan will tend to be based over the kitchen - but then this should not be the only consideration because you will also want to enjoy living in the caravan when you reach your destination and it is undoubtedly true that, sleeping accommodation permitting, more people seem to prefer an end kitchen than a centre one. The way to overcome the problem is simply to pack all of the heavy items in the middle and then repack them into the kitchen area as described in *Chapter 3, Using Your Caravan* when you arrive on site.

The logistics of living in a caravan won't fully occur to you until you actually try one out and after a fortnight away, intelligently planned cupboards, work tops, doors which open without disturbing the cooking area and so on will all be considered more valuable than a pretty fascia!

Quite a few caravans have a low front end to reduce drag when towing but check that this doesn't make the interior of the caravan claustrophobic and awkward for tall people. Those of us who *are* tall have known the agony of a day spent in the caravan in pouring rain, having to stand underneath the roof light in order to stretch out to full height!

BUYING GUIDE

You should also check out the ease of getting into seats and into the toilet compartment (which may well be fitted into the least accessible part of the caravan!) and consider the degree of agility of those who will be using the caravan. While on the subject of the toilet, don't be taken in by basins and trays that fold and flap, unless you are convinced that they really will be convenient - or at least tolerable - in daily use.

Equipment

Different caravans come with different levels of standard equipment, depending on their cost and size. Just about all modern caravans have electric lighting, running water and a gas powered hob in the kitchen. But not many have the facilities to hook up to all that the most advanced sites have to offer.

What you will require from a caravan will depend on where you want to go, who with and when. If you intend to visit only well-equipped caravan sites with their own shops, shower and toilet blocks and general amenities, you may not require as much equipment in the caravan.

If however, you prefer more basic sites with little more than a tap and drain on offer, you will probably require a better equipped caravan.

Similarly, if you are planning only to go away in your caravan over the summer months, heating and insulation won't be as much of a concern as if you intend to caravan through the winter as well.

Necessary Accessories

Whether you are buying a new or used caravan, don't forget the hidden extras that can add quite a few more pounds to the cost. You will certainly require a number of items of equipment that are pretty much essential before you can take your caravan away. These include gas bottles, a 12-volt leisure battery, water containers, a step to help you get in and out of the caravan, towing mirrors for your car and a number plate for the caravan.

Of course the shop at your local caravan centre will have displays of numerous other products designed to make caravanning a whole lot easier. But to start off with at least, stick to the basics and let time and experience help you decide what else you will need. After all, if you buy everything all at once, not only will you have an overloaded caravan but you might not have enough money left to pay for the holiday.

If you are buying your caravan from a dealer, you may be able to get some of these essentials thrown in as part of the deal. However, this is certainly a lot less likely with a private sale. Whichever, here's a checklist to help you make sure that you've got all the essentials.

In addition to the specialist accessories that are necessary for a successful caravanning holiday, it's easy to forget a few of those personal and domestic essentials. To help make sure that you don't forget anything, you will find a thorough checklist in Appendix 6, towards the back of this book. It's not a bad idea to copy this page and keep it in your caravan so that you can check off each item every time you go away.

Getting What You Pay For

CRIS

When buying a caravan built since 1991, make sure that you check the CRIS number. CRIS stands for Caravan Registration and Identification Scheme and is similar to a motor car's log. Every British built caravan since 1991 is given a unique 17 digit number which is etched on to all its windows and stamped on the chassis or A-frame.

If you are buying a new caravan, make sure to arrange with the dealer to have the Touring Caravan Registration Documents sent through to you. If you are buying a used caravan, check its CRIS number and make sure that the seller has the relevant documents relating to that specific van. When you then take ownership of the 'van be sure to fill in the transfer section of the document and send it to the CRIS office. They will then update the information on their computer and send you a new registration document.

It is strongly advisable that you keep your Registration Documents in a safe place and certainly not in the caravan, just in case it is stolen.

You should always insist on receiving a copy of the users handbook with the caravan, whether it is new or used. It has been a requirement that a handbook must be provided covering certain key information, since 1970. The information you should receive should cover at least: caravan type, dimensions, weights, wheels and tyres information, operating instructions and safety precautions. If a used caravan does not have one, contact the manufacturer and obtain another. If the manufacturer has gone out of existence, contact one of the caravan clubs or one of the caravanning magazines and see if the manufacturer has been taken over by another who may be able to help out. Much of the information contained in this book is dependent on your being able to obtain certain pieces of key information from the manufacturer's handbook and your ability to use the caravan safely will also be impaired if you can't obtain the right information. Strongly consider not purchasing a caravan for which no handbook is available.

It is not unknown for the vendor of a caravan to understate the age by quite an alarming number of years. Make sure that you have the CRIS number or the chassis number and contact the caravan or chassis manufacturer for its date of build. If the chassis number is missing, give that 'van a miss!

Making Comparisons

All of the caravan magazines run regular tests on caravans and it is possible in most cases to obtain back issues or copies of older tests from the publishers while the two caravan clubs also offer their members a road test photocopy service, if the particular 'van in which the member is interested has been tested by the club.

Finally some words of advice from The Caravan Club, whose assistance has been gratefully received in connection with this chapter: "You will part with a lot of money when you buy a caravan, and to be certain you obtain your money's worth, and exactly what you require, take time in making a decision. Time spent in looking is never wasted." In fact, time spent in looking can be almost as enjoyable as time spent in using your caravan, so have fun!

CHAPTER 3 - USING YOUR CARAVAN

Living in a caravan is more a matter of organisation and common sense more than anything else. Once set up on site it is similar to living in any modern house, but on a much smaller scale. During the first holiday away in a caravan, this new way of living might take a small amount of getting used to. But after a day or two to familiarise yourself, you will soon feel at home.

Caravanners are generally a friendly and helpful lot so if you do find yourself unsure of what to do on site, try asking your new neighbour for a hand. Chatting with other caravanners is certainly one of the best ways of getting to learn about the real ins and outs of caravanning. Plus, if you are lucky enough, it's a good way to pick up a few hints and tips.

INSIDE INFORMATION: A tip often followed by beginners and experienced caravanners alike, is to go away for a short trial run before embarking on a major excursion. Book in to a site no more than 20 or 30 miles from home for one or two nights and take an enjoyable short break while checking that everything works and getting to know the caravan's equipment. Remember to take a note pad, so you don't forget all those little foibles to be put right when you return!

PART I: EQUIPMENT

The best advice is to make sure that you've got a working knowledge of how everything works BEFORE you set off for the first time with your caravan. If you've got room, set the caravan up outside your house or wherever it's stored. The last thing that you want is to arrive on site and find that, for example, the water pump isn't working. Ideally you should give yourself a good two weeks leeway between checking your caravan over and going away for the first time each season. This will allow you plenty of time to get anything fixed that isn't working correctly.

As you go away more and more in your caravan, you'll get used to exactly how everything works and what you need to take with you. On a straightforward pitch on a good caravan site it shouldn't take you much more than 20 minutes to have your caravan pitched, connected up and fully ready to use. For the first time, however, there is a good chance that it might take you a good while longer, perhaps even an hour or two.

Try to make it easier for yourself by making sure that before you leave you have got everything with you. Check the route that you're taking to ensure that it's suitable for caravans, that is, with as few hills as possible and, where possible, keeping away from narrow lanes. Where you can, also try to travel outside of peak traffic times so that you're not adding to or involved in any of the congestion.

INSIDE INFORMATION: Make sure that you arrive good and early on site so that you're not groping around in the dark trying to get the caravan ready. And if you are caravanning with children, give each of them specific jobs to do. Perhaps, while one goes and fills the water containers, another could be winding down the corner steadies. It helps keep everybody busy, makes them feel involved and gets the work done more quickly.

Depending on their ages, caravans will have various levels of standard equipment. Older caravans might be quite basic, with just a basic hob and cold running water, unless a previous owner has uprated it. A more modern caravan, however, may well be fitted with many of the standard luxuries of home. However well equipped a caravan, getting to know the basics of how equipment works and how to use it properly is essential when caravanning.

Electrical System

While it is quite usual for older caravans to be fitted with a 12-volt electrical system only, most modern caravans will also have a 240-volt system.

The 12-volt system is powered by a single leisure battery which may look similar to the one fitted in your car. These leisure batteries are designed to provide 'deep cycling'. This means that they are capable of being completely discharged and recharged and have a longer life expectancy than a normal car starter battery used in similar conditions.

INSIDE INFORMATION: To maintain a leisure battery in good condition, it should be recharged outside the caravan every three months or so. Also check the electrolyte levels at the same time and, if necessary, top them up with distilled water. Remember to recharge the battery regularly in the winter months, as well as in the summer because batteries that are allowed to just 'stand' over the off-season period have much shorter life spans than those that are regularly charged.

The battery is generally located in a purpose built battery locker found in the exterior offside wall of the caravan and is accessible through a lockable locker door. It is important that the battery is held securely in place when the caravan is on the move and most caravans will have straps fitted for this purpose.

There are a number of different sizes of leisure batteries available for caravans and you should make sure that you get the one most suitable for your caravan. This will be partly dictated by the size of your caravan's battery locker and partly on which appliances the battery will be used to power. To do this calculate the power required by multiplying the Amp (current requirement) of each appliance by the typical number of hours it will be used for on a trip (AHR, or Amp Hour Requirement). Add all the AHRs together and check which battery's AHC (Amp Hour Capacity) exceeds that figure.

1. The Gunson's battery charger is designed to give the battery a 'trickle' charge but then to shut itself down when the battery is 'full', turning itself back on automatically when required, something that can't be done with a regular battery charger. Remove the battery before connecting up.

Guidelines on Power Requirements

The 12-volt system is generally responsible for powering the caravan's water pump, some interior lighting and the blown air heating system, plus any 12-volt accessories that might be fitted at a later date, such as a radio/cassette player. If you can discern the current required for each component - perhaps by looking at the rating plate - you may be able to use the following to work out the required current (the 'AHC') from your leisure battery.

Appliance	Current required	Hours used	AHC needed
TV - B/W	2	3	6
TV - colour	5	3	15
Light	2	4	8
Fridge	10	5	50
Water pump	3	.5	1.5

The Caravan Club uses a different method, shown below, of working out the current requirement from your leisure battery, based on the fact that much equipment is rated in Watts, and using the formula forgotten by generations of schoolboys and girls: Amps = Watts divided by Volts (i.e., 12 volts, in this case).

Appliance	Watts (example)	Hours Used	Watt Hours
3 strip lights	3 x 13 = 39	5	195
2 spot lamps	2 x 10 = 20	3	60
Portable TV	45	2	90
Water pump	35	0.25	7.5
		TOTAL WATT HOURS	352.5

If you then divide the total Watts by Volts, you get:

352.5 divided by 12, equals approx. 30 Ampere hours (the AHC figure mentioned above), indicating that a battery of 60 Ampere hours would provide power for two days without needing recharging. In practice, this only gives a rough guide, because the age of the battery, the condition of the wiring, the temperature and a number of other factors can throw out your calculations. The Club recommends building in a safety margin of about 25%.

Car-To-Caravan Electrical Cables

An important part of the 12-volt system are the black 12N (Normal) and grey 12S (Supplementary) cable connections to the car. These run from the caravan and are connected to the towcar for when the outfit is on the move. These cables supply a 12-volt current direct from the towcar's own electrical system to the caravan. See *Chapter 5, Servicing and Maintenance* for information on how to connect - or reconnect, when necessary.

The 12N cable powers the caravan's external road lights - brake lights, indicators, fog lights etc. The 12S cable, meanwhile, will supply power for the caravan fridge and internal lights, as well as keeping the caravan's battery charged up. Before setting off on a caravanning trip it is essential that you check that the 12N cable is working correctly. The best way to do this is for one person to operate the headlights, indicators, brake lights and fog lights in the car and for a second person to confirm that the same lights are working on the caravan. Towing a caravan with faulty road lights on the public highway is illegal and leaves the owner open to criminal prosecution.

NOTE: Some older caravans with a low equipment level may only be fitted with a 12N cable.

Electrical Distribution Panel

Inside all but the oldest caravan will be some form of electrical distribution panel which acts as a central control point for the 12-volt system. While the number of controls and meters will vary from caravan to caravan, operating this panel is very straightforward.

Almost all caravan's distribution panel will feature some form of rocker switch that selects the caravan's 12-volt power source. This is often labelled 'car', 'caravan' and 'off'. When the caravan is being towed out on the road, the switch should be in the 'car' position. When on site the 'caravan' position should be chosen. When the caravan is in storage, select the 'off' position.

Other common switch operations on this panel include one to isolate the submersible water pump and another for isolating the 12-volt lighting. There might well also be a battery power level indicator.

Modern caravans often combine this distribution panel to feature other facilities such as a 240-volt electrical and television aerial socket, as well as central heating and water heater controls.

Mains Electricity

As for the 240-volt system, this will allow most domestic mains powered electrical items to be used in a caravan. When fitted to a caravan it offers power for charging the battery, some interior lighting, the water heater and the fridge.

The 240-volt supply comes from hook-ups available on most caravan sites. A standard 25 metre orange lead is used to connect the site hook-up point to the caravan, with the caravan electrical inlet socket generally either being situated next to the battery in the battery locker or just under the caravan.

Depending on the site, the power supply available may vary quite considerably. While the average supply is 10 Amps, it can be as low as 4 Amps and as high as 16 Amps. It is important to check out what the supply is to make sure that you do not overload it by plugging in too many electrical appliances.

All caravans with a 240-volt mains electrical system should be fitted with some form of circuit breakers or trip switches. These are designed to protect the caravan and its inhabitants from power surges and overloaded supplies. These should be checked by an expert once a year and under no circumstances should they be bypassed.

Each time that you connect a caravan up to a mains supply inlet you should test these circuit breakers. This is a simple matter of pressing the 'T' (Test) button. If everything is working OK this will flick the circuit breakers to the 'Off' position. They can then be flicked back to the 'On' position for the mains supply to be reconnected.

If, however, this test procedure doesn't result in the supply being automatically turned off there is a fault in the system. If this occurs then disconnect the mains inlet lead and seek advice from a qualified electrician.

USING CYLINDERS

For identification Butane is supplied in BLUE cylinders and Propane in RED cylinders. **2A**

Gas System

Generally situated on the front, or on occasions, on the side of a caravan is an exterior gas bottle locker. This is where its LPG (Liquid Petroleum Gas) bottles are stored. A caravan's gas system can be used for the hob, grill, oven (if fitted), room heater and water heater.

SAFETY FIRST!
When either in use or in storage, a gas bottle should always stand on its base and never be allowed to rest on its side.

2A. Two types of gas are commonly used for caravanning - butane and propane. Butane is available in blue bottles and propane in red.

2B. Each requires its own type of regulator, which is a device that adapts the bottle pressure to one that suits the equipment in the caravan. These regulators are designed so that it is impossible to fit one to the wrong type of gas bottle. Propane regulators (centre) have a male thread; screw-on Butane regulators (right) have a female thread. See below (2D) for the left-hand regulator. (Illustration, courtesy Calor Gas Ltd.)

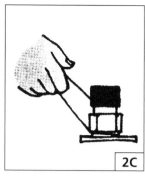

While butane is more readily available and burns hotter than propane, it will freeze when temperatures drop below 2 degrees Celcius. Propane, however, will not burn quite as hot but will remain usable at temperatures down to minus 40 degrees C. It is therefore common for caravanners to use butane during the Summer and Spring and Propane in the Winter and Autumn.

2C. As different types of regulators are used on different types and sizes of gas bottles, knowing how to use each one is essential. Before fitting either regulator though, the safety cap will have to be removed from the top of the cylinder. This is done by pulling the wire cage holding the cap in place to the side and taking the cap off the top of the cylinder. (Illustration, courtesy Calor Gas Ltd.)

BUTANE CYLINDERS
4.5kg size (handwheel valve)
This cylinder takes a regulator or flow controller which screws on to the valve outlet. Both have a connecting nut which incorporates a black sealing washer.

CONNECTING A CYLINDER

1 Check that the valve handwheel is OFF by turning clockwise.

2 Remove protective black cap and keep to replace later.

3 Inspect the black sealing washer for damage before connecting. Replace the washer if faulty.

4 Fit the connecting nut (left hand thread), to the cylinder using a Calor Gas spanner. Tighten firmly, but do not overtighten as this can damage the washer.

5 When gas is required, turn the valve handwheel anti-clockwise.

2D. To fit the regulators fitted to all propane and the small 4.5kg butane cylinders you will need to screw the regulator into place, remembering that it is a LEFT-HAND thread. After checking that the sealing washer is in place, hand-turn the nut ANTI-CLOCKWISE, then tighten firmly (but not over-tight) in the direction shown. A suitable spanner is used to secure the lock nut into position. Turn the gas tap fully anti-clockwise to start the gas flow and fully clockwise to stop the gas flow. (Illustration, courtesy Calor Gas Ltd.)

2E. With the 7kg and 15kg bottles, the procedure is slightly more complex, though no spanner is required. To attach the regulator to the bottle, check that the black sealing washer is fitted inside the cylinder valve, depress the spring catch in the middle of the regulator switch and turn the switch so that it's pointing downwards.

2F. Then put the regulator into position on top of the gas cylinder and turn the switch back 90 degrees anti-clockwise. This will attach the regulator to the cylinder without actually turning the gas on. To turn the gas on, turn the regulator switch a further 90 degrees anti-clockwise.

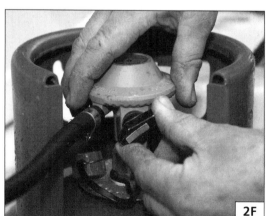

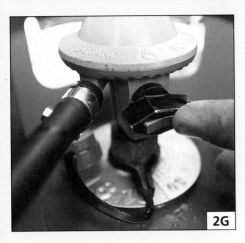

2G

2G. To release the regulator, depress the spring catch and turn the switch 180 degrees clockwise.

> **SAFETY FIRST!**
> *Never attempt to carry out any repairs or alterations to the gas system without first gaining the proper training. If your caravan develops any sort of problem with the gas system, turn the supply off immediately at the bottle, make sure all pilot lights are extinguished and seek expert help.*

INSIDE INFORMATION: Most caravan sites and dealerships will carry replacement gas cylinders for when the cylinders in your caravan run out. However, if your cylinder is running low, telephone ahead to the site you are travelling towards, to check that they stock the size, type and brand that you use, otherwise you may not be able to make the necessary switch.

Water System

No matter what the age of a caravan, basic water systems are always pretty similar to one another. The supply generally comes from an external container, filled from the site tap. The container then supplies the caravan either via a 1/2 inch pipe connected to an inlet point usually found at floor level on the offside exterior of the van or through a 12-volt submersible pump which is dropped into the water tank.

Older caravans will use a floor mounted manual foot pump to bring the water into the caravan. Modern caravans, meanwhile, will use one of two systems involving either microswitches or a pressure system.

With microswitches, the action of turning on one of the taps in the caravan will complete an electrical circuit causing a 12-volt submersible pump to come into operation. This will draw the water from an external container into the caravan.

A pressure system, however, works by the pump drawing water into the system as usual when a tap is turned on. When the tap is then turned off, pressure immediately builds up in the water system and activates a pressure switch which in turn switches the pump off.

Whichever type of water system is fitted to a caravan, you should make sure that the submersible pump is always completely submerged in water. Running a submersible pump out of water may well cause it to burn out.

Some modern caravans will be equipped with a removable water filter as standard. This will be situated next to the water inlet and the filter cartridge should generally be replaced after every 30 days use, or at the start of every season, in any case.

A few larger and more expensive caravans may be fitted with in-board water tanks. This is either filled by an external submersible pump being placed into a filled water container or by connecting the in-board tank directly up to a site water supply. Generally, caravans with an in-board water tank will also have a water level indicator as part of the caravan's main distribution panel.

Waste water is discharged from the caravan via waste outlets, generally found at floor at the rear of the caravan. These are connected to a waste water container through 3/4 inch pipes, either via individual pipes to individual containers, or by a 'Y'-shaped piece of pipe that allows two outlets to flow to a single container. When full, these waste water containers should only be emptied at the correct waste water disposal points.

PART II: GETTING READY TO GO!

Loading Up

Loading a caravan correctly is essential for ensuring that your outfit is safe and stable on the road. In fact, there are only really two things to consider. What goes where in your caravan and towcar, and noseweight. Remember that, if you want to ensure a stable and enjoyable 'tow', getting the load properly packed is paramount, once the basics such as tyre pressures are in place. You are trying, above all, to avoid the 'pendulum effect' of a lot of weight swinging from side to side as your car picks up speed, known as 'snaking'. The further back and higher up the caravan's load is situated, and the more unbalanced the car's own suspension is made, the greater the problem will be. Try to place the heaviest loads inside the car and, if at all possible, between the front and rear wheels, or as near to the rear wheels as possible. Other heavy loads, those which have to go inside the caravan, such as the awning, for instance, should be loaded in the centre of the caravan, as described on page 18.

GETTING READY TO GO!

INSIDE INFORMATION: If the weight limit seems too low, ask the manufacturer if the Maximum Laden Weight can be raised, so that you can safely load more into the caravan. The Caravan Club points out that limits are sometimes set artificially low and the unit could be modified to accept more - but you MUST check: making assumptions could be extremely dangerous!

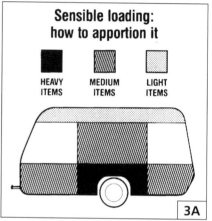

3A. The basic rule with what goes where in your caravan is that you should position as much weight as possible over the axle of your caravan, with a fairly equal loading on each side of the caravan. If there isn't enough space, place the heavier items in the centre and put lighter items towards the front of the caravan, but do remember that under heavy braking, items may slide forwards. Locate them as securely as possible. You should never put any heavy weights either towards the rear or high up in a caravan because either will make the caravan unstable. (Illustration, courtesy The Caravan Club.)

When putting any weight towards the front of the caravan, the main thing to consider is the noseweight. This refers to the maximum weight limit that should be exerted vertically downwards on a towing vehicles towball. This is dictated by the noseweight limit on the towcar's towing bracket and can vary from vehicle to vehicle. To find out the noseweight limit of a towing vehicle you can check the owners' manual, refer to the maker's plate on the bracket or consult your local car dealer.

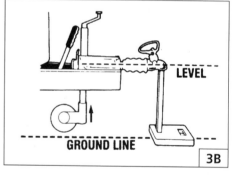

When loading your caravan, you should aim to get the noseweight as close to the car's limit as possible without exceeding it. To measure a caravan's noseweight you can either buy specialist noseweight gauges from your local caravan dealership, or use the DIY version.

3B. A DIY noseweight gauge means using a short length of broom handle and some bathroom scales. Put the bathroom scales beneath the tow hitch and put one end of the broom handle up into the hitch with the other end on the scales. Then take the weight of the hitch off the jockey wheel, letting it go on to the broom handle and take the weight reading from the scales. DON'T place the scales beneath the jockey wheel, otherwise a false reading will be given. The caravan must be level and on level ground.

3C. Alternatively, a specialist noseweight gauge can be placed under the caravan's hitch, taking the weight in the same way as the DIY version. With the specialist version, however, the caravan's noseweight can be read on a gauge. The main advantage of the specialist version is that you don't have to lug a pair of bathroom scales with you, so you can check before the journey home!

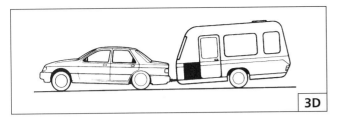

3D

3E

3D. Once your caravan is loaded and hitched up to your car, take a couple of minutes to stand back and admire your work. Ideally the outfit should be level, with, if anything, a very SLIGHT dip at the front of the caravan. If the caravan is either nose-up...

3E. ...or the back of the towcar is sagging badly, then you've got the loading wrong or your car's towball is too high. Recheck the noseweight and if that is correct, get a mechanic to check the towcar's rear suspension. It might be, however, that your car's rear suspension is just being asked to do too much, in which case the amount loaded into the car and even the nose weight could be reduced a touch from the recommended figure, in the short-term, while long-term, you may wish to consider having your car dealer fit uprated rear suspension (if available) or one of the proprietary brands of suspension assisters. (Illustrations, courtesy The Caravan Club.)

INSIDE INFORMATION: If your caravan has an end kitchen, the temptation will be to put heavy items, such as tins and bottles, into the storage provided, at the back of the caravan. Remember that this storage is intended only for use on-site, not when towing: or try dried foods instead of tin cans and melamine crockery in place of the best china!

To give a rough guide to how much various items of equipment weigh, The Caravan Club has published the following list:

Equipment	kg	lb
Awning complete	20	44
Battery (12v) and carrier box	20	44
Spare wheel and tyre (155 SR 13)	13	29
Spare wheel carrier (chassis mounted)	4	9
Portable TV	15	33
Porta Potti (empty)	6	13
Toilet fluid (2.5 litres)	2	4
Water carrier (rolling type) empty	4	9
Fire Extinguisher	2	4
Step	2	4
Lifting Jack	2	4
Chocks/packing pieces (wood)	4	9
Additional LPG above 15 kg allowance is total 2 full 7 kg cylinders	15	33
TOTAL	109	239
Additional weight of toilet full	12	26
Additional weight of water carrier full	26	57
TOTAL	147	322

NOTE: It is not recommended to travel with water container or toilet full.

It is very easy to accidentally exceed the maximum authorised weight of a caravan, and not only is this an offence, but you may also cause premature tyre failure, and damage other undergear components. The amount of payload offered with a caravan is therefore an important consideration.

4A

INSIDE INFORMATION: The Caravan Club recommends that you take your loaded-up caravan to a weighbridge - see Yellow Pages for your nearest - to check that you are not exceeding the Maximum Laden Weight, and that you check as often as required. But ensure that your local weighbridge is accurate with the (relatively) light weight of a caravan.

Hitching Up

Hitching a caravan up to a car is a job best done with two people, one to manoeuvre the car and the other to direct them. Make sure that both people know exactly what is expected and that they have agreed a system of communication.

4A. First of all, make sure that the caravan has its handbrake engaged and, if it is on a slope, that the caravan's wheels are chocked.

4B. Then, take care that all the caravan's windows and rooflights are closed and that there are no belongings loose inside the caravan.

4C. Next raise the caravan's corner steadies.

4D. Then carefully manoeuvre the towcar so that its towball is directly beneath the caravan's hitch. Do not lift the caravan hitch onto the towball. You will discover that by using the winder on the top of the jockey wheel, you can alter the height of the caravan's hitch so that a car's towball will fit beneath it. Once the towball is in position, use the winder to lower the caravan's hitch on to the towball.

There are four common types of hitches on modern caravans, all designed to work with the standard 50mm towball fitted to all modern towcars.

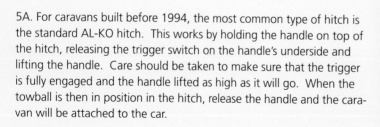

5A. For caravans built before 1994, the most common type of hitch is the standard AL-KO hitch. This works by holding the handle on top of the hitch, releasing the trigger switch on the handle's underside and lifting the handle. Care should be taken to make sure that the trigger is fully engaged and the handle lifted as high as it will go. When the towball is then in position in the hitch, release the handle and the caravan will be attached to the car.

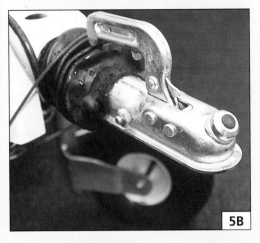

5B. For caravans built since 1994, most are fitted as standard with the AL-KO positive coupling indicator style of hitch. This is operated in exactly the same way as the standard AL-KO hitch but features the addition of a red button on its top. When the hitch is safely attached to a car's towball, this button rises slightly to reveal a green band. Similarly, once the hitch is disconnected, the green band will disappear.

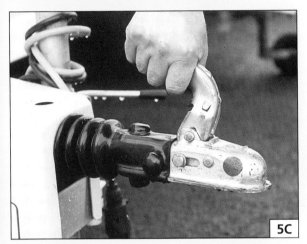

5C. The main alternative to the AL-KO hitches is the Albe variety. When engaging this hitch, the handle will already be locked in a raised position. When the towball is in the correct position, the handle will automatically snap down into position. To disengage the hitch the handle should be grasped, lifted as high as it will go and pressed forward.

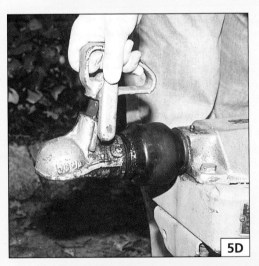

5D. Many older caravans will be fitted with a B&B style hitch consisting of a handle on the top and safety catch on the side. To engage and disengage this style of hitch, release the safety catch and lift the handle straight up.

INSIDE INFORMATION: You may find that the easiest way of connecting the caravan hitch to the car is to have an assistant guide you so that the car's towball is about level with the hitch, but alongside it. It is then easier to move the caravan from one side to the other with a rocking motion, aligning hitch and ball, rather than pull it or push it backwards and forwards.

Whichever type of hitch a caravan is fitted with, there is invariably a 'snap' as the hitch clicks into place. Double check by taking hold of the caravan near the front of its A-frame, near the coupling, and lifting it up slightly to make sure that the caravan is properly attached. With the caravan hitched up, it is time to connect up the different leads.

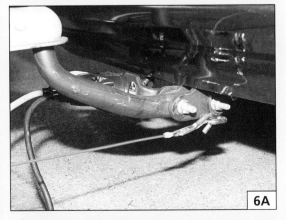

6A. The first one is the break-away cable. This cable is a safety device to stop the caravan from rolling away should it become detached from the towcar. It should be connected to a solid part of the car, but not the towing bracket itself. Then, if the caravan does become detached, this cable will pull the caravan brakes on before snapping and breaking free of the towcar.

GETTING READY TO GO!

6B. Then connect the caravan's black 12N and grey 12S cables to the matching coloured sockets on the towcar. In fact, some older towcars might not have a 12S socket. In this case, carefully knot the 12S cable around the winder of the jockey wheel so that it doesn't drag along the ground when the outfit is moving.

6B

6C. Now, wind the jockey wheel up as far as it will go.

6D. Loosen the jockey wheel's retaining bracket so that the wheel can be further raised off the ground and lock it into position.

6E. Release the caravan's handbrake and remove any wheel chocks.

6F. Make sure before you set off that all the car and caravan's road light are working and that the car's mirrors have been correctly adjusted. Don't forget to fit extension towing mirrors.

6C

INSIDE INFORMATION from The Caravan Club: After about 20 minutes driving, pull over and check:

Has a rooflight blown open?

Is everything in place inside the caravan?

Has anything fallen onto the floor?

Are the wheels cool? (If they feel hot to the flat of your hand, you may have a binding brake, which must be rectified before you go on, otherwise not only the brake but the wheel bearing could fail).

Do the tyres appear to be OK: still properly inflated

Are the 12 volt wiring connections dragging on the floor?

6D

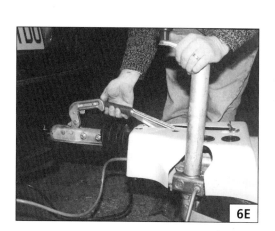
6E

6F

PART III: ON THE ROAD

Towing the Caravan

Towing is not as difficult as you may think. All it needs is some time, patience, a bit of thought and some practice. The first thing that you will notice is that the outfit needs more time for accelerating and braking. As a result, you should take care to leave far more time for overtaking and stay a greater distance from the vehicle in front than you would with a solo vehicle. It is also necessary to take a wider arc on corners and at roundabouts to stop the nearside wheel of the caravan catching the kerb, although the extra width is not usually as big a problem as beginners first imagine and you soon get used to it.

Snaking

When discussing the 'whys and wherefores' of towing a caravan, the subject of 'snaking' is always bound to come up. 'Snaking' refers to the excessive side to side swaying motion caused by a badly loaded outfit, excessive side winds or the change in air pressure caused by an overtaking high sided vehicle.

If this 'snaking' motion is allowed to continue it can result in the outfit going out of control. Curing a snaking outfit is a matter of keeping a cool head and knowing what to do. It's also a matter of keeping out of snaking situations, by not driving too fast for the outfit and keeping your eye on large vehicles that are approaching or are about to overtake you. If snaking recurs during the course of your journey, slow down! (But also stop somewhere safe to see if you have a puncture or some other physical reason for the snaking to be taking place.)

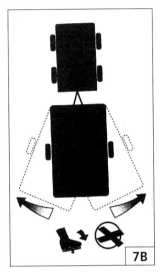

7A. If your outfit starts to snake, simply take your foot off the towcar's accelerator allowing the car to gently slow down, which will dampen out the snake.

If you are going down hill, it might be necessary to VERY GENTLY apply the car's brakes.

7B. Whatever you do, don't brake suddenly or try to accelerate out of the snake. In the majority of cases, neither of these actions will succeed in curing a snake.

*INSIDE INFORMATION: There's an old chestnut that has been around since the beginning of caravan time and if followed, it can be **EXTREMELY DANGEROUS**. You may well hear it said that the best way to get out of a 'snake' is to accelerate out of it. In fact, the faster you go, the more difficult it will be to regain control. In general, the best thing to do is sit it out, make the minimum amount of steering wheel movement (consistent with following the road and avoiding other traffic!) and take your foot off the accelerator pedal, or decelerate slowly if going up hill.*

Hill Starts

In general, you will have to resign yourself to slipping the clutch rather more than you would normally do when starting away on a hill. Your car's first gear is, technically speaking, too high for the extra load imposed on it for a hill start with a caravan, so you must compensate with extra clutch slipping until the combination is under way. But don't overdo it by slipping the clutch for prolonged periods, otherwise you'll end up with clouds of smoke and a burned-out clutch. NEVER hold the car and caravan on the clutch, to stop it slipping back; always use the parking brake.

With an automatic car, you won't have this problem: just give it a little extra gas and away you go!

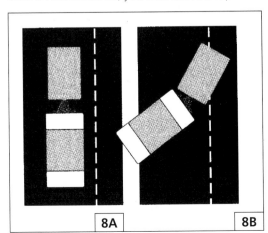

8A. *INSIDE INFORMATION: One other problem that might occur when towing a caravan is that you find that your towcar has difficulty pulling away on a steep hill. In this case, make some room behind the outfit by, if necessary, asking other motorists to move back a little. After all, they're probably not going anywhere until you can move!*

8B. *Then, very slowly, reverse the caravan back at an angle so that the outfit is facing slightly across the angle of the hill, with the caravan at slightly more of an angle to the hill than the towcar. This will allow the outfit to pull away across the hill, making it less steep than straight up the hill. Also, by having your caravan at more of an angle than the towcar, it will give the towcar a small amount of crucial slack as the caravan straightens up before taking on its full weight.*

CHAPTER THREE

Reversing the Car and Caravan

For many owners, the idea of reversing the unit brings them out in a cold sweat! However, while it is certainly not an impossibly difficult skill, it does require a bit more thought and practice, and should always be conducted at walking pace. You should also have an assistant keep an eye open behind the caravan, to ensure that small children, animals and obstructions aren't going to be at risk or in the way.

9A

9A. Remember that reversing with a caravan cannot usually be done in the smooth sweep that you can achieve with car alone. It takes place as a series of corrections, as the caravan tends to go too far in one direction or another. Start by going *very* slowly, making *very small* corrections as you go along and remember that over-corrections and vigorous movements will be your downfall as the caravan locks into a rapidly tightening curve.

When reversing in a straight line you should keep your eyes on the towing vehicle's wing mirrors. If the side of the caravan begins to appear in the left hand mirror, turn the steering wheel SLIGHTLY to the left until the caravan straightens up again.

Similarly, if the side of the caravan begins to appear in the right hand mirror, turn the steering wheel SLIGHTLY to the right until the caravan straightens up.

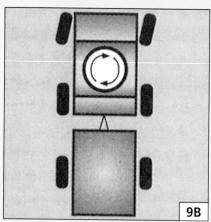
9B

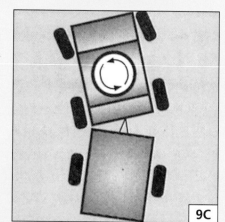
9C

9B. For reversing around a left-hand corner, start by turning the towcar's steering wheel to the right, until the caravan starts to turn to the left.

9C. Then change the steering direction to the left to maintain the caravan's smooth progression round the corner.

9D. As the caravan progresses around the corner, steer slightly back to the right so as not to turn the caravan too much.

9E. For reversing around a right-hand corner, start by turning the steering wheel to the left, until the caravan starts to turn to the right.

9D

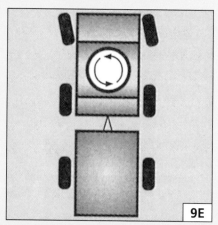
9E

9F. Then change the steering direction to the right to maintain the caravan's smooth progression around the corner.

9G. Finally, steer slightly back to the left so as not to turn the caravan too much.

If you find that the caravan has turned too much, then simply stop, drive forward just a couple of feet and start again. Don't try to over-compensate by making a large steering wheel correction in the opposite direction, because it will probably only make matters worse! Remember,

9F

9G

it's not a race and don't be embarrassed if you don't get it right first time. Just go back to where you started and have another go. And in the end, if you become too flustered to know which is left and which right (and it has happened to us all some time or other!), don't be afraid to unhitch the caravan and move it by hand, if the ground is level enough for you to do so.

INSIDE INFORMATION: There is no doubt that reversing a caravan is a skill quite separate from any other driving skill. If you are wise, you will try it out somewhere safe and with room to make mistakes, such as in a supermarket car park, after the supermarket has closed, or some other suitable space.

Towing Courses

Both of the major caravanning organisations in Britain, The Caravan Club and The Camping and Caravanning Club, run their own towing courses. These offer those new to the pastime the chance to learn the basic skills of towing a caravan in a safe environment before going out on to the open road. These are excellent courses and are highly recommended for caravanning beginners.

Similarly the Institute of Advanced Motorists have their own 'Caravan and Towing Test' that is available only to IAM members.

For further information on these courses, telephone The Caravan Club on 01342 326944, The Camping and Caravanning Club on 01203 694995 or the Institute of Advanced Motorists on 0181 994 4403.

PART IV: ON SITE

10A

Pitching

10A. When you get to a caravan site, the first thing that you are going to have to deal with is pitching your caravan. Many sites have quite strict rules concerning how exactly a caravan should be positioned, for example, which way it should be facing and where the car should be parked. There should also be minimum distance of three metres (or 10ft on Camping and Caravanning Club sites) between outfits in case of a fire.

If your reversing is up to it, simply reverse your caravan on to its pitch. If not, unhitch it as close to the pitch as possible and push it into place. It is not uncommon for other caravanners on site to give you a hand when manually moving a caravan.

10B

Unhitching your caravan is basically the reverse procedure that you went through when hitching it up. Follow the illustrations used for that sequence.

First, engage the handbrake.

Loosen off the bracket that holds the jockey wheel in place and then, once the jockey wheel has made contact with the ground, tighten the bracket up again.

Next disconnect the 12N and 12S cables, and the break away cable.

Then use the jockey wheel winder to raise the hitch away from the towball, making sure that you fully release the handle above the hitch at the same time.

10B. Don't forget to replace the cover over the car's towball. Otherwise it is a common occurrence to brush the greasy towball with your clothing.

Levelling the Caravan

With the caravan in position, the first thing to do is make sure that it is level. If the caravan isn't level not only does it make it awkward and uncomfortable when sleeping or sitting down inside, but it's also often difficult to get the fridge to work properly.

Most pitches on large caravan sites are pretty level in the first place so you probably won't have any great problems. However, for more basic sites you might have to spend more time in making sure that the caravan is level.

11A

11A. The first part of the job is to level the caravan front to back: simply a matter of winding the jockey wheel up or down until the van is horizontal. Place your spirit level on the A-frame. This one is fixed.

Levelling the caravan across the axle takes a little more thought. Whatever you do, DO NOT use the caravan's corner steadies to level it. This will only end up twisting the caravan's chassis.

ON SITE

11B. Levelling across the axle either means moving one or other of the caravan's wheels on to ramps or blocks by careful manoeuvring, or by using a specialist levelling aid, as described in *Chapter 6, Improving Your Caravan*.

11B

11C. When using blocks, make sure that they are as wide as possible so that they don't sink into the ground and that they are capable of taking the weight of the caravan.

Only when the caravan is level should you lower the corner steadies. Lower them until they just touch the ground and no more. If the ground is soft and the steadies sink in, place a piece of wood under each steady. This will help spread their weight and should stop them sinking in.

11C

*INSIDE INFORMATION: Always carry and use a spirit level to make absolutely sure that your caravan is level. You might **think** you can do it by using your senses, but you'll soon come to realise that you can be way out, leaving things to slide and roll alarmingly - and you may wonder why the fridge doesn't light!*

Connecting Up

With the caravan good and level, the next job is to connect up its various supply inlets and waste outlets.

While following a specific order is not strictly necessary, the general routine is water, waste, toilet, electricity, gas.

12A. Fill your fresh water container and place it near to the caravan's water inlet point. Then connect either the submersible pump (shown here) or inlet, depending on the caravan's age, and place them in the water container. Be sure that the water level completely covers the submersible pump.

12A

12B. Never run the submersible pump in an empty water container as it can cause the motor to burn out. Take in as much water as you need straight away: you can always top-up later! This caravan has an integral water level indicator.

Make sure that the water heater drain plug has been replaced if the caravan has been stored over winter.

12B

12C. Connect your waste water containers up to the waste outlets. Make sure that the top of the container is lower than the waste outlet point. Otherwise a situation occurs where old water sits in the waste pipe which, in time, can create an unpleasant smell.

After making sure that the gas cylinder is correctly connected, turn on the caravan's gas supply.

12D. Go inside the caravan and flip the 12-volt supply switch over from car to caravan.

12E. Plug the mains electricity supply cable into the caravan socket. Then plug the other end into the site hook-up point. On some sites you will have to ask the warden to turn on the power supply at a central point.

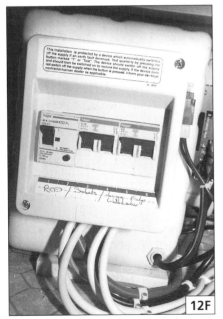

12F. Take time to check that the caravan's RCD devices (the power 'trips') are working properly.

SAFETY FIRST! and INSIDE INFORMATION:
You are recommended to use up to, but no more than, 25 metres of 3-core flexible cable, each core of 2.5mm. The cable should be orange, so that it can easily be seen in grass, and both end connectors (one male; one female) should be blue. If you buy ready made-up cable, ensure that it and the connectors are marked as being to BS 4343 (CEE17) standards.

12G. The following information is supplied by the Caravan Club to its members. The Club emphasises to its members that caravanners are personally responsible for the safety of all of the electrical appliances and equipment inside the caravan. (Illustration, courtesy The Caravan Club.)

TO CONNECT:

i) Before connecting the caravan installation to the mains supply, check that: a) the supply available at the caravan pitch supply point is suitable for the caravan electrical installation and appliances and b) the caravan mains isolating switch is in the OFF position.

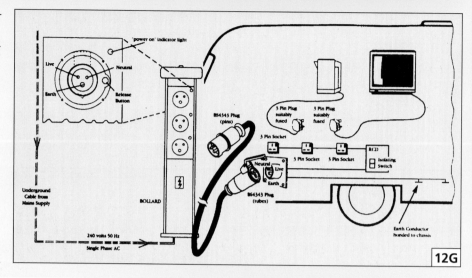

ii) Open the cover to the mains inlet provided at the caravan and insert the blue (female) connector of the supply flexible cable.

iii) Raise the cover of the electricity outlet provided on the pitch supply point and insert the blue plug (male) of the supply cable. (On Club Sites, turn plug clockwise until it locks.)

THE CARAVAN SUPPLY FLEXIBLE CABLE MUST BE FULLY UNCOILED TO AVOID DAMAGE BY OVERHEATING.

iv) Switch on at the caravan mains isolating switch.

v) Check the operation of residual current devices, if any, fitted in the caravan by depressing the test button.

IN CASE OF DOUBT OR, IF AFTER CARRYING OUT THE ABOVE PROCEDURE THE SUPPLY DOES NOT BECOME AVAILABLE, OR IF THE SUPPLY FAILS, CONSULT THE CARAVAN PARK OPERATOR OR HIS AGENT OR A QUALIFIED ELECTRICIAN TO DISCONNECT.

vi) Switch off at the caravan mains isolating switch, switch off at the pitch supply point and unplug both ends of the cable, site supply end first. (On Club Sites, press plug release button.)

In order to help with your calculations, this chart, reproduced here courtesy of The Caravan Club, gives some typical power consumption ratings of a number of appliances used in caravans. Be sure to check the specific ratings of the appliances you use.

Mains and 12V - Appliance Power Consumption in Amperes

Typical Appliance	Mains 240V AC	12V DC
Refrigerator	0.5	9.6
Black and White Television	< 0.1	1.25
Colour Television	0.2	4.2
Video Cassette Player	0.1	1.25 to 2.0
Microwave Cooker	5.0	
2 KW Kettle	8.3	
750 Watt Kettle	3.1	
1 KW Fan Heater	4.2	
Low Wattage Panel Heater	from 0.4	
Carver Water Heater	2.75	
Battery Charger	0.03	1.5
Carver Fanmaster	4.2 (slow) to 8.3	1.5 (max speed)
Water Pump		2 to 3
Fluorescent Lighting		0.5 to 1.5
Spot Lighting		0.8 to 1.75
TV Antenna		negligible
Powered Jockey Wheel		25 (running)
500 kg Electric Winch (500 lb load)		50 (typically)
Cassette Toilet Flush		2.3 max
Car Type Vacuum Cleaner		6 (typically)

PERIODIC INSPECTION: Preferably not less than once in every three years and more frequently if the vehicle is used more than normal average mileage, for such vehicles the caravan electrical installation and supply cable should be inspected and tested and a report on their condition obtained as prescribed in the Regulations for Electrical Installations published by the Institute of Electrical Engineers.

POWER CONSUMPTION LIMITS: Most Caravan Club Sites, for instance, have a pitch allocation of 16 Amperes, but always check the limit at whichever site you use.

INSIDE INFORMATION: You can calculate the capacity of equipment by using the formula: Amps equals Watts divided by Volts. Therefore, if you have a 2 kilowatt (2,000 watt) kettle, and a 240 volt supply, when you divide 2,000 by 240, you can see that you will be using up 8.4 of your 'allocation' of amps to boil up for a cup of tea - but you really should use a non-domestic low-wattage kettle.

SAFETY FIRST!
Also remember to ensure that you don't overload any of the circuits within your caravan. Have your caravan's electrical system and supply cable checked by a qualified electrician at least every two years, and carry out a visual check yourself far more frequently than that. See Chapter 5, Servicing and Maintenance.

The Refrigerator

Modern caravan fridges can be powered by any one of three supplies - 12-volt electricity, 240-volt electricity or gas. The 12-volt supply will come via the 12S cable from the car and should only be used when the outfit is on the move. Otherwise the fridge will run the car's battery down in less than an hour. 240-volt is generally used when a power supply is available on site.

Before setting out on a journey, it is best to start on gas to get the fridge down to an operating temperature before turning over to electricity, because keeping the temperature low takes less energy than getting it there in the first place.

Turn the power supply switch to gas and make sure that, if there's a voltage selector switch, it is set to '0'.

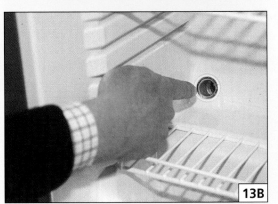
13A

13A. Then turn the gas supply knob to its highest setting and push it inwards towards the fridge. While it's being held in, press in the ignition button four or five times in quick succession.

13B

13B. As you're doing this look for the pilot light through a viewing glass usually in the bottom corner of the fridge. When this is alight, continue to hold the gas control knob down for a further 10 to 15 seconds and then release.

13C. To change the fridge over to mains 240-volt operation, turn the gas supply knob to '0' and select the mains voltage switch. In this case it's next to the transformer, beneath one of the beds. Check your handbook. Then turn the thermostat knob to the desired setting.

Caravan Heaters

There are two main types of heaters in a caravan, the variety incorporating a flue and the catalytic variety. Of the flued type, the most common by far are the Carver Trumatic 1800, 2000, 3000 and 5000 models.

A clear description of the Carver Trumatic heaters is given in the ABI Caravans Owners' Handbook. It explains that the heaters are completely room-sealed units based on a well proven and extremely efficient heat exchanger consisting of a pair of internally and externally fitted aluminium die castings.

The gas burner is situated at the bottom of a vertical passage which permits complete combustion of the gas before meeting the exchanger surfaces. The combustion products travel along the top horizontal section and then downwards through further galleries while transferring their heat to the caravan. They are kept moving by the thermal drive of the rising column of hot gases from the flame.

13C

ON SITE

The flue outlet of the heater is at the bottom of the heat exchanger ensuring that the majority of the heat is extracted from the combustion products before they leave the heat exchanger. The combustion path is completely sealed from the living space, all the air for combustion discharged through the adjacent flue.

Control and adjustment of the heater is by the gas control knob mounted on the top of the heater. Incorporated in the gas control is a flame failure device, so that if for any reason the burner flame is extinguished, the heater will automatically go to fail safe. Ignition is by piezo spark operated by pressing the ignition button mounted adjacent to the gas control knob.

All three have underfloor flues and, as a result, require unrestricted ventilation beneath the caravan. To allow the heater to work efficiently and safely it is essential that at least three sides of the vehicle must be open at one time. If the sides get blocked up by, for example, the build-up of snow, the heater shouldn't be used until the obstruction is cleared.

Using a Flued Heater

14A

14A. To switch on a caravan's standard gas heater, first make sure that the gas supply is turned on. Then turn the heater's thermostat control fully anti-clockwise and push the knob right in. While doing this, press the igniter switch several times.

14B. Keeping the thermostat depressed, look for the pilot light through the viewing hole near the heater's base. When the pilot light is visible, keep the thermostat held down for about 30 seconds and then release. The heater should now stay alight and can be adjusted to the desired heat setting.

To turn the heater off simply turn the thermostat to the 'Off' or 'O' position.

Using a Catalytic Heater

14B

14C. A cheaper, although much less efficient, alternative to the flued heaters fitted to most caravans is the catalytic variety. These differ from the Carver type of heater in that they don't require a vent for exhaust gases. Instead catalytic heaters are designed to burn off their own exhaust gases. However, if your caravan has one of these catalytic type of heaters fitted it is still strongly advised that the caravan is well ventilated whenever the heater is in use.

Blown Air Central Heating

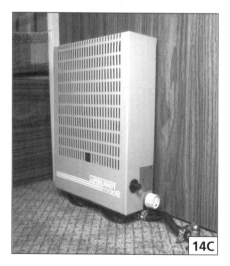
14C

Two common ways of uprating a caravan's heating are through the addition of blown air central heating and a Fanmaster device. Both of these are available either as standard equipment on newer and better equipped caravans or as kits to be fitted to older or more basic caravans.

Blown air central heating refers to an 12-volt electric fan system that can be fitted to the back of some caravan heaters and blows the heat through ducting out of vents situated throughout the caravan. There are two types of blown air central heating, the Senior and Junior systems.

The Junior fan is designed for use in smaller caravans. When combined with an 1800, 2000 or 3000 heater it provides an effective way of introducing blown air heating. A 12-volt distribution fan operates at two selectable speed settings. The Junior Fan can be operated while the heater is in operation or, on hot summer days, the fan can circulate air around the caravan. The Junior Fan is also very quiet on slow speed.

The Senior Fan incorporates a more powerful fan and is suited to larger caravans fitted with 3000 or 5000 heaters. The Senior Fan has two control options; 'Auto Fan' and 'Manual Fan'. Auto Fan monitors the temperature output of a gas heater and adjusts its speed accordingly, so that constant warm air is distributed around your caravan. Manual control allows you to set the speed of the fan, making it ideal for night-time use or in the summer for cool air distribution.

To operate the blown air heating, locate the 'Truma vent' control switch consisting off a circular thermostat control and a three-position switch. Leaving the switch in the 'O' position will turn the fan off. Putting the switch in the '.' position allows the fan to circulate cold air. The 'A' position, meanwhile, is automatic speed control which increases the speed of the fan as the thermostat control is turned to higher settings and decreases the speed of the fan as the thermostat control is turned to lower settings.

The Fanmaster System

15A

15B

15A. At the top end of the blown air heating range is the Fanmaster. Suitable for all caravans, it is compatible with Carver 1800, 2000 and 3000 heaters. It has a 230-volt AC heating element and a 12-volt DC distribution fan, giving blown air heating from the electric heating element or the on board heater. Alternatively, in the summer the fan may be operated without any heat input to distribute cool air around the caravan.

The Fanmaster is operated by a remote, wall-mounted control panel. When using electric heating the caravan temperature is regulated by the thermostat on the control panel but when using gas heating the temperature is regulated by the gas heater thermostat.

15B. The control panel contains a thermostat, 'On/Select' button, 'Off' button and five lights to show which mode is selected.

To turn the Fanmaster on press the 'On/Select' button once and the mode indicator light will show 'mode 1' selected, flash for a few seconds and then remain steady.

Pressing the 'On/Select' button further will select modes from 1 to 2 to 3 to 4 to 5 and then back to 1 again.

The thermostat on the control panel only operates when electric heating is selected. Movement clockwise increases the selected temperature. To switch the Fanmaster off, simply press the 'Off' button once.

As for the mode settings, different modes have different effects on the output of the heater. 'Gas Auto Fan Mode 1' distributes the heat produced by the gas heater and is controlled by the heater's thermostat. The Fanmaster speed tracks the temperature of the air being drawn into it from the heater. When the temperature is high the Fanmaster runs fast to distribute the heat around the caravan.

When the caravan temperature approaches the comfort level set on the heater thermostat, the gas input to the heater is reduced and the Fanmaster slows down to avoid producing cool draughts. When the heater thermostat then calls for more heat, the gas input to the heater increases, the air being drawn into the Fanmaster gets hotter and the fan speed rises to match it.

This mode may be used without a mains electric hook-up.

When 'Gas Slow Fan Mode 2' is selected the Fanmaster runs continuously at a low speed to distribute the heat from the heater.

In 'Fan Mode 3' the Fanmaster runs continuously at maximum speed. This can be used to maintain maximum air circulation whilst heating on gas only, or to circulate air without heating in the summer. When set at 'Electric Auto Fan Mode 4', the Fanmaster runs at maximum speed with the integral 2kW electric element operating. When the comfort level set on the Fanmaster control is achieved the electrical input is reduced to 1kW and the fan speed is reduced. If the temperature continues to rise the element is switched off but the fan continues to run at a slow speed. A drop in temperature will reverse the sequence.

A mains hook-up is needed for this mode and the maximum current will be approximately 8 Amps.

Finally, 'Electric Slow Fan Mode 5' means the Fanmaster runs continuously at low speed and the 1kW element is in operation. When the comfort level set on the Fanmaster control is achieved the element is switched off but the fan continues to run.

It is not recommended that electric and gas heating is used simultaneously with the Fanmaster system.

NOTE: For details of fitting blown air heating and the Fanmaster system to a caravan, see *Chapter 6, Improving Your Caravan.*

SAFETY FIRST!
i) Never block or cover the vents and grills at the top of the heater or outside the caravan. ii) Never leave the heater switched on when the caravan is on the move. iii) When children are in the caravan, position a safety guard around the heater at all times. iv) To prevent over heating of the Fanmaster system, at least one warm air outlet must be open at all times.

Water Heaters

For caravans with a water heater fitted as standard equipment, there are several different types such as the Carver Cascade 2, Carver Cascade 2 GE and the Maxol Malaga, which runs on gas or gas and electricity. The Cascade 2 uses gas to heat the water while the Cascade 2 GE uses either gas or mains electricity, or a combination of the two. Before using either, the relevant caravan taps should be turned on so as to fill the water tank.

Switching the Cascade 2 on is a simple matter of sliding the control knob down from the 'off' position to the 'on' position. If the heater is working satisfactorily a green light will come on. If, instead, the green and yellow lights come on together then there is a fault with the caravan's 12-volt supply and the battery will probably need charging. The heater will automatically switch itself off until the voltage is high enough.

If the green and red light come on the heater has either failed to ignite or has gone to safety shut down. This is usually due to failure of the gas supply or air in the gas system. If this occurs, switch the heater off and wait three minutes before trying again. If the problem is air in the gas system, it might take several attempts to light the heater.

If a caravan is equipped with the Cascade 2 GE heater, operation is basically the same although with one main differences. If using gas alone, follow the same procedure as the Cascade 2 heater. If using mains electricity, simply switch on the isolation switch. This will show a red light if the heater is working.

Using gas alone, the Cascade will take about 20 minutes to heat up a tank of water. This will increase to around one hour if using mains electricity alone. A combination of gas and electric will cut the time to about 15 minutes. It is generally recommended to initially heat the water with gas and then use the electricity only to keep the water up to temperature during the rest of the day.

A number of less common 240-volt water heaters are available to be fitted to caravans. These are generally operated through a simple on/off switch and adjustable thermostat. However, this type of water heater obviously requires a site with a sufficient mains electrical power supply.

INSIDE INFORMATION: Using a caravan's Fanmaster system and mains electric water heater at the same time will sometimes be too much for many site electricity supplies and may cause the supply to cut-out. Check with the staff on site, when you arrive, and where necessary, try not to use both appliances at the same time.

SAFETY FIRST!
Both the Cascade 2 and Cascade 2 GE must be switched off when the caravan is in motion.

Cooking Equipment

The gas cooking equipment in a caravan's kitchen works in very much the same way as that in most homes. But if your house is "all electric", here goes...

16A. When using a lighted match (or an igniter, as shown) to ignite a burner, put the match in position next to the burner before turning on the gas.

Then, depress the gas control before turning it anti-clockwise to the 'full' position. Hold down for five seconds, **with the gas alight** to allow the flame failure device to warm up. See 16B.

To turn the burner off, simply turn the tap clockwise until it won't go any further.

16A

For caravans fitted with automatic ignition, hold the ignition button down and then turn and hold down the gas control into the fully 'on' position as before. After the burner has lit, continue to hold the gas control down for 20 seconds. If there's no spark, check to see if the battery needs replacing.

SAFETY FIRST!
The hob, grill and oven must be turned off when the caravan is in motion.

Flame Failure Device

16B. All caravans built since 1994, and most high-spec models since 1992 will have flame failure devices fitted to all gas appliances. This will automatically turn off the gas supply should any of the cooking flames or pilot lights go out.

16B

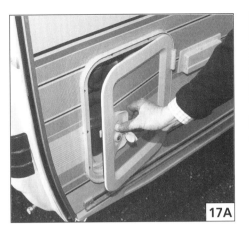

17A

17B

Cassette Toilet

Many caravans are now fitted with cassette toilets, so that you don't need to rely on site facilities, and the most common models are those produced by Thetford. The cassette toilet is a permanently fitted design which operates much like a domestic toilet, although generally with a turning flush knob rather than a push down lever.

17C

17A. To prepare the toilet for use, you have to go outside the caravan and open up the access hatch, generally found to the rear of the offside wall.

17B. Fill the toilet's water tank through a filler that folds out from the toilet compartment. This usually holds ten litres of water and should always be empty when the caravan is on the move.

17D

17C. A 'rinse' chemical should also be added at this stage. On some models fitted with an electric flush facility, a level indicator shows when enough water has been added.

17D. Next, remove the cassette, by releasing a large retaining clip at its base.

ON SITE

17E. Pull the cassette out of its compartment, stand the cassette on its end and add the required amount of toilet chemical, plus water, through the fold-out spout on the side of the cassette. A number of different type of toilet chemicals are available, plus a selection of powders which can also be used. Be sure to follow the instructions as different types will require different amounts to be added.

Put the top back on the spout and replace the cassette.

SAFETY FIRST!
Keep all toilet chemicals out of the reach of small children. It's advisable to wear protective gloves when using the fluid and if any gets into contact with your eyes, wash them immediately with cold water and seek medical advice.

17F. Before using the toilet it's a good idea to add a small amount of water to the bowl by pressing down the flush knob. To flush the toilet, press the flush knob down and turn it in an anti-clockwise direction.

17G. The cassette has a 20 litre capacity. A level indicator on the side of the toilet changes from green to red when the waste tank is full and requires emptying. As soon as this happens the cassette should be emptied. On no account should the cassette be allowed to become overfilled.

To empty the cassette simply open up the access hatch as already shown, release the retaining clip and take out the cassette.

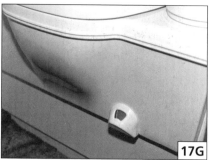

17H. Take the cassette to a specified cassette toilet disposal point and remove the spout cap. Next depress the air release valve button and empty the contents.

17I. As the cassettes can be quite heavy when full, there are a number of trolleys on the market to help you transport the cassettes from the caravan to the waste disposal point.

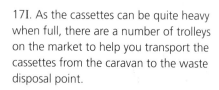

Sleeping Arrangements

While not considered as 'technical' equipment, constructing the caravan's bedding in the correct manner is essential for a good night's sleep. Making the main front seating area up into a double bed will either mean using the table top as a bed base to make up the gap between the two seating areas, or utilising the slatted bed base.

When the table top is used it will sit along narrow shelves situated on the edge of the bed bases. However, when using the table top as a bed base the problem of a build-up of condensation often occurs. This can be dealt with in one of two ways.

18A

Firstly, put a thick towel between the table top and the cushioning above to soak up any condensation. The second way is to use a slatted bed base.

18A. Most caravans today are fitted with slatted bed bases as standard. They are generally stored at the front of the caravan either beneath the seating or within the base of a chest of drawers.

18B. To use a slatted bed base, simply grasp the front rail and pull the assembly out along the holding rails until it is fully extended.

Slatted bed bases not only cure the problem of condensation but also generally offer better support for your back when in bed.

When using the caravan's seating cushions as mattresses, it is generally recommended to turn them upside down. This helps create a more even sleeping surface and saves wear on the upper fabric.

18B

18C. When a caravan is fitted with bunks, care should always be taken to follow the manufacturer's instructions to the letter of the law when constructing these. Also be careful to check the bunk's weight limit to make sure that it is capable of taking the weight of its occupant.

The Superpitch

19. An improved alternative to the usual pitching procedure for a caravan on site has become available over recent years. Superpitch is a system fitted to a number of new caravans that allows them to have all their services, gas, electricity, water and the cassette toilet, plus the option of satellite television and even a telephone line, connected up to their caravan through a single service point.

In order to work, the Superpitch requires the caravan to be placed on a specially developed pitch, and at present these are in relatively short supply. However, they are slowly increasing in popularity. For use on standard pitches, adaptors are available so that caravans with Superpitch facilities can be used as usual.

18C

19

Caravanning On The Continent

OVERSEAS REVERSED POLARITY: When caravanning on the continent, extra care should be taken when using mains electric hook-up points as the supply may be of reversed polarity. What this means is that the live and neutral wires may be reversed resulting in electrical equipment on board the caravan not being completely isolated when turned off.

The safest way to check for reversed polarity is to buy a simple tester, available from most caravan accessory shops. This simply plugs into any of the caravan's 240-volt sockets and shows whether the electrical input is of reversed or standard polarity.

If the input is of reversed polarity then you can either disconnect the supply and swap over the two wires in the caravan's inlet cable or use a polarity adaptor, available from most caravan accessory shops, between the site supply and caravan inlet cable. In either case, be sure to recheck the polarity when you move to a different site.

Caravans built since 1993 with mains electricity as standard have a double pole consumer unit fitted. In this case there is no problem with site electrical hook-ups which supply a reversed polarity feed.

20. **GAS CYLINDERS:** Another problem with caravanning on the continent is that the Calor type gas cylinders commonly used in Britain are not generally available. As an alternative, it is recommended to carry a Camping Gaz cylinder, either in addition or in place of the standard cylinders as it is readily available across the Continent. However, Camping Gaz cylinders require a different type of regulator to either standard propane or butane cylinders, so it is imperative that one of these is carried as well.

20

PART V: WINTER CARAVANNING

21. Time was when the on-set of winter meant that caravans were tucked away until the spring sunshine made it worthwhile coming out again. These days though, thanks to improved insulation, double-glazing and heating, many modern caravans are built for year-round touring. As a result, winter now presents two options.

Either follow the old ways and store your caravan away for the winter or get your full money's worth out of your purchase and continue caravanning through even the coldest spells. So, for those caravanners with a slightly more hardy disposition or who are looking to get the most out of their caravan, there are a number of steps to preparing your caravan for winter use.

As butane will freeze when the temperatures drop below 0 degrees centigrade, make sure that you change the caravan's gas supply over to propane. This will also necessitate changing the gas regulator. See Illustration No. 2.

If the water pipes run underneath the caravan where they'll be open to the elements, be sure to lag them to stop them freezing, cracking and causing leaks. You can buy suitable lagging material from some caravan accessory shops and most DIY outlets.

21

In order for a caravan's fridge to work effectively during cold weather it is necessary to fit covers over the vents. Electrolux market custom-made vent covers, available from caravan accessory shops. It is inadvisable to use home-made versions.

SAFETY FIRST!
UNDER NO CIRCUMSTANCES should the vents to the gas room heater or water heater be covered or blocked as this might cause potentially lethal carbon monoxide fumes to enter the caravan.

With the heating turned on and the windows kept tightly shut to keep out drafts, there's a good chance that condensation will start to build up, especially in an older caravan. To counter this, try to keep the roof-light open for short periods of time. Also, place towels beneath the windows to stop condensation dripping on to the upholstery.

While modern, high-spec caravans often have the benefit of improved heating equipment, older and more basic caravans generally have to make do with a basic space heater. However, it's not a difficult job to uprate these and for details on how to carry out the job, refer to *Chapter 6, Improving Your Caravan.*

Finally, make sure in advance that any sites you're planning to visit over the winter are open. Not all sites remain open all-year round and even some of those that do only have a limited number of pitches available for winter use.

PART VI: LEGAL & RECOMMENDED REQUIREMENTS

Please also check your Highway Code for any legal requirements or developments not mentioned below.

i) Driving licence
Although a special licence isn't required for towing a standard caravan, provisional licence holders are not legally permitted to tow a caravan.

ii) Speed limits
When towing a caravan you are restricted to a maximum speed of 60mph on motorways and dual carriageways, and 50mph anywhere else, unless there's a lower speed limit.

iii) Motorways
Caravans should not be towed in the outside lane of a three or four lane motorway, unless you're instructed to do so as the result of roadworks or an accident on the inside lanes.

iv) Number plate
A caravan must carry a number plate bearing the number of the towing vehicle and be illuminated at night.

v) Parking
Open land up to 15 yards from the highway is technically part of the highway. It is an offence to drive more than this distance on to any common and caravanning on many commons is expressly forbidden.

With the exception of motorways, parking on a roadside verge within 15 yards of the road is not an offence, though if it causes an obstruction the police can bring a prosecution.

A lay-by is part of the highway and a caravanner stopping overnight may be prosecuted for obstruction.

vi) The MOT Test
Although it isn't a legal requirement for your caravan to go through an annual inspection, (there is no statutory 'MOT' test for caravans), regular servicing is highly recommended

vii) Towing mirrors
You must be able to see the road behind the caravan. If the rear view through the caravan windows is inadequate, the law states that you must fit an additional mirror to the offside of the towing vehicle. However, it is also recommended that an extension mirror is also fitted to the nearside.

Any extension mirror must not project more than 200mm outside the width of the caravan when being towed or the width of the towing vehicle when driven solo.

viii) Weights
It is strongly recommended that the laden weight of your caravan doesn't excess 85% of your towcar's kerbweight. With some towcars, the manufacturer's towing limit may actually be lower than the 85% limit. In this case do not exceed the lower figure. If you do, you may well invalidate your towcar's warranty. Towing a badly loaded or overloaded caravan is against the law.

ix) Gas
Your caravan's gas supply should be turned off when the vehicle is on the road. It is also advisable to clearly mark on the exterior of your caravan both where the gas is stored and what type of gas it is (i.e. L.P.G.). This information could be crucial to the emergency services in the event of an accident.

x) Passengers
Passengers may not travel in a caravan under any circumstances, unless they are authorised test personnel working on behalf of a dealer or manufacturer.

xi) TV licences
TVs used in a caravan are covered by the users domestic licence, as long as they are not permanently installed.

CHAPTER 4 - TOOLS & EQUIPMENT

SAFETY FIRST!
There are, of course, important safety implications when working underneath any vehicle or trailer. Sadly, many DIY enthusiasts have been killed or seriously injured when maintaining their pride and joy, usually for the want of a few moments' thought. So - THINK SAFETY! In particular, NEVER venture beneath any vehicle or caravan supported only by a jack - of ANY type. A jack is ONLY intended to be a means of lifting a caravan or vehicle, NOT for holding it 'airborne' while being worked on.

Basic maintenance on any caravan can be carried out using a fairly simple, relatively inexpensive tool kit. There is no need to spend a fortune all at once - most owners who do their own servicing acquire their implements over a long period of time. However, there are some items you simply cannot do without in order to properly carry out the work necessary to keep your caravan in good condition. Therefore, in the following lists, we have concentrated on those items which are likely to be valuable aids to maintaining your caravan and in addition we have featured some of the tools that are 'nice-to-have' rather than 'must have' because as your tool chest grows, there are some tools that help to make servicing just that bit easier and more thorough to carry out.

Two vital points - firstly always buy the best quality tools you can afford. 'Cheap and cheerful' items may look similar to more expensive implements, but experience shows that they often fail when the going gets tough, and some can even be dangerous. And take care to look after your tools. Cleaning them after use and only using them for the job they have been designed for can mean that your tools will last for years. With proper care, good quality tools will last a lifetime, and can be regarded as an investment. The extra outlay is well worth it, in the long run.

The following lists are shown under headings indicating the type of use applicable to each group of tools and equipment.

Lifting:

It is inevitable that you will need to raise your caravan from the ground in order to gain access to the underside of it. However, remember that a manufacturer's jack is for emergency wheel changing ONLY and must NOT to be used as the sole means of support when working on or under the caravan. Often, a manufacturer will recommend a particular type of jack and a recommended jacking point in its owners' handbook. In this case, use only the manufacturer's recommended jack and jacking point. Where no such advice is given then it's a matter of you deciding which jack is most suitable for your caravan.

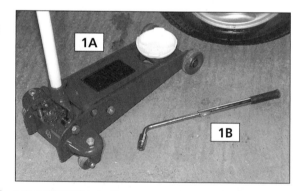

SAFETY FIRST!
i) NEVER, NEVER use bricks to support a caravan or car - they can crumble without warning, with horrifying results. Always chock both sides of the wheel or wheels not in the air, to prevent the caravan from rolling. ii) Make sure that the ground on which your jack and axle stands are placed is not so soft that they can tip. Always place a substantial plank beneath the jack and each axle stand to give it a firm base, and also lower all of the corner steadies to give yourself some extra protection, before going beneath the caravan.

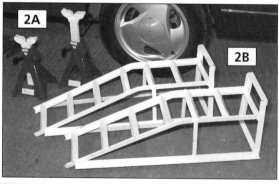

Thanks are due to Kamasa Tools for their kind assistance with this chapter.
Almost all of the tools shown here were kindly supplied by them.

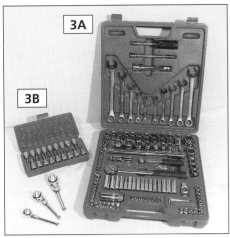

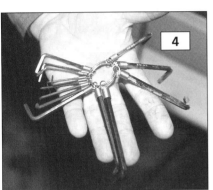

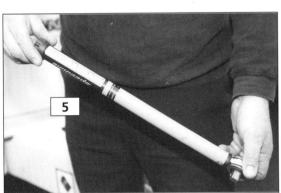

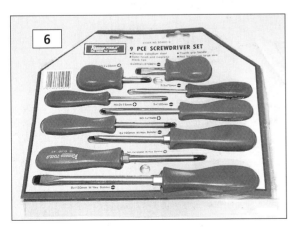

We strongly recommend that you invest in a good quality trolley jack, such as the Kamasa 2 1/4 ton unit shown here (1.A) while an excellent 'nice-to-have' is this extendible wheel nut spanner from the same company (1.B). This is also ideal for carrying in the car in case of punctures. If you've ever tried removing a wheel nut tightened by a garage gorilla, you'll know why this tool is so good!

Having raised the caravan from the ground, always support it under the axle, as near to the chassis as possible. Use only proper axle stands (2.A), intended for the purpose, with a solid wooden block on top, if necessary, to spread the load. These Kamasa stands are exceptionally strong and are very rapidly adjusted, using the built-in ratchet stops. Screw-type stands have an infinite amount of adjustments but are fiddly and time-consuming to use.

Frankly, car ramps are of no use when it comes to working on your caravan, but if you're also intending to work on your car and you don't need to remove the road wheels for a particular job, the use of car ramps (2.B) - generally more stable than axle stands - will provide the most stable supports of all.

In conclusion, here's a few more words on using and choosing jacks and supports.

Jacks: 'Bottle' jack - screw or hydraulic types - can be used as a means of lifting the caravan, in conjunction with axle stands to hold it clear of the ground. Ensure that the jack you buy is actually capable of locating securely on the caravan's axle without slipping.

Trolley jack - extremely useful, as it is so easily manoeuvrable, it will lift your caravan quickly, and the head provides a good, wide location point. Again, use only for lifting the caravan, in conjunction with axle stands to support it clear of the ground. Aim for the highest quality jack you can afford. Cheap types seldom last long, and can be VERY dangerous (suddenly allowing a car or caravan to drop to ground level, without warning, for example).

Axle Stands: Available in a range of sizes. Ensure that those you buy are sturdy, with the three legs reasonably widely spaced, and with a useful range of height adjustment.

Spanners:
INSIDE INFORMATION: Thread types vary enormously - and can even vary on the same caravan, although nowadays, almost all are metric. So, for most jobs, spanners in metric sizes, measured across the flats of the spanner in millimetres, will be required, with some items requiring the use of 'odd' spanner sizes, for which a good quality adjustable spanner will usually do the trick.

This Kamasa spanner set (3.A) is very unusual in that it includes many different types of spanner size in the same set. There are also 'stubby' ratchet handles available (3.B) for that cramped area where a normal ratchet just won't fit!

Note - in every case, ring spanners provide a more positive grip on a nut/bolt head than open-ended types, which can spread and/or slip when used on tight fasteners. Similarly, 'impact' type socket spanners with hexagonal apertures give better grip on a tight fastener than the normal 12 point 'bi-hex' variety.

You'll also need a number of other tools:
You'll need at least one adjustable spanner (9.A) - nine inch, to start off with (9.A) and an Allen key set. (4)
Torque wrench. This is a 'must-have' item for caravan owners and for any serious mechanic, (5). Prevents overtightening and shearing and stops caravan nuts and studs from being over - or under - tightened.

Screwdrivers: General-purpose set of cross-head variety and set of flat-bladed variety. (All available in various-sized sets.) (6)
Impact driver, useful for releasing seized screws. (7.A)

Sundry Items:
Tool box - steel types are sturdiest.

TOOLS & EQUIPMENT

Extension lead.

Small/medium size ball pein hammer this one part of the huge Kamasa range. (8.A)

Soft-faced hammer (available here, from Kamasa Tools, as a set). (8.B)

Copper-based anti-seize compound - useful during assembly of threaded components, to make future dismantling easier!

Grease gun.

Oil can (with 15W/50 multigrade oil, for general purpose lubrication).

Water dispellant 'electrical' aerosol spray.

Pair of pliers ('standard' jaw). (9.B)

Pair of 'long-nosed' pliers. (9.C)

Pair of 'side cutters'. (9.D)

Kamasa also sell pliers in sets, as this shoal indicates. (9.E)

Self-grip wrench or - preferably - set of three. (9.F)

Junior hacksaw.

Stud removing tools. A 'nice-to-have' when studs shear and all else fails. (7.B)

Tyre pump.

Tyre tread depth gauge.

Tyre pressure gauge.

Drifts - a set is an extremely useful 'nice-to-have'. (8.C)

Hub pullers, useful when you go beyond the straightforward servicing stage and could be necessary for some types of hub assembly. (7.C)

Electric drill. Not a servicing tool as such but a 'must-have' nevertheless. The Kamasa rechargeable drill (10) is superb, enabling you to reach tight spots without trailing leads - and much safer out of doors. Recommended!

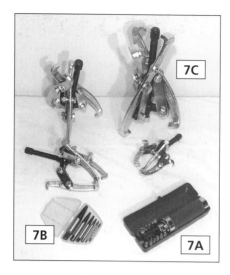

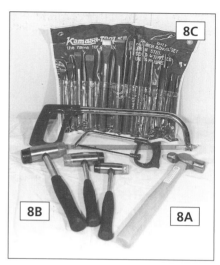

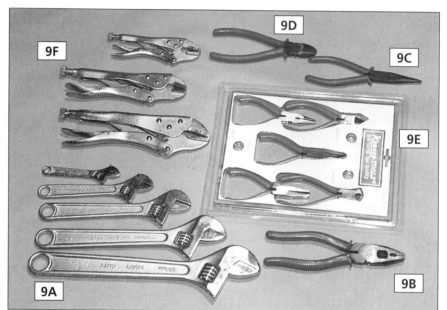

While it is doubtful that you will carry a full toolkit with you at all times when you are away in your caravan, it is recommended that you carry a selection of general tools, just in case you need to carry out 'on-site' maintenance.

Conversion Tables

When working on a caravan it is often useful to be able to convert data from one form to another, for example, from Imperial to Metric measurements. To help you, here is a list of useful conversion formulae and equations.

Inches to centimetres - multiply by 2.54

Centimetres to inches - multiply by 0.3937

Feet to metres - multiply by 0.3048

Metres to feet - multiply by 3.281

Pounds to kilograms - multiply by 0.4536 Kilograms to pounds - multiply by 2.205

Pounds to hundredweight - multiply by 112

Nm to Lbs.ft - multiply by 0.737

Amps = Watts divided by Volts

Volts = Watts divided by Amps

Watts = Amps multiplied by Volts

INSIDE INFORMATION: With all the calculations you may have to carry out, especially in connection with weight loading and electrical loading, to say nothing of the conversion tables mentioned here, you should consider adding a small pocket calculator to your travelling tool kit.

CHAPTER 5
SERVICING & MAINTENANCE

It's not only cars that need regular maintenance, caravans also need regular servicing if they are to operate efficiently and dependably over a number of years. There are hundreds of examples of caravans up to several decades old that have survived regular usage thanks to the efforts of their owners in keeping their caravans in good condition. Unfortunately, there are also many instances of caravans that have been poorly cared for, lasting only a fraction of their true potential lifespans.

Everyone wants to own a caravan that 'works' properly and lasts longer than the average. And there's no magic about how to put yours into that category; it's all a question of thorough maintenance! If you follow the Service Jobs listed here - or have a specialist workshop or mechanic do it for you - you can almost *guarantee* that your caravan will still be going strong when others have fallen by the wayside. This Service Schedule is just about as thorough as you can get; it's an amalgam of the maker's recommended service items plus all the 'INSIDE INFORMATION' from the experts that we could find. If you want your caravan to be as well looked after as possible, you'll follow the Jobs shown here, but if you don't want to go all the way, you can pick and choose from the most essential items in the list. But do bear in mind that *preventative maintenance* figures very high on our list of priorities. And that's why many of our service jobs have the word "Check..." near the start!

USING THE SERVICE SCHEDULES

At the start of each Service Job, you'll see a heading in bold type, looking a bit like this:

☐ **Job 14. Check indicator warning.**

Following the heading will be all the information you will need to enable you to carry out that particular Job. Please note that exactly the same Job number and heading will be found in *Appendix 4, Service History*, where you will want to keep a full record of all the work you have carried out. After you have finished servicing your caravan, you will be able to tick off all of the jobs that you have completed and so, service by service, build up a complete Service History of work carried out on your caravan.

You will also find other key information immediately after each Job title and in most cases, there will be reference to an illustration - a photograph or line drawing, whichever is easier for you to follow - on the same page. Where we feel that a little background information will make it easier to carry out the work, we include a box of **FACT FILE** information, relevant to the job in hand.

If the Job shown only applies to certain caravans, the Job title will be followed by a description of the type of system to which the Job title applies. For instance, where Job 39 applies to AL-KO TYPE BRAKES ONLY, the text in capitals tells you so.

Other special headings are also used. One reads *INSIDE INFORMATION.* This tells you that here is a Job or a special tip

that you wouldn't normally get to hear about, other than through the experience and 'inside' knowledge of the experts, such as those at The Caravan Club and The Camping and Caravanning Club, and others, who have helped in compiling this Service Guide.

Another is **SPECIALIST SERVICE**, which means that we recommend you to have this work carried out by a specialist. Prime examples of this are the gas appliances fitted in a caravan. There may be other areas about which you don't feel competent and in those cases, once again, leave it to the experts. Where we think you are better off having the work done for you, we say so! But if you decide to 'have a go', with the help of this book, but want to be sure that your work has been carried out correctly, have a qualified engineer check your work over for you, perhaps at your home or wherever it is that you store the caravan, before using it on the road or on site.

It is also important that you take your caravan along to an approved dealer once a year to get it fully checked over, especially important in case any safety recalls have been issued. When you're doing this it's also recommended that you mention to the dealer any work that you might have carried out on the caravan that you're not too sure about. However, there are still a large number of service procedures that a caravanner should be able to carry out quite competently on his or her own caravan - and that is exactly where this book comes in.

SAFETY FIRST!
This special heading is the one that could be the most important one of all! SAFETY FIRST! information must always be read with care and always taken seriously. In addition, please read the whole of Chapter 1, Safety First! before carrying out any work on your caravan. There are a number of hazards associated with working on a caravan but all of them can be avoided by adhering strictly to the safety rules. Don't skimp on safety!

The 'Catch-up' Service

When you first buy a used caravan, you never know for sure just how well it's been looked after. So, if you want to catch-up on all the servicing that may have been neglected on your caravan, just work through the entire list of Service Jobs listed here, and your caravan will be bang up to date and serviced as well as you could hope for. Do allow several days for all of this work, not least because it will almost certainly throw up a number of extra jobs - potential faults that have been lurking beneath the surface - all of which will need putting right before you can 'sign off' your caravan as being in tip-top condition.

The Service History

Until now, it hasn't been possible for the owner of an older caravan to keep a formal record of servicing but now you can, using the complete tick list in *Appendix 4, Service History.* In fact, there's the extra bonus that there is space for you to keep a record of all of those extra items that crop up from time to time. New and replacement parts; extra accessories: where can you normally keep a record of those? Now you can, so if your battery goes down only 11 months after buying it, you'll be able to look up where and when you bought it. All you'll have to do is remember to fill in your Service Schedule in the first place!

Raising a Caravan Safely!
When working on various areas of a caravan you will find that it's often necessary to jack the caravan up. It is essential that you follow the correct procedure for this and use the recommended tools. It is also advisable that, whenever working under a caravan, you make sure that somebody nearby knows what you're doing so that they can regularly check on you to make sure that everything's OK.

I. Make sure that the caravan is on firm and level ground.

II. Apply the caravan's handbrake. If you're carrying out work on the brakes or wheels, however, it might well be necessary to release the handbrake. In this case, be sure to chock the wheel that's not being raised off the ground.

III. Lower the caravan's corner steadies on the side that is going to be raised. DO NOT use the corner steadies to raise the caravan.

IV. Place an axle stand under the axle. DO NOT rely instead on bricks or odd pieces of wood as these have a potentially hazardous habit of crumbling and giving way at a crucial moment.

V. If the caravan has its own jacking point, use that to raise the caravan. If not place a jack under the caravan's axle, as close to the chassis as possible and raise the caravan. Note the plywood pad beneath the foot of this jack.

INSIDE INFORMATION: Use a jack made for caravan use: it will fit the axle tube profile. (Illustration, courtesy AL-KO Kober Ltd)

VI. With some caravans, you are able to jack or support the caravan beneath clearly visible axle-to-chassis mounting points. NEVER jack beneath the centre of the axle: you could easily distort it. (Illustration, courtesy Knott.)

VII. Further lower the corner steadies on the raised side of the caravan so that they just touch the ground.

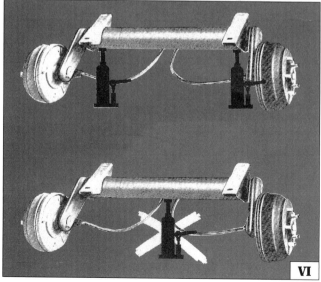

Changing a Wheel

It can happen at any time and for a variety of reasons so it's always useful to know the correct procedure for changing a wheel on a caravan. It might be that the tyre has suffered a puncture or simply deteriorated as a result of being stored too long in the sun. Either way, using the correct equipment and procedure is essential.

As with a car, it is recommended that you always carry a suitable spare wheel and jack in your caravan in case of punctures or wheel damage.

When faced with having to change a caravan's wheel, try to get the caravan as far away from other road traffic as possible, giving yourself as much room to work safely as possible. A ruined tyre is worth a lot less than a ruined life! Also don't forget to use some sort of warning device, such as a reflective triangle, so that other motorists are aware in advance that there's a hazard further up the road.

If, however, you're in a position where carrying out any roadside work on the caravan would be a dangerous act, use the safer alternative and call in the likes of the AA and RAC. If possible though, don't be tempted to leave the caravan unattended at the roadside while you go off for help.

IV

VIII

To change the wheel on a caravan -

I. Ensure that the caravan's handbrake is fully applied. If the outfit is parked at the roadside, it is also advisable to leave the car and caravan hitched up.

II. Lower the jockey wheel so that it can take some of the caravan's weight when the wheel is being removed.

III. Chock the wheel on the opposite side of the caravan to the one that you are intending to change.

IV. Using a wheel brace, just slacken off the tightness, but do not undo any further, the wheel nuts of the wheel to be changed. If you try to do so after the wheel has been raised, the wheel will turn instead of the nut.

V. Position a caravan jack either at the caravan's specified jacking point (details of this will be in the owners' handbook) or along the caravan's axle, as close to the chassis as possible. Raise the jack sufficiently to allow the wheel to be removed.

INSIDE INFORMATION: If there isn't room to get the jack under the caravan because of a flat tyre, drive the afflicted tyre carefully up one of your levelling ramps.

VI. Lower the caravan's corner steadies on the same side only as the wheel that you are about to remove. Under no circumstances should you attempt to use the corner steadies to jack up the caravan. If you have them, it's also strongly advisable to place axle stands under the caravan. Never rely on the jack alone to hold the caravan.

VII. Remove the wheel nuts and wheel, being sure to store the wheelnuts in a safe place.

VIII. Put the replacement wheel on to the wheel drum and fasten the wheel bolts finger tight. Then, with the wheel lowered to the ground, using a torque wrench, tighten up the wheel nuts to the figures shown below - but check your caravan handbook for specific requirements. (Obviously, you're not likely to have your torque wrench with you if you have a puncture on the open road, in which case UNDO each nut/bolt in turn and RETIGHTEN with the torque wrench as soon as you can.)

IX. Tighten bolts or nuts in the sequence 1, 2, 3, 4, in the accompanying illustration. (Illustration, courtesy AL-KO Kober.)

IMPORTANT NOTE: AL-KO Kober recommend that their wheel nuts are tightened to 8.0kg/m (62ft.lbs.), and bolts to 9.0kg/m (65ft.lbs.). Peak Trailers recommend the following settings for wheel nuts:

IMPERIAL STUDS	METRIC STUDS
3/8 in. UNF - 45 ft.lbs.	M12x1.5 - 75 ft.lbs.
1/2 in. UNF - 80 ft.lbs.	M16x1.5 - 145 ft.lbs.

TIGHTENING SEQUENCE

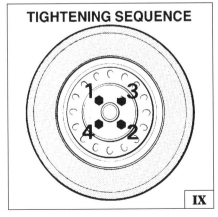

IX

So, *check your handbook for the specific requirements for your caravan.* Note also that overtightened nuts/studs can be just as dangerous as those that are not tight enough.

SERVICING & MAINTENANCE

X. Raise the caravan's corner steadies, lower the jack, remove the wheel chocks and raise the jockey wheel.

XI. After driving a further 20 to 50 miles, it is important to stop and recheck the torque settings of the wheel nuts. Then remember to recheck them regularly, preferably before each journey with your caravan.

INSIDE INFORMATION: A torque wrench only checks the torque when tightening a thread; never when unscrewing it. To check the torque effectively, it is essential that the nut or bolt is backed off, that the thread is clean and free-running, and the torque setting is made as the nut or bolt is being retightened.

XII. TO USE A TORQUE WRENCH: You set the scale on the wrench to the torque figure required and then use the wrench with a regular socket spanner and extension, if needed. When the nut or bolt reaches the required torque, the torque wrench 'lets go' and, instead of turning the thread any further, makes a clear clicking sound as the wrench is turned.

Never attempt to use your towcar's spare wheel on your caravan, or vice versa, as the types of wheels and tyres used on cars and caravans are rarely the same. Before fitting a new wheel, always check it for distortion or damage. If you find any, do not fit the wheel.

There are a number of aerosol products now available that can be sprayed into a punctured tyre through its valve, designed to seal a puncture and reinflate the tyre. If used, these products should not be relied upon to keep the tyre inflated over long distances and the tyre should be properly repaired or replaced as soon as is possible. Bear in mind that they are suitable for emergencies only: The tyre will probably be unrepairable, and the aerosol puncture repairer will not work when a tyre has been split or badly damaged by a kerb or rock, so don't rely on a can of this stuff in place of a spare wheel!

PREPARING FOR THE START OF THE SEASON

Before using the caravan, you will have to fit it back out with all the soft furnishings you may have removed, refit the wheels if you have taken them off and generally check that everything works properly before setting off. The jobs listed below don't include too much that is completely obvious, and if some of them *seem* obvious, please use them as an *aide memoire* to help you make sure that everything gets done.

Also, before using the caravan, you should carry out the checks listed as **EVERY WEEK, OR BEFORE EVERY LONG JOURNEY**, as well as those for the towcar listed below, as well as ensuring that your car is serviced in accordance with the manufacturer' schedules bearing in mind that with some makes, there may be shorter service intervals for driving in 'arduous conditions', including towing!

☐ Job 1. Check interior for damp.

1. Check the interior of the caravan – by looking and 'sniffing' – to ensure that neither damp nor mould has taken a hold. Wash off mould, if necessary, and check all seams, if necessary, to cure leaks. See Jobs 53 and 54.

☐ Job 2. Prepare refrigerator.

2A. It is likely that the fridge it will often require a good clean-out and this is certainly something that you don't need to be an expert to do! You'll no doubt do this as part of your domestic chores, but it should certainly be done before a caravan is to be stored over a long period and before it is used again after being brought out of storage. It may also be necessary if there are spillages from food and drink stored in the fridge. Generally all that is needed to clean the fridge out is the use of plain warm water and a clean cloth.

2B. Check that the fridge flue vent has not become blocked by leaves or spiders' webs: check the cooker flues, too!

INSIDE INFORMATION: i) If the fridge has a persistent smell, something that can happen if it is left turned off with the door closed for any period of time, mix in a teaspoon of bicarbonate of soda with a cup of warm water and use that to clean out the fridge. This is an excellent way of getting rid of most odours. Once you've washed the fridge out, be sure to dry it well with a clean cloth. ii) Once cleaned

out, if you're not planning to use the caravan for some time always make sure that you leave the fridge door in the storage position. This means positioning the retaining pin into the outer of the two holes in the top of the door. In this way air is allowed to circulate through the fridge preventing odours forming and stopping any condensation turning to mould. Use a proprietary mould remover, or bleach, for stubborn mould marks: never abrasives.

Before carrying out several of the following Jobs, you will need to reconnect the gas and leisure battery.

Also, with the caravan on level ground, check that the fridge works, and check that it also works off the 12 volt system from the car.

Job 3. Check water system.

Check that the water pump/s work and flush through the water system. (See Job 28.)

Job 4. Change water filter.

4. You should replace the water filter at the start of every season and then as often as the manufacturers recommend. (Illustration, courtesy Carver)

Job 5. Clean paintwork.

5. Over the winter months, it is possible for mould to bloom on your caravan's bodywork and seams. Spray mould remover - available from your DIY or garden centre (it's used for greenhouses) - over the affected area and wash off before washing again with car wax/wash.

Job 6. Check interior lights.

With the leisure battery reconnected, check the operation of the interior lights and replace bulbs and strip lights, as necessary.

Job 7. Check awning.

Get out the awning and erect it. IMPORTANT: Only do so when the weather is dry, as putting it away again wet will cause mould to form and could rot the fabric.

Check that you still have all the poles and bits-and-pieces(!) and that there is no corrosion or damage. Check to see if any mould has formed, in which case try brushing or washing it off. Dry thoroughly and reproof.

Job 8. Check 12 volt connectors.

Check both 12 volt wiring connectors at the front of the caravan. Ensure that neither has been damaged over the winter and that there is no corrosion around the pins - clean off if necessary. Park the towcar near to the front of the caravan and connect up the wiring connectors. If there is any problem with any of the exterior lights, or with the accessories inside the caravan when running off the car battery, open up each connector, as appropriate, and check the wiring.

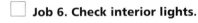

1. Left-hand indicator
2. Rear fog lamp
3. Common return (earth)
4. Right-hand indicator
5. Right-hand side/tail
6. Stop lamps
7. Left-hand side/tail

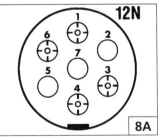

1. Reversing lamp
2. Battery charging
3. Common return (earth)
4. Interior lights
5. Sensing device
6. Fridge
7. Spare

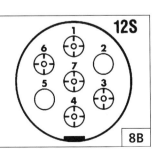

8A. This is the normal, standard layout of the terminals for the 12N, the black connector, viewed from the rear of the plug. (Illustration, courtesy The Caravan Club.)

8B. These are the usual terminals for the 12S, the white or grey accessory connector, viewed from the rear of the plug. (Illustration, courtesy The Caravan Club.)

SAFETY FIRST!
Ensure that your car and caravan are wired in this way. (Sometimes, the 'bodgers' may have been at work!) Incorrect wiring could cause a fire.

8C. Unscrewing the two screws holding the two halves of a 12-volt caravan plug together.

8C

8D

8D. The wiring connections are made to this block, which locates inside each half of the plug.

8E. Check *each* connection to ensure that: i) none of the wires have pulled loose, or have just a few strands of wire remaining ii) there are no expanses of bare wire - the insulation should just butt up against the entrance to each screw connector iii) there is no white or green corrosion in the plug. If so clean off thoroughly. Strip off a fresh 'end' if necessary.

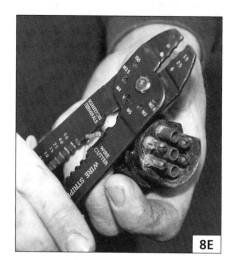

8E

8F. Make certain that the wire clamp is tight, otherwise it is all too easy to pull the wires out of the plug as it is disconnected from the car. In this case, the clamp is placed *uselessly* over the wires, not the insulation sheath. Also make sure that the rubber shroud seals correctly. Replace if necessary.

CHECKS TO THE TOWCAR

The following checks should be made in addition to the regular servicing requirements of your car.

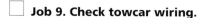 **Job 9. Check towcar wiring.**

9. You can carry this out in conjunction with Job 8 above, of course. You may find a problem inside one of the towcar sockets.

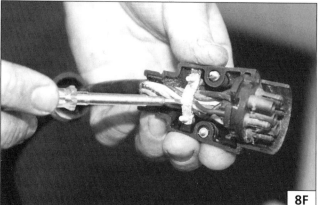

8F

INSIDE INFORMATION: There are two 'favourite' wiring problems that might have occurred over the Winter months: i) If water has got in through the backs of the sockets, clean up the sockets (replace them, if necessary) and when refitting the wiring grommet, use silicone seam sealer around the grommet, and around the back of each socket to seal them of properly. ii) Check that the earth lead from the socket has not become dislodged where it is bolted inside the car, usually in the spare wheel well, beneath the car or inside the boot/hatch area. Also, remove if necessary, clean up the surfaces to bare metal, treat with copper-impregnated grease and refit.

9

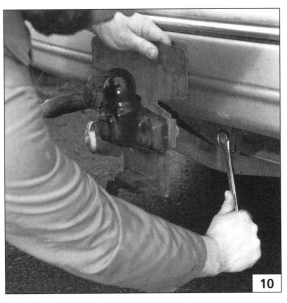

10

☐ Job 10. Check towbracket mountings.

10. Go over all of the towbracket and towball mountings on the car with spanners and a torque wrench and check that all are fully tight to the maker's recommendations. Also look for evidence of cracking around the mounting points. If any is found, **SPECIALIST SERVICE:** Have the car repaired before towing and check with your local main dealer that you have the correct, manufacturer-recommended towbracket for your car. Some cheap 'n' cheerful ones are believed to put inappropriate stresses on the car. IMPORTANT NOTE: From 1 January 1996, all new car tow-brackets are European Type Approved. A good thing!

☐ Job 11. Check rear suspension.

While in this area of the car, check the rear suspension. A towing car takes more of a pounding in this area than most cars so: check rear shock absorbers for leaks; check springs for sagging (measure the ride height of both sides of the car and compare).

☐ Job 12. Check car tyre pressures.

Ensure that the rear tyre pressures are suitable for driving the car when fully laden, if you intend to do a lot of towing. See your car's handbook for details. If you only tow occasionally, do this before each journey and restore pressures to 'normal' afterwards.

☐ Job 13. Check headlamp alignment.

If, when you are towing at night, oncoming traffic 'flashes' at you because your headlights are dazzling them, have your head-lamps set a little lower, but not so low that they are unsafe, illegal or will fail an MoT. This is a **SPECIALIST SERVICE** job and must be carried out by a garage with beam-setting equipment: DON'T GUESS IT!

☐ Job 14. Check indicator warning.

Check that, when the car is connected to the caravan by the 12N plug, and the indicators are operated, the caravan indicator warning light or buzzer inside the car operates correctly. This is a legal requirement!

☐ Job 15. Check towing mirrors.

Dig out those towing mirrors and make sure that they haven't been cracked over the winter, and that all the fixings are still there.

EVERY WEEK, OR BEFORE EVERY LONG JOURNEY

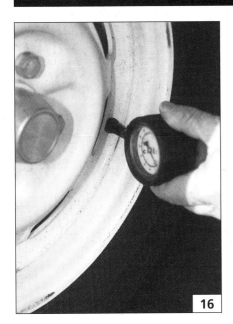

16

☐ Job 16. Check caravan tyre pressures.

16. Check each of the tyre pressures with the tyres cold, before the caravan is used. As a tyre 'works', it heats up and this increases the pressure inside the tyre, giving a false reading.

Also check the tyre valves for damage.

SERVICING & MAINTENANCE

FACT FILE: TYRE PRESSURES

RECOMMENDED CARAVAN TYRE PRESSURES:
The Caravan Club has issued the following tyre load and pressure chart for 82/85 series radial ply tyres commonly used on trailer caravans.

Tyre Size	Max Axle Load If Speed Kept Below 62 mph		Max Axle Load If Speed Above 62 mph		Recommended Tyre Pressure PSI (at max load)	
	kg	cwt	kg	cwt	Below 62 mph	Above 62 mph
145 R 13	825	16.2	750	14.7	35	32
145 R 13 Reinforced	935	18.4	850	16.7	42	39
155 R 13	935	18.4	850	16.7	35	32
155 R 13 Reinforced	1045	20.6	950	18.7	42	39
165 R 13	1045	20.6	950	18.7	36	33
165 R 13 Reinforced	1166	22.9	1060	20.8	45	42
165 R 13 C 6 PLY	1290	25.3	1230	24.2	54	*54
175 R 13	1166	22.9	1060	20.8	36	33
175 R 13 Reinforced	1276	25.1	1160	22.8	45	42
175 R 13 C 6 PLY	1407	27.6	1340	26.3	54	*54

* Where tyres carry below the maximum permitted axle load, pressures may be adjusted to between 45-54 psi to improve handling. But check with your tyre dealer to see if this applies to 'your' brand of tyre.

IMPORTANT NOTE: You should refer to your caravan owners' handbook for any variations concerning tyre sizes and pressures.

17A

17B

17C

Job 17. Check caravan tyres condition.

17A. When running on the road, and especially when pulling on and off a site, cuts or bulges in the tyres can occur, especially if you happen to go over rough ground or a kerb. Check *both sides* of each tyre with great care, rotating the wheels so that all of the tyres' treads and sidewalls can be examined. If any lumps or bulges appear in the sidewalls, the tyre must be scrapped. If you find any cuts, ask your local tyre dealer to take a look. Very shallow cuts may be OK; deeper ones probably call for a new tyre.

17B. Look for cracking or crazing on the tyre walls. Caravan tyres rarely cover the mileage of car tyres and they are usually scrapped before the treads are worn out. Sunlight and ozone cause all tyres to go cracked and brittle. Check carefully and if the tyres show signs of starting to deteriorate, replace them.

17C. Also, check for abrasion of the tyre wall, which can take place either in conjunction with bulging, or by itself. This invariably results from an impact, such as the tyre striking the edge of a kerb or a pothole in the road. If you find abrasions on your caravan's tyre you should take advice from a tyre specialist as to whether the tyre will require replacing.

SAFETY FIRST! and INSIDE INFORMATION:
*Tyres generally have a life expectancy of around five years, and they should **certainly** be scrapped and replaced after seven years - or less if they are worn out, of course!.*

Thanks are due to Dunlop/SP Tyres for the use of all the tyre photographs used here.

FACT FILE: WHEELS AND TYRES

CARAVAN TYRES require the same level of care and attention as those on a car. They are also covered by the same laws. So make sure that there is at least a minimum of 1.6mm of tread in a continuous band across three quarter s of the tyres width. In practice, you should replace tyres before they get near this level, and certainly if any of the tyre tread falls below the recommended level.

17D. UNDER INFLATION. If the outer edges of the tread are noticeably more worn that the centre, the tyres have been run under inflated, which not only ruins tyres, but increases fuel consumption, causes poor handling and is illegal.

OVER INFLATION causes the centre part of the tyre to wear more quickly than the outer edges. This is also illegal as well as making the tyre more susceptible to concussion damage and reduces grip.

17D

TYRE TYPES Caravans may be fitted with either tubeless or tubed tyres. Make sure that the correct type is fitted to the wheels of your caravan. Tubeless tyres must only be fitted to safety-type rims. For older caravans with non-safety rims, tubes must be fitted with 'tubeless' radial tyres. SPECIALIST SERVICE: It is not always possible to fit modern tyres to very old rims (wheels). If you have any doubt about what tyres should be fitted to your caravan, consult your local caravan dealer or tyre specialist.

RECOMMENDED TYRES The publishers of this book recommend the use of appropriate radial-ply tyres in preference to cross-ply tyres because of their superior grip qualities and resistance to 'following' the shape of the road, which may reduce the risk of snaking under some circumstances. Under NO CIRCUMSTANCES should cross-ply and radial-ply tyres be mixed on the caravan (or car!). If you wish to switch from cross-ply to radial-ply tyres, consult your local tyre depot, caravan dealer or the manufacturer of your caravan for specific advice on tyre-to-wheel fitments.

INSIDE INFORMATION: i) It is also advisable to have the same type of tyres fitted on all wheels of both the caravan and the towing vehicle. ii) Some older caravans may be equipped with cross-ply tyres, which are no longer available. When a change is required, radial-ply tyres will have to be fitted, and we recommend that the change is made as soon as possible, because of the great superiority and improved safety of radial-ply tyres. iii) When having new tyres fitted, DO NOT FORGET THE CARAVAN'S SPARE TYRE. The spare tyre is liable to exactly the same rules and regulations as the other tyres on your caravan (when fitted), so don't leave yourself with a spare that isn't compatible with the tyres on the caravan.

SPEED RESTRICTIONS On British roads caravans are restricted to a top speed of 60mph on motorways and dual carriageways, and 50mph on other roads except, of course, where lower overall speed limits are applied. However, if you're caravanning abroad the speed limits can vary. It is therefore essential to check the speed rating of your caravan's tyres to make sure that it is safe to tow at higher speeds. If you are unsure of the speed rating of the tyres on your caravan you should either consult the owners' handbook or your local tyre service centre.

TYRON SAFETY WHEELS Increasing numbers of new caravans are now being fitted with Tyron Safety Wheels as standard equipment. These allow you to maintain greater control of the caravan in the event of a puncture occurring at speed. This is achieved by the Tyron preventing the deflated tyre from entering the well of the wheel and causing the caravan to go out of control. Instead the tyre is locked on to the rim of the wheel, maintaining its shape. It also allows the caravan to be towed FOR A SHORT DISTANCE to a place where it's safe to repair the puncture. For details of Tyron Safety Wheels, contact Tyreservices Great Britain (see Appendix 3) or go along to your local caravan dealership.

INSIDE INFORMATION: these wheels must regularly be checked and re-balanced by your local tyre specialist.

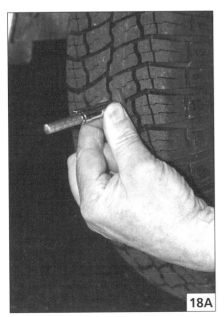

18A

☐ **Job 18. Check caravan tyres' tread depth.**

18A. Use a proper tyre tread depth gauge to check the tyre treads. The legal minimum in the UK is 1.6mm across the centre 75% of the width of the tyre. (In practice, many police officers are said to regard with a jaundiced eye the sight of any of the width of a tyre's tread below 1.6mm!).

SERVICING & MAINTENANCE

18B. Modern tyres have tread wear indicators built in to the tread grooves (usually about eight of them, spread equidistantly around the circumference of the tyre). When the tread depth wears down to 1.6mm, these appear as continuous bars running across the tread. There will be distinct reduction in wet weather grip well before the tread wear indicators begin to show, and you should replace the caravan's tyres well before they get to this stage, in our opinion.

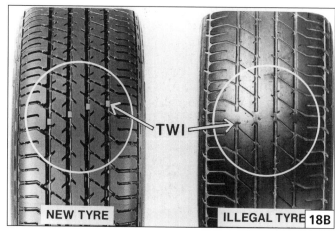
NEW TYRE | ILLEGAL TYRE 18B
TWI

☐ **Job 19. Check wheel rims.**

19. Wheel rims can also be damaged, especially when driving on or off site or over rough ground. Rim damage can cause rapid tyre deflation with catastrophic consequences. Have your local tyre centre or caravan dealer take a look. Slight damage can be repaired; otherwise a new wheel will be needed.

INSIDE INFORMATION: Unfortunately, it is unlikely that you will find a wheel to fit your caravan at a car scrapyard. Not only are the diameter and stud hole positions crucial, the 'offset' of the wheel - the amount by which the rim sticks out from the line of the hub - is not likely to be the same as anything you can find on a car. In addition, the load requirements are different. It's back to your caravan dealership, it seems!

19

☐ **Job 20. Check wheelnuts for tightness.**

Use a torque wrench to check that the wheel nuts (or bolts) are sufficiently tight - but not too tight, which can be just as bad, because bolts or studs can shear if over-tightened.

SAFETY FIRST!
See Changing a Wheel towards the start of this chapter for vital information on tightening caravan wheels. Refer to your caravan handbook for specific information on wheel nut or bolt torque settings.

FACT FILE: WHEELNUTS

For some time, there has been some concern in caravan circles that caravan wheelnuts are much more prone to coming loose than those fitted to cars. Aluminium wheels are often considered to be more prone to coming loose than steel wheels, though no one quite seems to know why! However, the fact is that if a wheel comes off your caravan, the results could be horrific. This is a case where it would make sense to pay out the money required, buy a torque wrench, so that the correct tightening force required can be accurately measured, and check your wheel nuts regularly, even if it means taking off awkward wheel trims to get at them. Check 20 to 50 miles after changing a wheel *and* after delivery of a new caravan.

☐ **Job 21. Check exterior lights.**

Connect the towcar electrical connectors to the caravan and try out all of the exterior lights, both front and rear, not forgetting any auxiliary lights that may be fitted.

INSIDE INFORMATION: If a rear fog light or fog lights have been fitted to your caravan, they are subject to the same Construction & Use regulations as those fitted to your car. Ensure that they work properly and that the correct wattage bulb is fitted.

21A. Almost all caravan light lenses are easy to remove and bulbs are simple to replace. Clean the lenses, inside and out, while they're off and check that seals are effective. If not, the insides of the lamp housings and the bulb holders will quickly deteriorate.

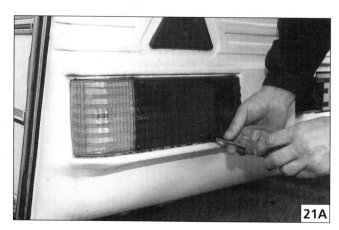
21A

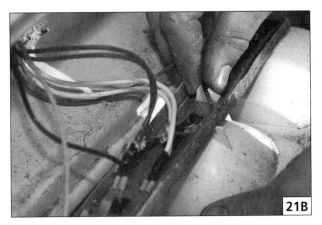

21B. The common, wrap-around 'Jokon' light units contain a separate internal bulb holder. Squeeze together the two clips...

21C. ...and lift away, *but take enormous care not to break the left-hand bulb* - it's a tight squeeze!

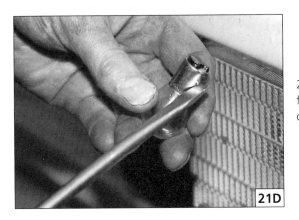

21D. Note that tail/stoplight bulbs have offset pegs to prevent their being fitted the wrong way round (brake lights are brighter than tail lights, of course).

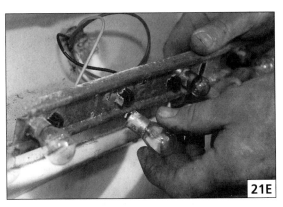

21E. Fitting is quicker, once you suss this simple fact! Make sure terminals are clean!

Most caravan lighting problems stem from one of two sources: connections to the caravan plug or car socket, or earthing problems within the caravan lamps themselves. To solve the latter problem, remove each lens and check for good connections between the lamp units and the caravan body; check for corrosion-free bulb holders; check for sound wiring connections.

☐ Job 22. Check break-away cable.

22. The breakaway device should be checked every month for signs of damage and wear. Pay particular attention for signs of the cable kinking or splitting.

Also, make sure that the clips, including the ring clip that attaches the cable to the handbrake is in good working order. If any faults or damage are discovered, make sure that the cable is replaced with the correct part. DO NOT be tempted to use some old piece of cable that you might have lying around. IMPORTANT NOTE: The use of a break-away cable might, by now, have become a legal requirement, as expected.

☐ Job 23. Check caravan battery.

One item which is essential to keep well maintained on just about all caravans is the 12-volt leisure battery. Forgetting or ignoring to maintain the battery could well cause it to fail, potentially leaving the caravan without power for the items such as the light and water pump.

22

FACT FILE: BREAKAWAY CABLE

One essential but often ignored part of a caravan's braking system is the breakaway cable. When the caravan is hitched up to a towcar, this cable should be attached to a solid part of the towcar, but preferably not the towing bracket. Ask for advice from your caravan specialist if you're not sure how to attach it.

In the extremely unlikely event that the caravan should 'break away' from the car, the breakaway cable will become taut and pull on the caravan's brakes. Immediately that the cable has engaged the brakes it is designed to snap. The result will be that the caravan comes to a halt instead of either careering off down the road out of control or flailing about behind the towcar while connected solely by a piece of cable.

SAFETY FIRST!
When servicing the battery: i) Unhitch the caravan from the towing vehicle. ii) Always switch off the battery charger and disconnect the caravan's mains electrics hook-up and 12N/12S cables. iii) Make sure all the electrical components in the caravan are turned off. iv) Always disconnect the battery's negative terminal (earth) first and, when the servicing is complete, reverse the procedure by re-connecting the negative terminal last. v) Never smoke nor allow a spark anywhere near a battery, especially when it is being charged, as it gives off explosive fumes. vi) Wear gloves and goggles when handling non-sealed type batteries and if any battery electrolyte (acid) is spilled onto skin or eyes, wash off with copious amounts of cold, running water and immediately seek medical advice.

23A

23A. If the caravan does not have its own battery charger, the battery should be removed every three months, or in the winter every month, and recharged outside of the caravan. For this purpose use only a battery charger designed for the job and preferably one that sets its own, correct charging rate automatically. Not all car-type chargers are suitable.

23B. While the battery is disconnected, make sure that its terminals are clean, secure and in good condition. If not clean them off with sand paper, back to a shiny surface, both on the battery and the terminals. Protect the surfaces with copious amounts of Vaseline. Similarly check the battery leads and connectors in the caravan for signs of wear, damage or corrosion and check the battery casing for signs of cracks or damage.

INSIDE INFORMATION: Deposits of white 'fur' will wash off if, after the battery has been removed, you pour a kettle of hot water over the terminals taking care to keep it out of the battery cells.

23B

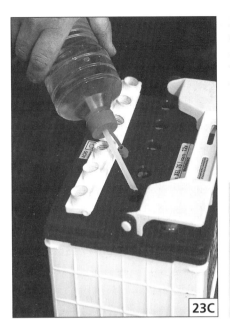

23C. If the battery is of the non-sealed variety, check the electrolyte levels and, if necessary top them up with distilled water. Distilled water is generally available from car accessory shops. This won't be necessary if the battery is of the sealed variety. Wipe the top of the battery casing - dirt or grease on the top of the casing can help 'furring' to occur.

23D. Make sure that the vent in the battery box is clear and, if the battery is fitted with one, that the breather pipe is clear. When the battery is returned to the storage locker make sure that it is strapped or clamped securely into place so that it can't move about when the caravan is on the move.

SAFETY FIRST! and INSIDE INFORMATION:
i) Always keep a battery safely out of reach of children and somewhere that it's unlikely to get knocked or dropped. However, try not to place it on the floor as a battery stored on a concrete floor will slowly discharge itself. If the battery is removed from the caravan for any length of time, for example, while the caravan is stored over the winter period, make sure that it is never left in a discharged condition.

Job 24. Check mains electricity system.

24. Examine the cable used to connect the caravan to the on-site mains supply and pay special attention to the connector on each end. Ensure that only the outer sheathing is visible where it enters each plug, not the inner cables and that the cable is clamped tight and cannot move in and out of each plug. Check that the cable itself is not abraded or split - if it is, renew it; DON'T tape it up!

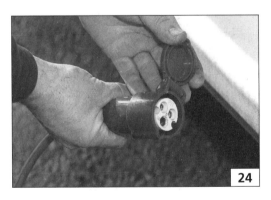

Look inside the caravan to make sure that all of the electrical connections appear sound, that all of the fixed appliances and the internal supply and trip unit (the RCD unit) are securely mounted.

SPECIALIST SERVICE. If any work is needed on your caravan's mains wiring system, entrust it to a qualified, CORGI-registered electrical engineer familiar with the requirements of caravans.

SAFETY FIRST!
Before carrying out any work on a caravan's mains electrical system, ensure that both the mains supply cable and the 12N and 12S cables from the towcar are disconnected. Under no circumstances should you attempt to alter, modify or bypass any part of a caravan's mains electrical system without the guidance and advice of an authorised expert. If you are in the slightest doubt about any problem that occurs with a caravan's mains electrical system you should immediately disconnect the power supply and seek expert help from an NICEIC or ECA registered contractor.

Job 25. Check fridge vents.

Apart from regular cleaning, the only point to consider with the fridge is to check that the vents are kept clear. It's quite uncommon for the vents to become blocked but if they do, it can seriously affect the efficiency of the fridge..

SPECIALIST SERVICE: Like any gas appliance, the fridge in a caravan should be serviced only by a qualified engineer, every 12 months.

SERVICING & MAINTENANCE

Job 26. Check heater flue.

Servicing the heater is most certainly a **SPECIALIST SERVICE** item. However, if the heater flue or the air inlets become blocked, the heater could be lethal in operation, so check that they are clear.

Job 27. Clean out cassette toilet.

27. One important area that's often forgotten when servicing or storing a caravan is cleaning the cassette toilet. In fact, little work is required, as the toilet's own chemicals help to keep it clean when the caravan is in use.

Even so, it's not a bad idea to rinse and empty the toilet and waste tank, washing it through with warm water and Milton 2 or Chempro SDP sterilising fluid. DO NOT use strong household cleaners or any solutions containing chlorine, solvents or acid, as these might well damage the toilet. A mild soap solution can be used to clean the toilet bowl, seat and cover, as well as the outside of the toilet and cassette.

Job 28. Clean out water system.

The difference between having water that tastes good and water that tastes awful in your caravan, water filter or no water filter, can be a matter of simply keeping the water clean and in good condition. What this *doesn't* mean is flushing it through with disinfectant. This will undoubtedly clean it out, but it will almost certainly also leave a nasty taste in the pipes that will be extremely difficult to remove.

INSIDE INFORMATION: Before cleaning the water system through, make sure that the in-line filter system is removed, if one is fitted. If the system has the popular Carver Crystal Filter fitted, put an old filter temporarily in place, as the cleaning process could reduce the effectiveness of a new filter.

Fill the caravan's water container with drinking water and a add a mild steriliser, such as Milton 2 or Chempro SDP. Both of these should be available from your local chemist. Then, turn on the caravan's taps and let the solution run through the system. Allow some of it to stand in the system for a while so that it can get to work on the insides of the pipes. Next, wash the system through with *up to six containers of fresh drinking water*, before finally refitting the water filter.

While cleaning the water system, take time to check for leaks - particularly at pipe connections - and check for damaged pipes. Even a minor leak left unrepaired can cause serious damage over a surprisingly short period of time, right from mould and rotten upholstery, through to serious rot in structural timbers and delamination of floorboards.

28. Check that all the jubilee clips are tight - without actually damaging the pipes or your hands if you slip! - and check that the electrical terminals on the water pump inlet aren't corroded.

INSIDE INFORMATION: If the Jubilee clip on a pipe is difficult to tighten try i) using a screwdriver with a 'square' end, rather than the usual rounded-off job you find in the back of the kitchen drawer; ii) holding a hot, wet rag around the joint just before tightening it. This will soften the plastic and allow the clip to tighten further, especially if you also lubricate the threads on the clip. (Illustration, courtesy Carver)

Job 29. Adjust water pressure.

PRESSURE WATER SYSTEMS ONLY

If your caravan is fitted with a pressure water system, it might need adjusting occasionally. If it does, this is usually due to variations in the power source, generally caused by a drop in battery power. If this is the case, refer to the specific instructions in your caravan's handbook. With most models, there is a simple procedure to follow:

29. Locate the adjusting nut. This is usually to be found on the back or the top of the pressure switch, depending on model. Turn one of the caravan taps on and turn the adjusting nut slowly in an anti-clockwise direction until you hear a click. Then turn it a further half-turn in the same direction, and the setting should be correct.

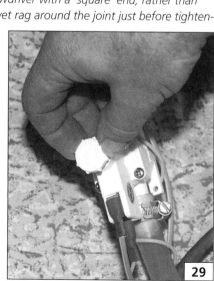

FACT FILE: PROBLEMS WITH SWITCHES

If there's a problem with your water pump system, check the following points:

Most caravans equipped with pressure switches will have an isolation switch fitted. This is used a safety precaution to stop the pump running dry and burning out, should the pump develop a fault, such as a leak. Check out the isolation switch.

If your caravan has a microswitch attached to the tap, this will occasionally fail and need replacing. Signs of switch failure are commonly: that the water pump fails to cut out even though the tap has been turned off; or there is a notable delay between the tap being turned off and the pump cutting out.

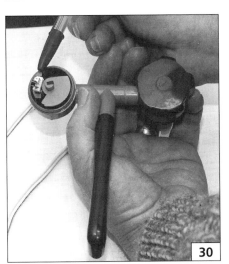

☐ **Job 30. Replacing a microswitch.**

WHEN NECESSARY

Because so many different types of tap have been fitted to caravans over the years, it is impractical to detail the procedures for replacing all of the varieties of microswitch fitted. Probably the commonest type to be found is made by Whale and, in those cases, it makes sense to refer to the detailed instructions that Whale supply with their replacement microswitches.

INSIDE INFORMATION: Because of the great variety in types of switch available, you should always take with you the old switch when buying or ordering a replacement. Also, quote the make model and year of your caravan to help in narrowing down the possibilities - take with you the appropriate **Caravan Data-Base** *information from the front of this book.*

However, there is much that is common to the majority of non-Whale switches, as detailed below.

30. After disconnecting the caravan's 12-volt battery, carefully remove the control cap on the top of the tap to gain access to the microswitch assembly. Disconnect the microswitch wires from beneath the tap mounting and remove the microswitch.

After fitting the new microswitch and reconnecting the wires, the tap control cap can be refitted and the caravan battery can be reconnected.

☐ **Job 31. Clean drainage system.**

A mild detergent is ideal for cleaning the drainage and waste water points. And while you're at it, don't forget that the same solution can also be used to clean out the waste water containers, otherwise they can really start to smell, particularly after being stored away.

TWICE A SEASON, OR EVERY THREE MONTHS

FACT FILE: CARAVAN CHASSIS

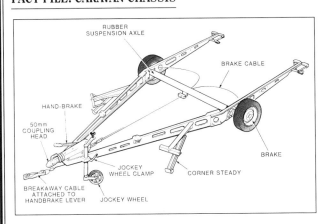

RUBBER SUSPENSION AXLE

BRAKE CABLE

HAND-BRAKE

50mm COUPLING HEAD

BRAKE

JOCKEY WHEEL CLAMP

CORNER STEADY

BREAKAWAY CABLE ATTACHED TO HANDBRAKE LEVER

JOCKEY WHEEL

A typical modern, lightweight but strong, caravan chassis layout. (Illustration, courtesy AL-KO Kober)

READ THIS FIRST!

Very few, if any, modern caravan manufacturers produce their own chassis. In the days when it was common for them to do so , proprietary parts such as the brakes, wheels and so on would be bought, and

more - or less - of the manufacturers own parts, such as the brake linkage or hitch, would be added, according to the size and resources of the manufacturer. It is therefore impossible to be specific about every make of older caravan. However, small-volume production components are generally easy to understand and almost all will follow the broad outlines indicated here.

Nowadays, the German companies AL-KO Kober, Knott, and BPW dominate the component market, with AL-KO having by far the largest share. If a caravan manufacturer needed to produce a run of, say, 40 of a particular model of caravan, the order would go out to AL-KO Kober or Knott (pronounced KER-NOTT) for 40 "chassis kits" consisting, typically, of complete chassis (more or less broken down for assembly by the caravan manufacturer, according to type); axles, including hubs and brakes; hitch assemblies, brake rods, linkages and cables. So, with a modern caravan, there is much more uniformity and the instructions shown here are likely to be much more relevant to most modern caravans. With older caravans, the B&B chassis was most common, and that is the main type of older chassis featured here.

SERVICING & MAINTENANCE

☐ Job 32. Lubricate over-run.

32A. With any type of hitch, find the grease points - two in this case - located on the top part of the hitch, and apply grease using a standard grease gun.

32B. Check to see if there is a third grease point on the underside of the hitch, and on the over-run lever and again, treat with a grease gun.

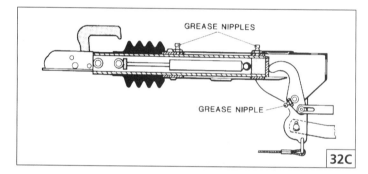

32C. These are the three grease points on the AL-KO hitch. (Illustration, courtesy AL-KO Kober)

☐ Job 33. Lubricate jockey wheel.

33A. Lubricate all moving parts of the jockey wheel using light oil. Locate a small hole in the operating handle of many earlier hitches and apply some oil and/or lube the top bearing. Wipe off the excess. IMPORTANT NOTE: Some older jockey wheels were fitted with a grease nipple towards the top of the shaft, in which case, apply grease with a grease gun.

33B. Apply more oil to the centre of the jockey wheel itself and to the threaded handle...

33C. ...and the clamp that holds the jockey wheel to the side of the A-frame.

□ Job 34. Lubricate corner steadies.

34A. Taking each corner steady at a time, clean off any dirt that might have been thrown up from the road and lightly grease the threads...

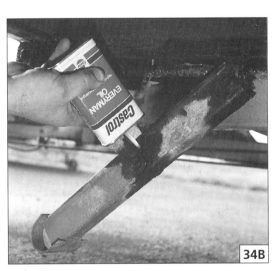

34B. ...and all the moving parts of the mechanism.

□ Job 35. Lubricate braking system external parts.

35. Lubricate all external moving and sliding parts of the braking system, taking care to keep any grease or oil away from contact with the surface of the brake shoes.

SERVICING & MAINTENANCE

☐ Job 36. Check and lubricate car towball.

36A. While you're dealing with the lubrication points on the caravan, don't forget the towcar's towball. Clean off any dirt and apply a thin layer of multipurpose grease EXCEPT where a friction head stabiliser, such as the AL-KO AKS2000, is fitted. When the caravan's unhitched, don't forget to replace the towball cover, otherwise the greasy towball has a nasty habit of rubbing against your clothing!

36A

36B. **SPECIALIST SERVICE:** Unless you possess appropriate measuring equipment, have your specialist measure the tow ball. AL-KO Kober recommend a minimum diameter, at any point, of 49.61mm. If the ball is worn below this point, REPLACE IT BEFORE TOWING THE CARAVAN.

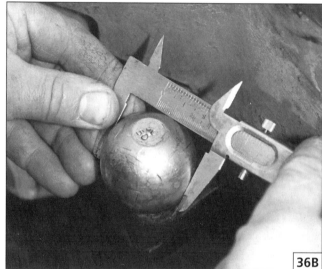

36B

☐ Job 37. Lubricate caravan coupling head.

37A. Lightly grease the inside of the towball coupling, except where a friction head stabiliser, such as the AL-KO AKS2000, is fitted.

37B. Now oil all the other moving parts of the coupling head (Illustration, courtesy BPW)...

37A

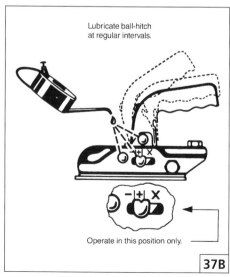

Lubricate ball-hitch
at regular intervals.

Operate in this position only.

37B

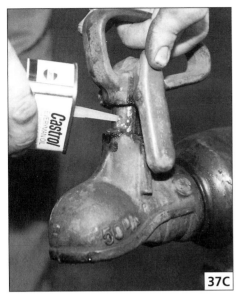

37C. ...paying particular attention to the plunger assembly on the B&B-type hitches. Wipe off the excess.

37C

☐ Job 38. Lubricate external hinges and locks.

38. Take the oil can to all of the door hinges, catches and locks, and the window hinges and catches. Push the door key into the lock so that the protective 'door' on the lock is held open (if fitted) and inject a little oil into the barrel. Spray in releasing fluid if the key feels stiff in the lock.

38

ONCE A SEASON, OR EVERY THREE THOUSAND MILES, IF SOONER

CARAVAN BRAKING SYSTEMS

Adjusting the brakes is a matter of adjusting BOTH the brakes at the wheels AND the handbrake/over-run linkage, because both have to work in conjunction with one another. In some case, the brakes at the wheels are adjusted first; in some case the over-run and rod/cables are adjusted first. See the information below.

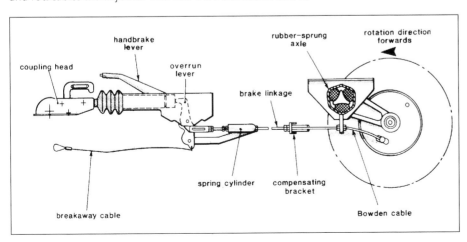

IMPORTANT NOTE: When adjusting the brakes, turn the wheel only in a forwards direction (i.e., the direction in which the wheel will turn when the vehicle is travelling forwards). As described below, caravan brakes are designed only to work properly in that direction, because the automatic reverse facility, disabling the brake comes into operation when the direction of rotation is reversed and you will not be able to adjust the brakes when turning the wheel backwards. Do not use excessive force during adjustment. (Illustration, courtesy AL-KO Kober)

SERVICING & MAINTENANCE

FACT FILE: BRAKING SYSTEMS

IT IS ESSENTIAL THAT YOU READ THIS FACT FILE BEFORE ATTEMPTING TO WORK ON YOUR CARAVAN'S BRAKING SYSTEM.

SAFETY FIRST AND SPECIALIST SERVICE!

i) Obviously, your caravan's brakes are among its most important safety related items. Do NOT dismantle or attempt to perform any work on the braking system unless you are fully competent to do so. If you have not been trained in this work, but wish to carry it out, we strongly recommend that you have your local caravan specialist workshop or qualified mechanic check your work before taking the caravan on the road. See also the section on BRAKES AND ASBESTOS in Chapter 1, Safety First! for further information. ii) Remember that brake dust can contain asbestos and in the case of older systems, it most certainly will. Since asbestos can kill: ALWAYS spray a proprietary brand of aerosol brake cleaner on to the brakes after removing the hub (available from your local auto accessory store); ALWAYS wear an efficient particle mask, gloves and a hat, and wash your hands and arms after doing the job; ALWAYS dust yourself off thoroughly out of doors; ALWAYS dispose of the old shoes, wiping rags and wiped-up dust in a sealed plastic bag, and keep children and pets away from the work area. iii) Always replace the brake shoes in sets of four - never replace the shoes on one wheel only. Keep all traces of oil or grease off the friction surfaces. iv) When adjusting the brakes, it is necessary to adjust one side first and then the other. In both cases it will be necessary to work underneath the caravan and it is therefore essential that the correct safety procedure is followed for raising and supporting the caravan. See the section on 'Raising A Caravan Safely' earlier in this chapter. v) Always specify and use ASBESTOS FREE brake linings.

BACKGROUND INFORMATION: The braking system on a caravan is far simpler than that on the modern car. Even so, it is essential that the braking system is kept in perfect working order for the safety of all road-users. This is particularly so because if the caravan's brakes fail to work properly they will, at least, throw more strain on the towcar's brakes than they were designed for.

Although occasional exceptions do occur, you will probably find one of three types of braking systems on caravans - those made by AP Lockheed and fitted to a large number of earlier British chassis - some with rod operation and some with cable operation; those fitted on the AL-KO chassis from 1983 onwards (now accounting for around 75% of all UK systems), and Knott brakes and their close cousins, BPW brakes. Although new systems can appear at any time, the main three types are covered here. In addition, we touch briefly on the much earlier AP Lockheed system with manual reverse lock: all of the others lock out the over-run braking system automatically when the car is reversed - see below.

All caravans feature a similar type of braking system, designed to respond to the braking of the towcar. The caravan's tow hitch is mounted on a shaft which is spring loaded /hydraulically clamped into the front of the caravan's A-frame. When the towcar brakes, the weight and momentum of the caravan causes it to press forwards against the force of the spring, pushing the shaft back into the A-frame. This movement is transmitted through the caravan's braking system, by rods and/or cables, causing the brake shoe mechanism at the wheel to operate. Later models are fitted with a damper and this must work efficiently.

Incorporated into the caravan's braking system is a mechanism that automatically allows the caravan to be reversed without the braking system being engaged. As the car starts to reverse, the drawbar shaft is compressed, as normal, but then the brake mechanism inside the drum senses that the wheel is rotating backwards and the brake is disabled. On much older caravans, the driver or assistant had to manually lock-out the over-run brake, using a reversing catch on the tow hitch, before reversing could be carried out.

When the caravan is unhitched on site, the handbrake mounted on the A-frame is engaged to lock the brakes in position. It is essential that you follow the instructions in the handbook supplied with your caravan when applying the parking brake. For instance, when applying the very popular AL-KO handbrake on a reverse slope or steep hill, it is necessary to push the caravan back an inch or two while applying the brake to ensure that it holds. Use chocks to stop the caravan moving too far and perhaps running away!

☐ **Job 39. Adjust brakes at the wheel.**

AP LOCKHEED AUTOMATIC REVERSING BRAKE (EARLY MKI) MODELS ONLY

FACT FILE: 'B&B', AP LOCKHEED and

PEAK TRAILER BRAKES

At one time, B&B chassis were pre-eminent in Britain - and there are large numbers of them still in use today. B&B used mainly AP Lockheed brakes and so, these brakes are often referred to as 'B&B brakes': a commonly used term but, to be pedantic, incorrect! Then B&B were taken over by AL-KO, who are now by far the largest manufacturer of caravan chassis and brakes in use in the UK, and B&B are no more.

However (there's always a 'however'...), most AP Lockheed brake components continue to be available, apart from the earliest non-automatic reversing lock brakes. But most AP Lockheed trailer brake parts are now made under licence by Peak Trailers. So, do you call them, 'B&B', 'AP Lockheed' or 'Peak Trailers' brakes? We prefer AP Lockheed - because no matter whose chassis they were fitted to, AP Lockheed is what they are! The contact addresses for all of these companies can be found in *Appendix 3*, at the back of this book.

39A. Park the caravan on level ground. Having decided which wheel you are going to adjust first, raise that side of the caravan, as described in the section *'Raising A Caravan Safely'* earlier in this chapter.

39B. Disengage the handbrake and pull the caravan drawshaft forwards, away from the A-frame. Make sure that there's slack in the brake rod. If the handbrake lever is prevented from disengaging fully because it fouls the fibreglass fairing, adjust the fairing or trim the fibreglass so that it can release properly.

> **SAFETY FIRST!**
> **Fibreglass dust is extremely dangerous if breathed in. Always wear an efficient particle face mask when cutting or sanding fibreglass.**

39C. Remove any wheeltrims. If the caravan is fitted with the original wheels, locate a small hole towards each wheels's centre and between two of the wheel stud holes. If there's not a hole in the wheel (or the wheel has been put back in the wrong place!), remove the wheel and locate the hole in the drum.

Turn the wheel/hub until the hole in the front of the hub exposes the adjuster screw. Turning the screw pushes both brake shoes out until they push against the sides of the drum. Use a large screwdriver and turn until the hub is locked.

39D. Operate the handbrake a couple of times, and then fully release it again, to centralise the shoes, then try the adjuster screw again.

INSIDE INFORMATION: The adjuster screw bears directly on the front shoe but the rear shoe is only pushed open via the sliding expander (See Job 42 - Part I). This can be a little difficult to move by the action of the adjuster alone, if there is corrosion or a build up of brake dust on the backplate; which is why you need to centralise the shoes using the handbrake.

Now back off the adjuster one 'click' stop at a time until the brake drum is *just* completely free to rotate when turned only in a *forwards* direction.

*INSIDE INFORMATION: The **very slightest** amount of rubbing at one or two points in the drum's location is acceptable, but no more.*

IMPORTANT NOTE: Should the amount of adjustment seem excessive, remove the brake drum and ensure that the carrier shoe is in the correct position. See Job 42.

Don't forget to examine the rubber boot on the backplate (when fitted) and renew if necessary.

Replace the wheel and lower the caravan.

Repeat the procedure on the opposite wheel.

'STANDARD' AP LOCKHEED - NON AUTOMATIC REVERSE BRAKES ONLY

These brakes predated the later 'automatic' AP Lockheed brakes. Not all spares are available.

39E. When 7 in. brakes are fitted (only in a tiny number of cases), the adjustment is by a starred wheel adjuster (see AL-KO brakes), accessed from the front of the drum, with the wheel removed. (Illustration, courtesy Peak Trailers.)

39F. When 8, 9, or 10 in. brakes are fitted, the adjuster is identical to that shown for the automatic brake system. (Illustration, courtesy Peak Trailers.)

ADJUST AL-KO TYPE BRAKES AT THE WHEEL

AL-KO point out that all servicing must be carried out by an authorised dealer throughout the period covered by the chassis warranty.

Ensure that there is some end float in the brake rod and spring cylinder. Make sure that the drawshaft is fully extended: pulled out as far as it will go and that the handbrake is fully 'OFF'.

If the handbrake lever is prevented from disengaging fully because it fouls the fibreglass fairing, adjust the fairing or trim the fibreglass so that it can release properly.

SAFETY FIRST!
Fibreglass dust is extremely dangerous if breathed in. Always wear an efficient particle face mask when cutting or sanding fibreglass.

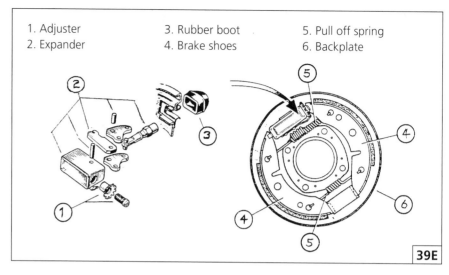

1. Adjuster
2. Expander
3. Rubber boot
4. Brake shoes
5. Pull off spring
6. Backplate

39E

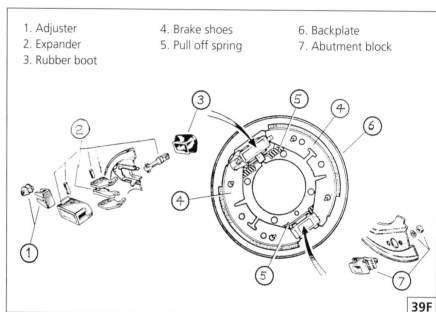

1. Adjuster
2. Expander
3. Rubber boot
4. Brake shoes
5. Pull off spring
6. Backplate
7. Abutment block

39F

39G. Jack the caravan up and remove the wheel, following the lifting procedure as described before adjusting the AP Lockheed brakes...

39H. ...with the axle stand underneath the outer end of the axle and placed on a firm, level surface.

39G

39H

39I. At the back of the wheel hub, remove the inner of the two plastic blanking plugs.

39J. Take a look at the back of the hub and you will see an arrow stamped there. (You may have to clean off the dirt and sand off the rust!) Insert a flat-head screwdriver into the hole revealed by having removed the blanking plug, and turn the star wheel inside...

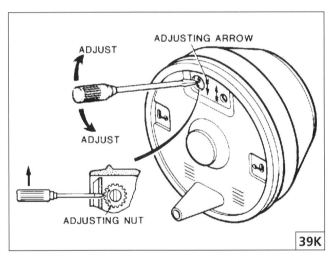

39K.   ...turning the star wheel until there is resistance when you try to rotate the road wheel by hand. IMPORTANT INFORMATION: always rotate the roadwheel in the forward direction, NEVER backwards. Now slacken the star wheel once again until the road wheel just begins to turn freely in the FORWARD direction.

Repeat the procedure on the other side of the caravan. (Illustration, courtesy AL-KO Kober.)

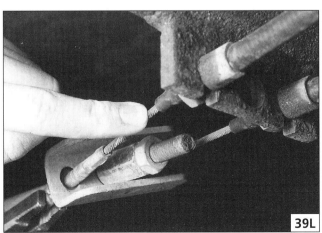

ADJUST COMPENSATOR, AL-KO-TYPE BRAKES

39L. Next, locate the brake compensator, where the brake cables pass through a bracket on the centre of the axle. Using a pair of pliers to hold the cable steady, pull the inner cable out and check how far it extends. It should extend between 5 and 8 mm. This applies to each Bowden cable, i.e. the one from each road wheel. IMPORTANT NOTE: this check and adjustment (see Job 39M) does not apply when a gas strut hand brake is fitted.

SERVICING & MAINTENANCE

39M. Ensure that the compensator is pulled evenly - apply and release the handbrake three or four times to centralise the brake shoes.

INSIDE INFORMATION: Check that the brake rod support bar which is fixed to the caravan floor is actually supporting the brake rod evenly and not just at one end.

Adjust the brake rod so that the over-run lever butts up against the end of the towing shaft, leaving no clearance. Tighten up all brake rod locking nuts. (Illustration, courtesy AL-KO Kober.)

39N. Adjust the locking nuts to give 1 mm clearance ONLY on the spring cylinder. (As we said before, if the over-run is fitted with a gas strut handbrake, this does not apply because there is no spring cylinder fitted.

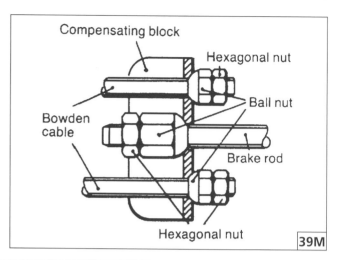

39M

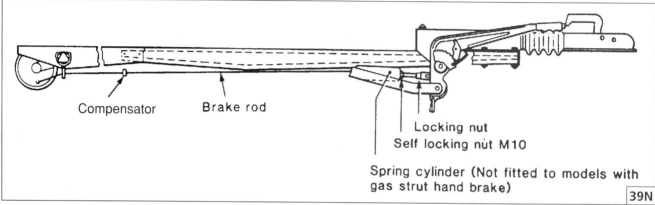

39N

Correct adjustment of the linkage is checked by operating the handbrake lever so that a slight braking force is felt when you attempt to turn the wheels by hand when the handbrake is on the second or third tooth of the ratchet. IMPORTANT NOTE: if either the wheel brakes or linkages are over-adjusted, reversing will be difficult or impossible. (Illustration, courtesy AL-KO Kober.)

39O. Before replacing each wheel, remove the second (outer) plastic plug at the rear of the wheel hub and check the condition of the brake shoes. If they appear damaged or worn down to a thickness of less than about 2 mm, replace them as shown in Job 42 - Part II.

Assuming that all is well with the brake shoes, replace the wheel, retighten using a torque wrench to 65 lbs/ft or 90 Nm - on all M12 wheel bolts in the correct sequence of north, south, east, west. Now lower the caravan back to ground level.

39O

KNOTT AND BPW BRAKES (PLUS LATER (MKII) LOCKHEED BRAKES) ONLY

IMPORTANT NOTE: Where Knott and BPW brakes are fitted in conjunction with their standard Bowden cable brake system, follow the cable adjustment procedures for AL-KO brakes, above.

N.B. The type of adjustment at the road wheels shown here is also applicable to Lockheed trailer brakes *with automatic reverse*. Please note that the adjuster on these later Lockheed brakes is a small squared shaft and is best adjusted with a proper brake adjuster tool, available from your auto accessory store.

39P

39P. After lifting both caravan wheels off the ground and supporting the caravan with an axle stand under the end of each axle, and lowering each corner steady, turn the brake adjusting nut, as illustrated, with a 17mm ring spanner in a clockwise direction until the wheel locks up. Do not force it! (Illustration, courtesy BPW)

INSIDE INFORMATION: Because this type of adjuster is external, it can suffer from the thread rusting solid. Spray it with a little releasing fluid a few hours before commencing work.

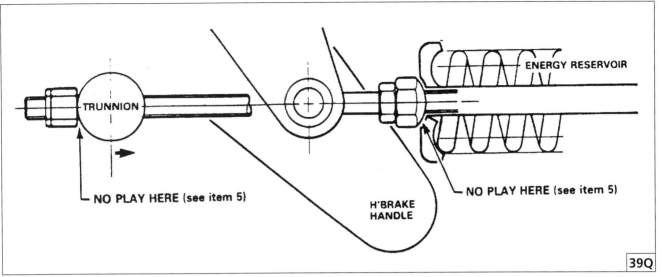

ENERGY RESERVOIR

TRUNNION

NO PLAY HERE (see item 5)

NO PLAY HERE (see item 5)

H'BRAKE HANDLE

39Q

39Q. When these brakes are fitted in conjunction with the Peak Trailers 4700 Series coupling, the linkage has next to receive some attention. Check that the linkage is free and properly lubricated and ensure that the linkage is free from slack. Pull the central brake rod forward to take up all the free play and at the same time, push the brake rod trunnion (illustrated) on the hitch back to its rear position. There should now be no clearance between the rear of the nut and the trunnion, as shown. Adjust the nut to take up any clearance, as necessary.

Also, check the spring pack assembly, and adjust the domed nut, as necessary, so that there is no clearance between it and the locating plate, as shown. IMPORTANT NOTE: The overall length of the spring pack is factory set and should not be interfered with.

Now, go back to the wheels and back off each adjuster until each wheel just turns freely with no binding. Check the adjustment by pulling on the handbrake one or two 'clicks' until the brake is just starting to work.

INSIDE INFORMATION: With the Knott system, it is advisable to gently tap the adjuster with a hammer to ensure that it has seated correctly.

There should now be an identical amount of 'drag' from each brake. If not, adjust by slackening off the 'tight' brake, not by tightening the 'loose' one: binding brakes can be dangerous and damaging. DO NOT compensate by adjusting the brake cables. Adjusting the brakes in this way, with this system, ensures that the correct amount of play is present in the Peak Trailers linkages. (Illustration, courtesy Peak Trailers.)

☐ Job 40. Adjust handbrake and over-run.

IMPORTANT NOTE 1: Before adjusting any of the handbrake systems shown here, it is essential that the wheel brakes, cables and compensator are correctly adjusted, as described in Job 27.

IMPORTANT NOTE 2: Until recent years, there were as many different types of brake operating mechanism as there were chassis manufacturers, it sometimes seems! AP Lockheed brakes, for instance, were fitted to several different types of chassis, each with its own operating mechanism. For instance, the Peak Caravans rod operated mechanism consisted of simple rods which followed the line of the lengthy A-frame which reached right back to the axle-line, while some CI chassis operating mechanisms were complex in the extreme! The B&B system described here is one of the most common types and can be taken as a guide. If necessary, obtain specific information from the original manufacturer (see list towards the back of this book) or from your local caravan dealership.

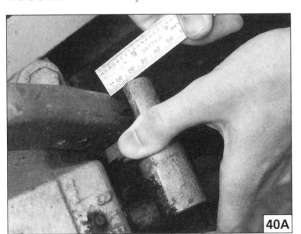

40A

B&B-TYPE HANDBRAKE ONLY

Once you have adjusted the drum brakes, don't forget to check the handbrake. The handbrake/over-run mechanism is an important part of the system and works in conjunction with the wheel brakes.

Make sure that the drawshaft is fully extended and that the brake rod is in good condition and not bent or twisted.

40A. Pull back the over-run lever and measure the distance between it and the handbrake. Ideally it should be 5 - 10mm.

40B. If necessary, adjust it by moving the nuts on the front-end of the brake operating rod.

Once you've done this, check the brakes by engaging the hand-brake and pushing the caravan backwards on smooth, level ground. A 'click' should be heard from each brake and then you should not be able to move the caravan any further. If the brake fails to hold the caravan, readjust the brake rod until it does so.

If you do have to readjust the brake rod, check that, with the brakes disengaged, there is no drag when the caravan is pulled forward. Best of all, raise each wheel in turn from the ground and check for 'drag' when turning each wheel forwards by hand.

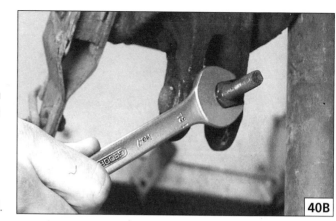

40C. Locate any grease nipples on the brake linkage, such as underneath the caravan behind the wheels and at the front, depending on the type of linkage fitted, and regrease using a grease gun with Castrol LM grease. Also grease any grease nipples that may be fitted to brake cable 'outers'.

AL-KO TYPE HANDBRAKE ONLY

IMPORTANT NOTE: It is essential that the brakes are adjusted correctly at the wheel, and the brake compensator correctly set. Do NOT attempt to adjust the handbrake until the these jobs have been correctly carried out.

The handbrake will be 'right' when, with both wheels off the ground, there is a braking effect when the handbrake is on its second or third 'click' of the ratchet. It is important that the braking effect you can feel (by turning each wheel in the direction it will go in when the caravan is travelling forwards) is equal on each wheel. If one wheel is tighter than the other, slacken that brake off *at the wheel* (not at the cables or rod) until the 'tight' brake just matches its colleague. DON'T adjust by tightening the 'loose' brake, because it can be dangerous to have binding brakes.

☐ **Job 41. Replacing a Bowden cable, when necessary.**

KNOTT AND BPW BRAKES ONLY

41A. This type of cable can be replaced without dismantling, just by lifting off the upper shroud, as shown. (Illustration, courtesy BPW.)

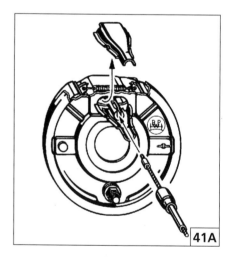

AL-KO BRAKES ONLY

41B. To replace an AL-KO cable of the type fitted to the later, asbestos-free brakes, these can also be inserted externally. After removing the steel sleeve from the support collar, the upper part of the cable support can be detached.

41C. The nipple is pressed in to the insertion eye, pulling back the cable 'outer' so that the nipple engages correctly.

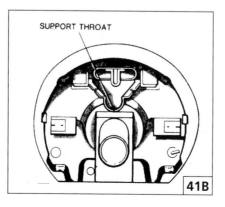

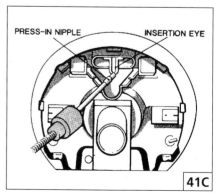

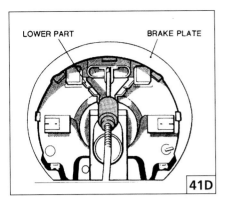

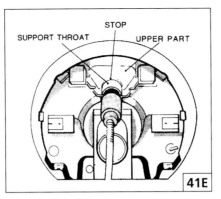

41D. The upper part of the cable support is inserted into the brake plate opening, flush with the lower, welded part of the brake support.

41E. Now the cable end-bush is pushed over the support throat as far as it will go.

41F. Once you are certain that the nipple is inserted correctly, it only remains to tighten the wire of the cable. (All five illustrations, courtesy AL-KO Kober)

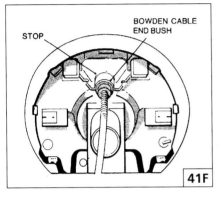

AP LOCKHEED MKII AUTO REVERSE & EARLY KNOTT BRAKES
Raise the caravan and remove brake drum, as shown earlier. Beneath the 'van, disconnect the forward ('pulling') end of the cable and release the outer case from the anchor/abutment plate. At the brake, prise the expander lever towards you as you can release the cable eye. Withdraw from the rear, fit a new cable, reassemble and readjust the brakes.

INSIDE INFORMATION: Pull the handbrake on hard, several times, before final adjustment.

☐ **Job 42 (PART I). Replace AP Lockheed MKII and early Knott brake shoes (when necessary).**

If, during the servicing of a caravan's braking system, you discover that the brake shoes are worn or damaged, it will be necessary to replace them. The main things to look for when deciding if a brake shoe requires changing are any signs of excessive wear, damage or less than 2mm thickness on the shoe's friction material. While you should be able to buy replacement brake shoes from most of the larger caravan dealerships, older brake shoes can sometimes be a bit more difficult to get hold of. If this is the case, the recommended route is to contact your local AP Lockheed service centre (or see Peak Trailers, in the Appendix to this book) where it should be possible to have your existing brake shoes relined.

SAFETY FIRST AND SPECIALIST SERVICE!
i) Obviously, your caravan's brakes are among its most important safety related items. Do NOT dismantle or attempt to perform any work on the braking system unless you are fully competent to do so. If you have not been trained in this work, but wish to carry it out, we strongly recommend that you have a your local caravan specialist workshop or qualified mechanic check your work before taking the caravan on the road. See also the section on BRAKES AND ASBESTOS in Chapter 1, Safety First! for further information. ii) Remember that brake dust can contain asbestos and in the case of older systems, it most certainly will. Since asbestos can kill: ALWAYS spray a proprietary brand of aerosol brake cleaner onto the brakes after removing the hub (available from your local auto accessory store); ALWAYS wear an efficient particle mask, gloves and a hat, and wash your hands and arms after doing the job; ALWAYS dust yourself off thoroughly out of doors; ALWAYS dispose of the old shoes, wiping rags and wiped-up dust in a sealed plastic bag, and keep children and pets away from the work area. iii) Always replace the brake shoes in sets of four - never replace the shoes on one wheel only. Keep all traces of oil or grease off the friction surfaces. iv) When adjusting the brakes, it is necessary to adjust one side first and then the other. In both cases it will be necessary to work underneath the caravan and it is therefore essential that the correct safety procedure is followed for raising and supporting the caravan. See the section on 'Raising A Caravan Safely' earlier in this chapter. v) Always specify and use ASBESTOS FREE brake linings.

IMPORTANT NOTE: Before dismantling the brake shoe assembly, take notes, sketches and even a photograph or video of the spring assembly. It is *essential* that all springs are re-attached in their correct locations. As well as examining the brake shoes for wear, carefully examine the brake springs. If any appear stretched - if the coils appear open at any point, or the hooked ends appear open - replace them with a complete new set of branded parts. DO NOT substitute any other springs! Look out for oil staining on the brakes and backplate. If any is found, the oil seals must be renewed.

It is *essential* that the hub nut is neither over-tightened nor under-tightened. We recommend having your local caravan dealer check the work when you have finished and before taking the caravan on a trip. It is also *essential* that a new split pin is used on the hub castellated nut each time it is removed. See Job 49 for details.

INSIDE INFORMATION: Before replacing the brake drum, check it for damage, cracking or excessive scoring from brake shoes. If the drums are deeply scored, see if you can have both drums lightly skimmed by an engineering workshop. Otherwise, replace them with new drums. IF THE SCORING IS DEEP, OR YOU SUSPECT THAT THE DRUMS HAVE PREVIOUSLY BEEN SKIMMED, REPLACE THEM WITH NEW. Also, hang up each drum by a piece of string or similar and tap lightly with a hammer. You should hear a clear ringing sound. If the sound is dull and flat, the drum is cracked and should be scrapped immediately and replaced with new.

REPLACING AP LOCKHEED AUTO REVERSE BRAKE SHOES ONLY

MKI ROD OPERATED VERSION

42A. The AP Lockheed brake has a conventional mechanical expander with sliding links, a micram type adjuster on the leading shoe and a carrier on the trailing shoe. When the caravan is travelling in a forward direction as the brakes are operated, the shoes are forced into contact with the brake drum and by virtue of the trailing shoe moving in the carrier and the expander being able to slide on the backplate a duo-servo braking effect is achieved.

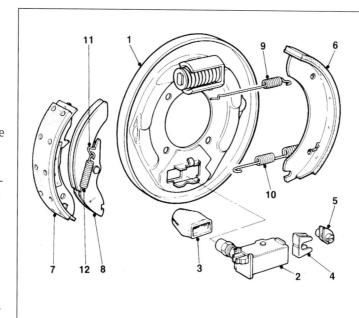

1. Backplate
2. Expander
3. Rubber boot
4. Mask
5. Micram adjuster
6. Leading brake shoe (2)
7. Trailing brake shoe (2)
8. Trailing shoe carrier
9. Pull-off spring (Black) Single coil R.H.
9. Pull-off spring (Red) Single coil L.H.
10. Pull-off spring double coil R.H.
10. Pull-off spring double coil L.H.
11. Carrier link (2)
12. Carrier spring (4)

42A

When reversing, as the brake shoes contact the drum the trailing shoe is immediately pulled around the carrier away from the expander. With the shoe moving in this direction, the design of the contact area between the shoe and carrier allows the shoe to move inwards, away from the drum, thus the braking effect is negligible and the wheel moves freely. When reversing ceases and the load is removed from the actuating mechanism, the trailing shoe is immediately pulled back into position by two return springs.

The fitting opposite the expander is fixed for the leading shoe, but the trailing shoe seats onto a powerful coil spring which acts as a torque limiter. During heavy forward braking, reaction through the trailing shoe/carrier assembly compresses the spring at a given torque thus allowing the shoe to move away from the drum and limit the brake. Note that the whole assembly is often turned, with the spring usually on the right-hand side rather than at the top.

BRAKE SHOE REMOVAL

42B. Securely chock the caravan wheel, loosen the wheel nuts on the appropriate side and jack up the wheel supporting the caravan on an axle stand. Lower the corner steadies. Fully release the handbrake, ensure that the hitch is fully extended and remove the road wheel.

42B

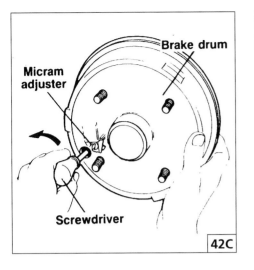

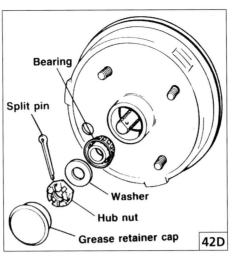

42C. Line up the hole in the brake drum with the slotted head of the micram adjuster. Back off all brake adjustment with a suitable screwdriver by turning the micram fully anti-clockwise.

42D. Prise off the hub grease retainer cap and remove the split pin, hub nut, washer and bearing. Withdraw the brake drum from the stub axle. TAKE CAREFUL NOTE OF THE SPRING AND SHOE POSITIONS.

INSIDE INFORMATION: Take care that the bearing doesn't fall out.

42E. Release the *double coil* pull-off spring, indicated here, from behind the hook on the back plate, adjacent to the expander.

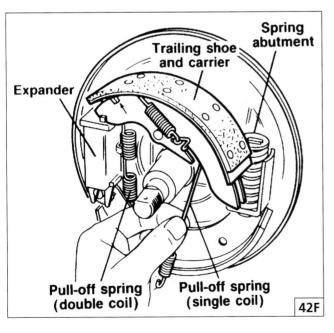

42F. At the opposite end lift the carrier and shoe away from the spring abutment and disconnect the *single coil* pull-off spring, as shown, from the leading (lower) brake shoe.

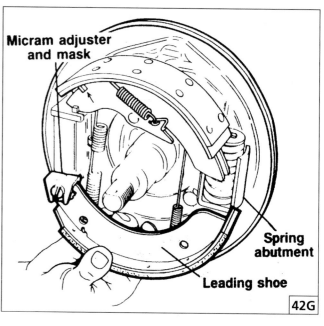

42G. Lift the leading shoe from the spring abutment and slide the adjuster and mask off the expander body. Remove both shoes from the backplate.

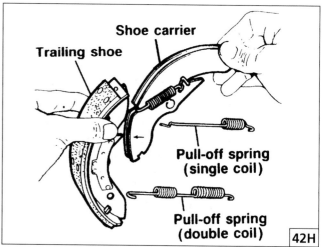

42H. Slide the carrier assembly from the trailing shoe to expose both pull-off springs. Note their positions and remove them.

INSIDE INFORMATION: The double coil spring is not interchangeable with the one on the opposite brake.

42I. This is the way in which the trailing shoe is seated in the carrier.

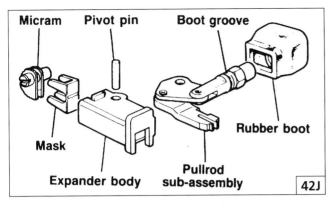

Micram · Pivot pin · Boot groove · Mask · Expander body · Pullrod sub-assembly · Rubber boot

42J

EXPANDER REMOVAL AND REPLACEMENT

42J. Disconnect the pullrod and remove the rubber boot. Withdraw the expander assembly from the backplate, push out the pivot pin and extract the pullrod sub-assembly from the expander body. Remove all dust and deposits from the backplate using an aerosol car brake cleaner and a clean rag. *Do not blow out with an air line. Do not use petrol or paraffin.*

Before replacing, lubricate the pullrod sub-assembly *using only approved brake grease,* fit into the expander body and insert the pivot pin. Fit the expander assembly onto the backplate and check that it slides freely in the slot. Pack the rubber boot with Lockheed Rubberlube (Part No. LPK 102), and slide over the pull-rod up to the backplate. Ensure that the boot lips locate correctly over the backplate tabs, and also seat into the pullrod boot groove.

42K

42K. Assemble the new shoes, carrier and springs by reversing the removal procedure.

*INSIDE INFORMATION: The easiest way of doing so is to put springs in place on the trailing shoe and carrier (top) and the leading shoe, then hook the shoes onto the expander **without** the adjuster assembly in place.*

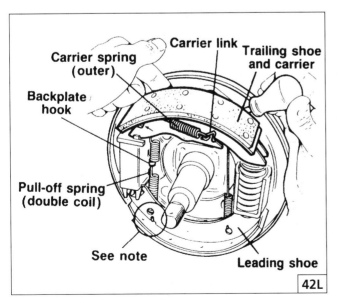

Carrier spring (outer) · Carrier link · Trailing shoe and carrier · Backplate hook · Pull-off spring (double coil) · See note · Leading shoe

42L

BRAKE SHOE REPLACEMENT

42L. Using only an approved brand of brake grease (not ordinary grease), very lightly smear all metal to metal contact points such as brake shoe and carrier tips, the abutment faces, the areas of the backplate against which the shoe webs rest, also the surface of the carrier roller. *Avoid contact of grease with shoe linings, rubber parts and the friction surface of the brake drum.*

SERVICING & MAINTENANCE

42M. You can then pull the brake shoe assemblies into place on the spring assembly, one shoe at a time. Don't despair if it takes a few goes before you manage to get the shoes back on with the springs still in place! Trying to fit the springs with the brake shoes in place is a hopeless task.

*INSIDE INFORMATION: Taking care **not to grip the friction lining material,** grip the end of the last brake shoe to be fitted with a mole grip or adjustable spanner, to give yourself the extra leverage needed to pull against the force of the spring.*

You will also have to lever the expander-end of the lower shoe away from the expander in order to fit the adjuster assembly.

42M

42N. SAFETY FIRST!
1. It is ESSENTIAL that the springs are in their correct positions. After shoe replacement ensure that the carrier springs are correctly located. The outer spring is easily seen, but the shoe and carrier should be eased away from the backplate so that the inner spring can be felt to confirm correct positioning. IMPORTANT NOTE: The double coil pull-off spring hook is located into the slotted hole adjacent to the leading shoe platform. Also ensure that the spring is behind the hook on the backplate.

2. Ensure the carrier link locates onto the spur on the trailing shoe web. Near the heel on the trailing shoe web will be seen a metal tab. Stamped into the carrier in this area is an arrow. The shoe is correctly located in the carrier when the arrow and the tab line up exactly. (See 'Carrier shoe location check' in drawing 42N.) Check the shoe action in the carrier by pushing the shoe against the carrier springs. When released the shoe should freely spring back to the marked position. Also note that, when checking the brake adjustment, the tab and arrow position must always be checked through the hole in the drum before brake adjustment is carried out.

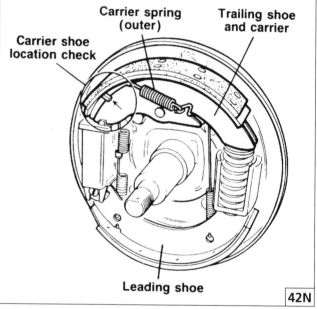

Carrier spring (outer)

Trailing shoe and carrier

Carrier shoe location check

Leading shoe

42N

42O. Ideally, follow the caravan manufacturers instructions concerning hub lubrication. As a general guide the bearings should be liberally coated with a good quality hub grease but *do not overpack the hub as this could lead to contamination of the brake linings.* (Illustration, courtesy Indespension.)

Refit the drum, bearing, washer and hub nut. Tighten nut to the torque recommended by the caravan manufacturer. Fit a new split pin and bend the ends over against the nut. Replace the hub grease retainer cap. (See Job 49.)

KNOTT AND BPW BRAKES ONLY

INSIDE INFORMATION: Always rotate the drum forwards whilst tightening the hub nut. This ensures that the taper roller bearings are seated correctly and unlikely to become loose.

Carry out the brake shoe adjustment procedure as shown in Job 39, but remember to turn the drum in the forward direction only when doing so.

42O

1. Backplate
2. Expander assembly
3. Adjuster assembly
4. Shakeproof washer (2)
5. Hexagonal nut (2)
6. Leading brake shoe (2)
7. Trailing brake shoe (2)
8. Trailing shoe carrier
9. Pull-off spring single coil (2)
10. Pull-off spring double coil (Red)
10. Pull-off spring double coil (Black)
11. Bias spring (2)
12. Carrier spring (4)

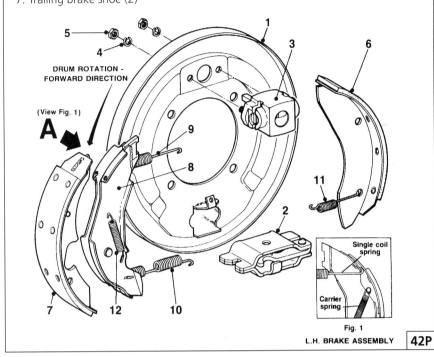

DRUM ROTATION - FORWARD DIRECTION

(View Fig. 1)

A

Single coil spring

Carrier spring

Fig. 1
L.H. BRAKE ASSEMBLY **42P**

AP LOCKHEED AUTO-REVERSE MKII CABLE OPERATED VERSION

42P. The AP Lockheed cable operated brake has a conventional mechanical expander into which fits the toe of the leading shoe and the trailing shoe carrier. In the forward direction of travel when the cable operated the expander lever, the shoes are forced into contact with the brake drum and by virtue of the trailing shoe moving in the carrier, and the expander being able to slide on the backplate, a duo-servo braking effect is achieved.

The brake features a single point adjuster with an aluminium body housing two slopping tappets and a threaded square stem that protrudes behind the backplate.

In a reverse direction when the brake shoes contact the drum the trailing shoe is immediately pulled around the carrier away from the expander. With the shoe moving in this direction, the design of the contact area between the shoe and carrier allows the shoe to move inwards, away from the drum, thus the braking effect is negligible and the wheel moves freely. When reversing ceases and the load is removed from the actuating mechanism, the trailing shoe is immediately pulled back into position by two return springs.

BRAKE SHOE REMOVAL

42Q. Securely chock the caravan wheel, loosen the wheel nuts on the appropriate side and jack up the wheel supporting the caravan on an axle stand. Lower the corner steadies. Fully release the handbrake, ensure that the hitch is fully extended and remove the road wheel.

With a suitable spanner back off all brake adjustment by turning the square adjuster screw stem behind the backplate fully anti-clockwise.

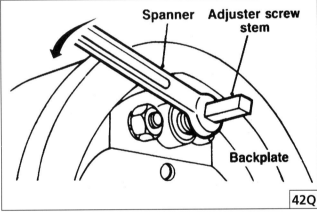

Spanner   Adjuster screw stem

Backplate

42Q

*INSIDE INFORMATION: The brake adjuster frequently seizes solid and the stem rounds off before it turns. **Always** use a proper brake adjuster, which you can buy from your local auto-accessory shop. Spray releasing fluid onto the thread **the day before you start work,** applying more fluid several times over a 24 hour period. 'Work' the adjuster backwards and forwards until the thread frees off. The adjuster assembly can be replaced if necessary, by removing the two nuts holding it to the backplate.*

42R. Prise off the hub grease retainer cap and remove split pin, hub nut, washer and bearing. Withdraw the brake drum from the stub axle.

NOTE: A different design of double coiled pull-off spring and a new design bias spring are incorporated in Spring kit LK 17056. For details of their correct location refer to Job 42S.

Bearing
Split pin
Washer
Hub nut
Grease retainer cap
42R

42S. After taking careful note of the spring and shoe positions pull the heel of the leading shoe, followed by the toe of the carrier, out of the adjuster tappet slots. Disconnect the single coil spring from the leading shoe web. Release the *double coil* spring from behind the metal tab on the backplate, then ease the leading shoe out of the expander slot. Remove the bias spring, and the double coil spring from the leading shoe web. *Make a written note of the spring hook positions* then remove the springs from the carrier. Disconnect both carrier springs and remove the trailing shoe from the carrier.

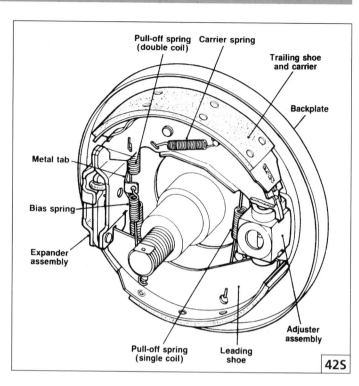

EXPANDER REMOVAL AND REPLACEMENT

42T. Disconnect the eye end of the operating cable and remove expander from backplate. Remove all dust and deposits from the backplate. *Do not blow out with an air line, it could be harmful to inhale the dust, but remove with an aerosol car brake cleaner and a damp cloth. Do not use petrol or paraffin.*

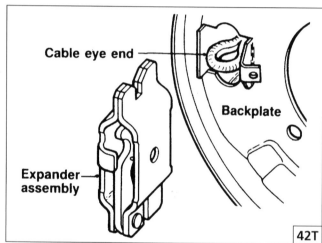

42U. Before replacing the expander, lubricate the expander operating lever and pivot pin *using only an approved brake grease* (not ordinary grease) and also smear a *very* small amount onto the area of the backplate on which the expander slides. Fit the expander against the backplate. It is particularly important to check that the brake shoes are fitted the correct way round. In the case of the left-hand brake assembly (illustrated) the expander operating lever stop faces towards the adjuster assembly. On the right-hand brake assembly it faces away from the adjuster, then the shoes are fitted accordingly.

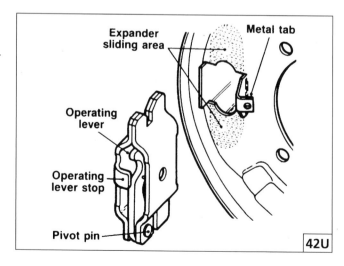

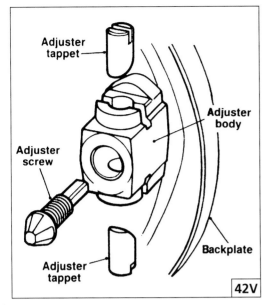

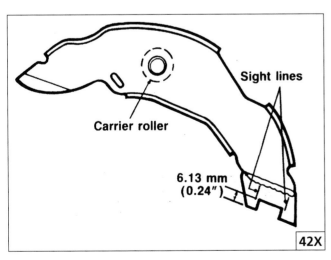

42V. If the adjuster thread has freed off nicely, the adjuster body need not be removed from the backplate. However, if the whole thing is thoroughly seized, you should replace with new. If not, it is highly advisable to strip and rebuild the adjusters when the shoes are replaced. Extract the adjuster tappets - they just pull (or fall!) out, and unscrew and withdraw the adjuster screw from the front of the adjuster. Thoroughly clean the parts, then smear tappets and adjuster screw threads *very lightly* with brake grease or with copper impregnated grease. Screw the adjuster fully into place (to provide minimum adjustment for when the brake shoes are refitted).

INSIDE INFORMATION: To help prevent seizing in future, ensure that the threads of the adjuster stem exposed behind the backplate are well coated with grease after assembly.

Insert the tappets into the adjuster body, the sloping ends matching the tapered angle of the adjuster screw.

BRAKE SHOE REPLACEMENT

42W. Using *only an approved brand of brake grease* (not ordinary grease), very lightly smear all metal to metal contact points such as the brake shoe and carrier tips, the carrier roller, the areas of the backplate against which the brake shoe platforms rest, and the adjuster tappet slots. *Be certain not to get the slightest amount of grease on the brake shoe linings or the friction surface of the brake drum.*

Assemble the trailing shoe to the carrier and secure with the two springs. Refit the shoes, carrier and pull-off springs by reversing the removal procedure.

IMPORTANT NOTES:
i) It is important that the brake shoes are fitted the correct way round. On the left-hand brake assembly (illustrated), the operating lever stop faces towards the adjuster. On the right-hand brake assembly, it faces away from the adjuster. The shoes are now fitted accordingly.

ii) Ensure that the double coil pull-off spring link is located *behind* the metal tab adjacent to the expander assembly.

iii) Check that the single coil pull-off spring is hooked into the carrier correctly as shown in illustration 42L, Fig. 1. This is a view from direction of arrow 'A' with the brake shoe assembled to the carrier.

iv) Certain chassis manufacturers fit the brake with the leading shoe in the top position. In this case the bias spring (4) is unnecessary and is not fitted.

42X. IMPORTANT NOTE: **BRAKE SHOE CARRIER** Two types of shoe carrier design have been used with this brake assembly. The later design has an increased adjuster location recess depth of 6.13 mm (0.24 in.) as illustrated. It is important that the newer carrier is only used with the later type adjuster assembly that has deeper body slots to accommodate the new carrier shape. The new adjuster assembly if required is available under AP Lockheed Part No. 4158-133, and can be identified by the Body Casting No. 3144-310 C.

Ideally follow the caravan manufacturer's instructions concerning hub lubrication. As a general guide the bearings should be liberally coated with good quality hub grease. *Do not overpack the hub as this could lead to contamination of the brake linings.* Refit the drum, bearing, washer and hub nut. Tighten nut to the torque recommended by the caravan manufacturer (see Job 49). Fit a new split pin and bend the ends over the nut. Replace the hub grease retainer cap. Carry out the brake shoe adjustment procedure described in Job 39 but remember to turn the drum in the forward direction only during this operation.

42Y. LOCATION OF LATER TYPE OF BIAS SPRING. The design and method of fitting of the bias spring has been changed from the original design. Compare your spring with those shown below and assemble accordingly.

42Z. LOCATION OF LATER TYPE OF PULL-OFF SPRING. The design and method of fitting of the pull-off spring has also been changed from the original design. Compare your spring with those shown below and assemble accordingly.

AP LOCKHEED ('STANDARD') NON-AUTOMATIC REVERSE BRAKE SHOES ONLY

Please see the drawings and parts lists detailed with Jobs 39E and 39F and read carefully all of the instructions contained within Job 42.

Thanks are due to AP Lockheed for their kind permission to use the information and drawings in this section. See Appendix 3 for information on where to obtain parts for AP Lockheed brakes.

☐ **Job 42 (PART II). Replace AL-KO brake shoes, (when necessary).**

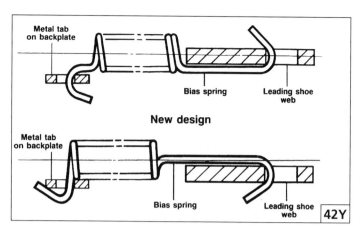

42Y

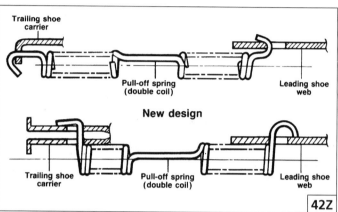

42Z

SAFETY FIRST AND SPECIALIST SERVICE!
i) Obviously, your caravan's brakes are among its most important safety related items. Do NOT dismantle or attempt to perform any work on the braking system unless you are fully competent to do so. If you have not been trained in this work, but wish to carry it out, we strongly recommend that you have a your local caravan specialist workshop or qualified mechanic check your work before taking the caravan on the road. See also the section on BRAKES AND ASBESTOS in Chapter 1, Safety First! for further information. ii) Remember that brake dust can contain asbestos and in the case of older systems, it most certainly will. Since asbestos can kill: ALWAYS spray a proprietary brand of aerosol brake cleaner onto the brakes after removing the hub (available from your local auto accessory store); ALWAYS wear an efficient particle mask, gloves and a hat, and wash your hands and arms after doing the job; ALWAYS dust yourself off thoroughly out of doors; ALWAYS dispose of the old shoes, wiping rags and wiped-up dust in a sealed plastic bag, and keep children and pets away from the work area. iii) Always replace the brake shoes in sets of four - never replace the shoes on one wheel only. Keep all traces of oil or grease off the friction surfaces. iv) When adjusting the brakes, it is necessary to adjust one side first and then the other. In both cases it will be necessary to work underneath the caravan and it is therefore essential that the correct safety procedure is followed for raising and supporting the caravan. See the section on 'Raising A Caravan Safely' earlier in this chapter. v) Always specify and use ASBESTOS FREE brake linings.

AL-KO brakes are now by far the commonest found on newer caravans, but even so, there are a number of different types. The main ones are covered here. The greatest differences arise between the earlier brakes and those fitted to the newer so-called Euro-Axle brakes. See below for details.

IMPORTANT NOTE: Before dismantling the brake shoe assembly, take notes, sketches and even a photograph or video of the spring assembly. It is *essential* that all springs are re-attached in their correct locations. As well as examining the brake shoes for wear, examine carefully the brake springs. If any appear stretched - if the coils appear open at any point, or the hooked ends appear open - replace them with a complete new set of branded parts. DO NOT substitute any other springs! Look out for oil staining on the brakes and backplate. If any is found, the oil seals must be renewed.

It is *essential* that the hub nut is neither over-tightened nor under-tightened. We recommend having your local caravan dealer check the work before taking the caravan on a trip. It is also *essential* that a new split pin is used on the hub castellated nut each time it is removed. See Job 49 for details.

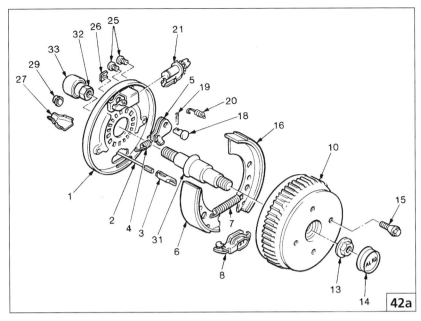

42a. In the case of the Euro-Axle, no split pin is fitted. Instead, a 'one-shot' locknut is used and it is important that a new one is always fitted after the old one has been removed. DO NOT RE-USE THESE HUB NUTS as they could then come loose, shedding the wheel/hub assembly as the caravan is travelling along. **SPECIALIST SERVICE.** Work on the Euro-Axle hub - and therefore brake replacement - is beyond the scope of most DIY repairers because the locknut (42a.13) requires a massive torque tightening figure 214 lbs/ft (290 Nm) - both plus or minus about 3% - well beyond the capacity of most workshop torque wrenches. (Illustration, courtesy AL-KO.)

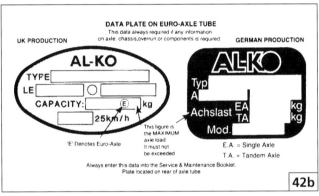

42b. All AL-KO Euro-Axles can be identified by looking for the data plate on the rear of the axle tube. In addition, the brake backplate has a gold coloured finish. (Illustration, courtesy AL-KO Kober.)

THE FOLLOWING INSTRUCTIONS RELATE ONLY TO THE AL-KO NON-EURO-AXLE BRAKES.

42c. Taking one side of the caravan at a time, jack the caravan up and support it with its corner steadies and axle stands, as described earlier in this chapter. Remove the wheel. Chock the opposite wheel, release the caravan's handbrake and make sure the hitch assembly is fully extended. IMPORTANT NOTE: See Job 39 on adjusting the brakes. Turn the star wheel as far as it will go in the *opposite* direction to the arrow on the backplate, so that the brakes are backed right off.

42d. Remove the split pin, hub nut and washer and withdraw the wheel drum from the hub. As well as examining the brake shoes for wear, examine carefully the brake springs. If any appear stretched - the coils appear open at any point - or the hooked ends appear open, replace them with a complete new set of branded parts. DO NOT substitute any other springs!

Wash off the brake backplate assembly with a proprietary brand of aerosol brake cleaner before dismantling and once again when all the parts have been removed.

1. Backplate
2. Bowden cable
3. Link
4. Tension spring (handed)
5. Transmission lever (handed)
6. Brake shoe
7. Tension spring
8. Expanding clutch
9. Inner bearing
10. Brake drum
11. Outer bearing
12. Split pin
13. Castle nut
14. Grease cap
15. Wheel bolt
16. Brake shoe (right)
17. Oil seal
18. Pivot pin
19. Split pin
20. Pressure spring
21. Leaf spring
22. Adjusting screw
23. 'Starred wheel' adjuster
24. Pressure clip
25. Screw
26. Cover plate
27. Cable cover (upper not shown)
28. Bush
29. Lockwasher (not fitted to 2051 brake unit)

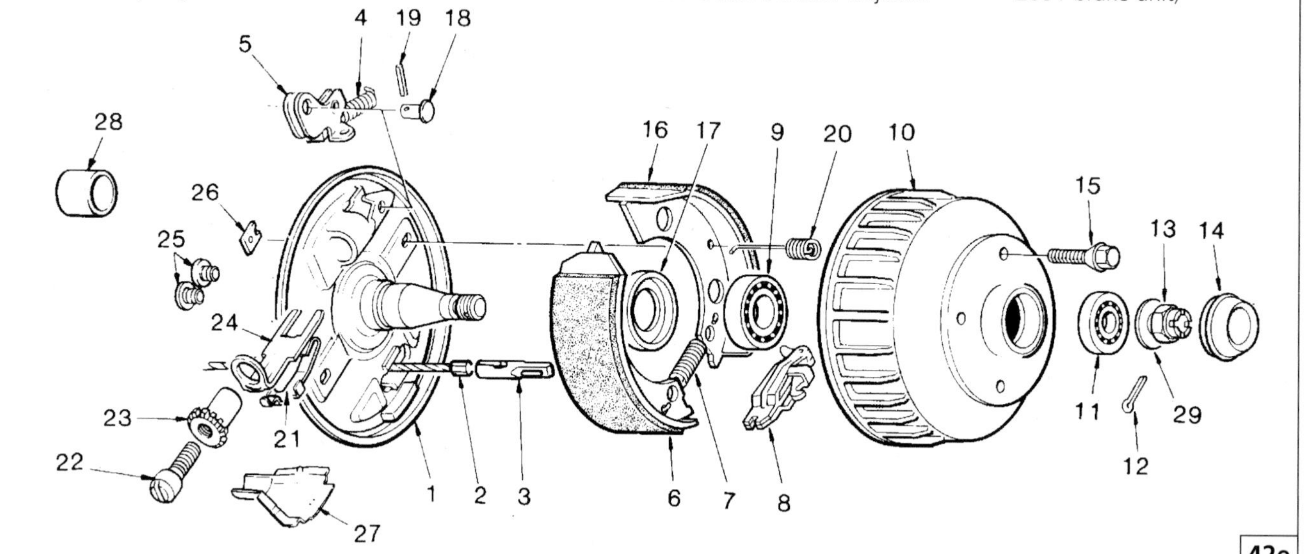

42e. The layout of the AL-KO brake types 1637 and 2051 is as shown here. NOTE THAT PART NO. 29 IS NOT FITTED TO THE 2051 BRAKE. This drawing is applicable to several different sizes of brake.

INSIDE INFORMATION: Be sure to take the old parts with you to your AL-KO stockist when ordering new parts. (Illustration, courtesy AL-KO.)

42f. This is the layout of the following AL-KO brake types: 1635, 1636, 2035, 2050 and 2350. (Illustration, courtesy AL-KO.)

1. Brake drum
2. Wheel bolt
3. Castle nut
4. Grease cap
5. Lock washer
6. Split pin
7. Outer taper roller bearing
8. Expanding clutch
9. Tension spring
10. Brake shoe
11. Cover plates
12. Backplate (handed)
13. 'Starred wheel' adjuster
14. Adjusting screw
15. Pressure spring
16. Transmission lever (handed)
17. Split pin
18. Pivot pin
19. Oil seal
20. Inner taper roller bearing
21. Bowden cable tension spring

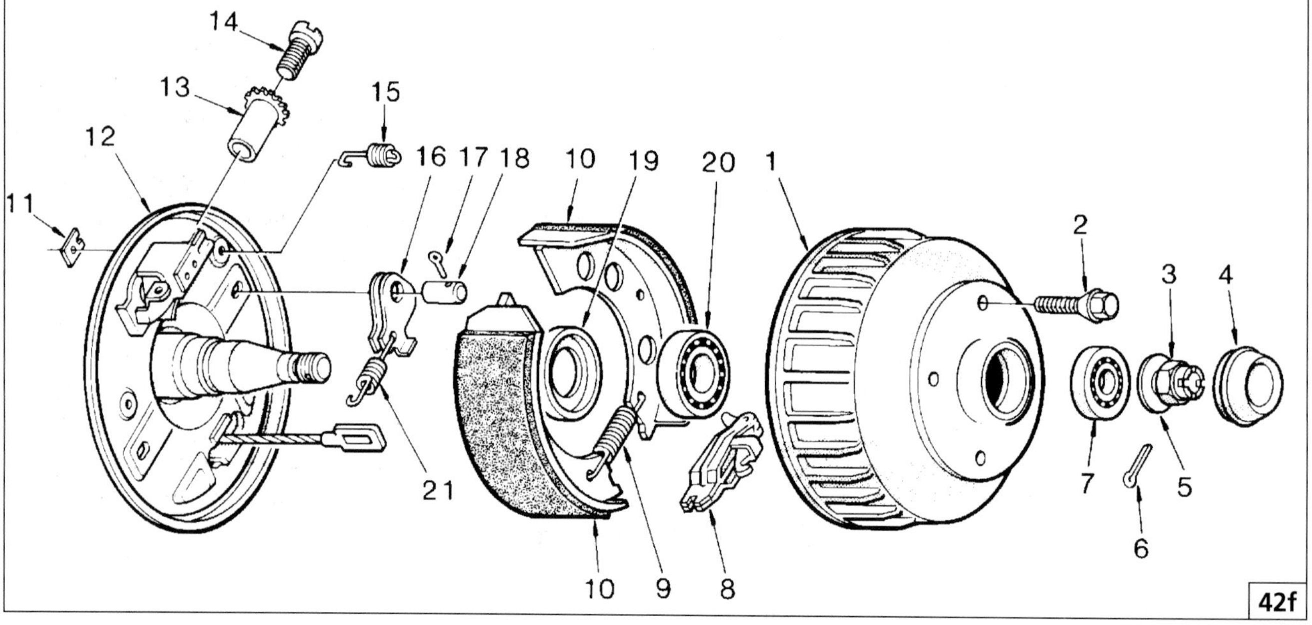

42g.

42h.

42g. Push in the brake shoe retaining springs and remove the sprung retaining clips at the rear of the hub. Take care not to lose these clips.

42h. You can now remove the brake shoes from the hub.

42i. Replace the old shoes with the new ones, making sure that you put them on the right way up. Look out for the embossed marking arrows on the Type 1625 and 1627 brake shoes. *The brakes will not work if the shoes are fitted to the wrong side.* For brake Types 2051 and 2361, the left and right shoes are identical. See 42e and 42f to help you identify which type of AL-KO Kober brakes you have and, if in any doubt, consult your dealer.

42i.

Reposition the brake shoes on to the hub and replace the retaining springs and their retaining clips. Ensure the CORRECT POSITIONS OF BRAKE SHOE SPRINGS! Refer to the other side of the caravan, if necessary.

Use a *very small* amount of *brake grease* on all metal contact areas - don't use ordinary grease and DON'T get any lubricants onto any of the friction areas or the inside of the brake drum.

INSIDE INFORMATION: Before replacing the brake drum, check it for damage, cracking or excessive scoring from brake shoes. If there is excessive scoring, replace them with new drums. Also, hang up each drum by a piece of string or similar and tap lightly with a hammer. You should hear a clear ringing sound. If the sound is dull and flat, the drum is cracked and should be scrapped immediately and replaced with new.

Replace the drum, washer, hub nut and refit a new split pin. See Job 49 for details. Replace the wheel and carry out the same job on the caravan's other wheel, then readjust the brakes.

☐ **Job 42 (PART III). Replace Knott brake shoes (when necessary).**

SAFETY FIRST AND SPECIALIST SERVICE!
i) Obviously, your caravan's brakes are among its most important safety related items. Do NOT dismantle or attempt to perform any work on the braking system unless you are fully competent to do so. If you have not been trained in this work, but wish to carry it out, we strongly recommend that you have a your local caravan specialist workshop or qualified mechanic check your work before taking the caravan on the road. See also the section on BRAKES AND ASBESTOS in Chapter 1, Safety First! for further information. ii) Remember that brake dust can contain asbestos and in the case of older systems, it most certainly will. Since asbestos can kill: ALWAYS spray a proprietary brand of aerosol brake cleaner onto the brakes after removing the hub (available from your local auto accessory store); ALWAYS wear an efficient particle mask, gloves and a hat, and wash your hands and arms after doing the job; ALWAYS dust yourself off thoroughly out of doors; ALWAYS dispose of the old shoes, wiping rags and wiped-up dust in a sealed plastic bag, and keep children and pets away from the work area. iii) Always replace the brake shoes in sets of four - never replace the shoes on one wheel only. Keep all traces of oil or grease off the friction surfaces. iv) When adjusting the brakes, it is necessary to adjust one side first and then the other. In both cases it will be necessary to work underneath the caravan and it is therefore essential that the correct safety procedure is followed for raising and supporting the caravan. See the section on 'Raising A Caravan Safely' earlier in this chapter. v) Always specify and use ASBESTOS FREE brake linings.

Please read the IMPORTANT NOTE before Job 42a on page 76.

SERVICING & MAINTENANCE

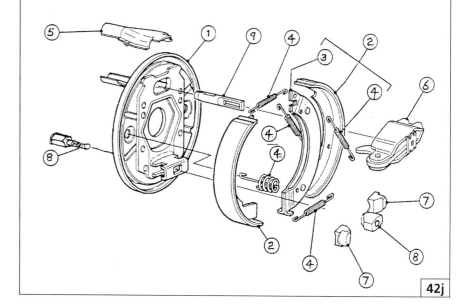

1. Backplate pressing
2. Brake shoes
3. Auto-reverse brake shoe carrier
4. Brake spring set
5. Cable shroud
6. Brake expander
7. Adjustment shoe-post
8. Adjustment wedge and bolt
9. Torpedo connector

42j. This is the layout of the main Knott brake system. Please read carefully all of the notes, information and *Safety First!* relating to the other brake systems described here. (Illustration, courtesy Knott)

☐ Job 43. Check for chassis damage.

43A. A caravan's chassis should last the life of the caravan itself. However, it's certainly worth checking it occasionally for evidence of damage. Up to 1982 most caravans were built on painted, non-galvanised steel box-section chassis. In this case, if damage is discovered it is possible to get it repaired by a skilled welder, although it's always advisable to have any damage checked by a qualified caravan expert. With the galvanised steel chassis fitted to a majority of caravans after 1982, any sort of damage should be immediately referred to a caravan dealer.

> **SAFETY FIRST!**
> **Home welding of galvanised steel should not be attempted because of the toxic nature of the fumes given off.**

43B. You should also check all of the chassis assembly and mounting bolts for tightness. (Illustration, courtesy BPW.)

A smaller number of caravans have been built on aluminium chassis and while, like the other types, in a majority of cases these should last for good number of years, problems can occur. In the main with aluminium chassis watch out for the appearance of hair-line cracks where some members of the chassis meet, particularly around the axle and A-frame. You'll need to clean the chassis carefully before checking. If cracks are discovered, the caravan must be taken to an approved caravan dealership for specialist repair.

INSIDE INFORMATION: If steel components are bolted to an aluminium chassis, there should be a gasket to keep the steel and aluminium apart and prevent electrolytic corrosion. Check!

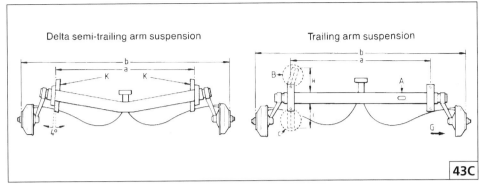

Delta semi-trailing arm suspension   Trailing arm suspension

43C. AL-KO also recommend that you should check the axle tube for damage. (Illustration, courtesy AL-KO Kober.)

43C

43D

43D. INSIDE INFORMATION: *Severe chassis damage, such as would be caused by an accident, could lead to one or more wheels running 'out of true', and this would clearly show up as a tyre worn more heavily on one side than the other.* **SPECIALIST SERVICE.** *If this is something you suspect, have your caravan dealer look over the chassis for you.*

☐ Job 44. Check chassis corrosion.

EARLY, NON-GALVANISED CHASSIS

Examine the chassis to see if there is any evidence of corrosion, especially likely on earlier, non-galvanised chassis. If any is found, wire brush, sand or scrape off the rust back to shiny metal and apply a coat of wax-based chassis protection, brush-on or aerosol.

INSIDE INFORMATION: *The cheaper, black, brush-on type of underseal can be worse than useless. Over the years it will dry out, allowing moisture to creep beneath and make matters worse rather than better. Most of the wax-based 'underseals', such as Waxoyl, won't go brittle and contain corrosion inhibitors.*

GALVANISED CHASSIS

Light deposits of 'white rust' can be removed using a hard nylon or wire brush, and the affected area is best treated with a brush-on wax-based underbody sealer or, if you want to preserve the appearance, with a zinc-rich paint.

> **SAFETY FIRST!**
> **Under no circumstances should any holes be drilled in the chassis. This could seriously affect the integral structural strength of the chassis and will also cause a break in the galvanised protection.**

FACT FILE:

GALVANISED CHASSIS CORROSION

One problem that has caused concern with owners of caravans with galvanised chassis is 'white rust'. In fact this term has very little in common with rust as the term applies to steel. Instead it refers to the formation of a soft, porous, light grey oxidisation layer on the chassis and, although it's not to be welcomed, it is evidence that the zinc galvanising is doing its job. When zinc and steel exist next to each other, the zinc acts as a 'sacrificial anode' in the corrosion process. In other words, it 'lays down its life' in order to protect the steel in the chassis. However, if the galvanising is thin, scratched or abraded away, or the corrosion is very severe, rust will eventually take hold of the steel in the chassis as the galvanising is 'used up'.

☐ Job 45. Check suspension springs.

EARLY MODELS WITHOUT RUBBER SUSPENSION ONLY

Check that the coil springs are in good condition with no signs of breaks or sagging. Is the caravan lower on one side than the other, when parked on level ground and evenly loaded? If so, **SPECIALIST SERVICE:** you may need to have both springs renewed.

CARAVANS WITH RUBBER SUSPENSION ONLY

There is very little to go wrong with rubber suspension. Check that the steel housings for the suspensions rubbers have not corroded; that the rubber has not gone soft, allowing the caravan to be lower on one side than the other when standing on level ground and when evenly loaded; that the rubber has not gone soft and started to 'ooze' out of its housing. When the suspension units need replacing, this may be a SPECIALIST SERVICE job.

INSIDE INFORMATION: *the life of the suspension rubbers will be prolonged by supporting the caravan on axle stands during the winter months (if it is not to be used, of course!). Fitting 'winter wheels' will take the load off the tyres but not off the suspension, of course.*

Servicing & Maintenance

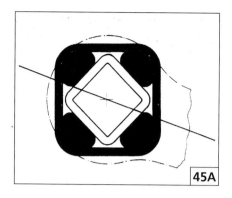

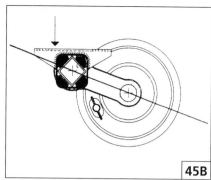

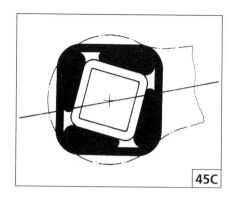

45A. In principle, rubber suspension operates quite simply. Rubber strips are pressed into a cavity between two steel tubes, one at an angle to the other. These BPW springs use square tubes and four rubber strips, AL-KO units tend to use three strips and different shaped tubes.

45B. As a downward force is placed upon the suspension...

45C. ...the rubber strips compress. They do not wear and cannot be replaced. Of course, all rubber deteriorates over a long period of time, so check older caravans for suspension sagging. (All three illustrations, courtesy BPW.)

FACT FILE: RUBBER SUSPENSION

Rubber suspension is excellent for caravans and, in most applications, does not require the use of separate shock absorbers, although some modern caravans do also have them fitted.

□ **Job 46. Check hydraulic shock absorbers.**

OLDER MODELS AND SOME OTHERS

46A. If your caravan is fitted with car-type telescopic shock absorbers, check the body of each shock absorber for leaks or for corrosion. In either case, it will need replacement.

46B. If telescopic shock absorbers are fitted, check the rubber bushes at the top and bottom end of each shock absorber. Grasp each end of the shock absorber in your hand and try to move it, TAKING CARE NOT TO PULL THE CARAVAN OFF ITS SUPPORTS. If the bush has 'spread' or is missing, and if any wear is evident, fit new bushes.

EVERY 12 MONTHS, OR AT THE END OF EVERY SEASON

47A

☐ **Job 47. Check stabiliser.**

BLADE-TYPE STABILISER

47A. The most popular type of stabiliser - the blade-type - has to have a certain amount of resistance at the damper. Use bathroom scales to ensure that the stabiliser gives about 60 lbs. (28 kg) of "push" before the blade starts to move. Check the maker's instructions for the exact figure for your stabiliser.

47B

47B. Adjust the adjusting nut and bolt as appropriate.

AL-KO AKS2000 STABILISER

Like many other caravan accessories, the AL-KO AKS2000 stabiliser does require occasional maintenance and servicing. The main point to consider is the brake pads within the stabiliser. A guide on the side of the stabiliser shows if the pads need replacing by the position of three numbers, two on the casing and one on the pivot. If, as the handle on the stabiliser is engaged, No.1 is between No.2 and No.3, the pads are OK. If, however, No.1 is next to No.2, then the pads need replacing.

Servicing the AKS2000 stabiliser is a job that requires specialist tools and, as a result, will need to be referred to a AL-KO approved caravan dealer.

NOTE: Do not oil or grease a towcar's towball when this type of AL-KO stabiliser is fitted, as this will make the AKS2000 ineffective and decompose the pads.

LUBRICATION POINTS

There are a number of points on a caravan that require regular lubrication, either with Castrol LM grease or light, general purpose oil. For a floor plan showing all the lubrication points see Appendix 1: Lubricants on page 115. Keeping these various areas well lubricated is an essential part of keeping a caravan in good working order. For all lubrication it is recommended that you use general purpose grease and oil from a top-quality company such as Castrol. Although there will be differences between different models, the general principles remain the same. You just have to find the right lubrication points for your particular model.

☐ **Job 48. Check wheel hub for wear.**

48

SAFETY FIRST!
Follow the safety information at the start of this chapter and in Chapter 1, Safety First! regarding safe procedure when working underneath a caravan supported off the ground.

Hub bearings can and do wear out. Lift each wheel in turn off the ground and try spinning the wheel. If you hear a rumbling sound, it is very likely that a wheel bearing has worn and will need replacement. This may be a **SPECIALIST SERVICE** job.

48. You should also check the wheel bearings by grasping the wheel top and bottom and trying to rock the wheel. If there is any sign of movement, this is probably an indication that the bearing is worn depending on type. It may need adjustment or replacement.

INSIDE INFORMATION: Have an assistant look at the inside of the wheel/hub assembly to check whether there is discernible movement in the hub bearings, or whether the whole assembly is moving on the suspension.

SPECIALIST SERVICE. If you suspect that there is too much free movement, have your specialist take a look. It really needs the eye of experience to tell for sure just how much play is too much!

SERVICING & MAINTENANCE

☐ **Job. 49. Replace wheel bearing.**

AL-KO EURO-AXLE

Many caravans built since 1992 were based on an AL-KO Euro-axle. These are manufactured with sealed for life bearings which are maintenance free. Therefore no attempt should be made to replace or service these bearings. This is similarly the case with the less common Knott axles built from 1991. SPECIALIST SERVICE: If excess wear is found in these items, consult your local caravan specialist workshop.

SERVICEABLE-TYPE HUBS, WHEN NECESSARY

For caravans not fitted with an AL-KO Euro-axle, checking and servicing the hubs on different types of caravans is basically similar. In each case, the brake drum has to be removed.

49A

SAFETY FIRST!
Brakes are commonly fitted with brake shoes containing asbestos. As a result, when removing the dust from the wheel: i) NEVER use a brush or blow the dust out with an airline. ii) ALWAYS spray a proprietary brand of aerosol brake cleaner onto the brakes and wipe with a damp cloth. ii) Seal dust and used wet cloths in a plastic bag immediately after you have finished with them and dispose of safely. iii) Always wear an efficient particle face mask. ASBESTOS DUST KILLS!

49B

49A. Taking one side at a time, jack the caravan up and remove the wheel. It is *essential* that you slacken off the brake adjusters so that the brake shoes don't prevent removal of the drum. See Job 39.

49B. Remove the grease cap, levering and tapping until it comes free, but taking care not to damage it and take out the split pin from the castellated hub nut. Remove the hub nut.

49C

49C. Taking care not to lose the central collar (when fitted), remove the brake drum. The drum may need to be tapped free using *only* a soft-faced mallet, used on the edge of the drum.

49D. Using a proprietary brand of aerosol brake cleaner and a rag, wipe away any brake dust from the brake drum and wheel hub. DO NOT BLOW THE DUST OUT AND ALWAYS WEAR AN EFFICIENT PARTICLE FACE MASK.

49D

49E. Check the condition of the brake shoes. If they appear worn or damaged, or the rivets are near to the surface of the shoes, replace them. See Job 42.

49F. Remove the outer bearings from the brake drum and renew the oil seal/s, taking care not to nick or damage the rubber lip as the seal/s are tapped home. Repack the inside of the bearing housing with Castrol LM High Melting Point grease, taking care not to overfill it.

On models with an inner bearing race, that will also have to be removed and replaced taking note of the above information regarding oil seals. **SPECIALIST SERVICE.** If the bearing is a pressed fit, it won't be possible to replace the bearing at home, but you may be able to complete the job by having a specialist engineering workshop press out and replace the bearings for you.

49G. Replace the outer bearing, pushing grease into the bearing race. In the case of some hubs, including some B&B units *without* taper roller bearings, you should tighten the hub nut up to 26lb/ft (3.7kg/m) using a torque wrench. *It is essential that you check your caravan manual for details as to the correct procedure for your model.*

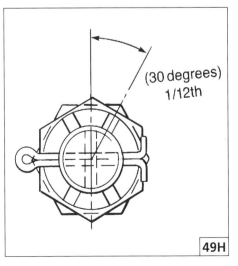

49H. With many hubs, including AL-KO non-Euro-Axle hubs, you tighten the hub nut until the hub movement *just* feels impaired when you turn it; no more. Then back the nut off *one flat* (30 degrees) and make certain that the hub can spin without feeling tight or impaired. If it does feel tight, back off one more flat until it *just* runs free. Always fit a new split pin. (NEVER reuse the old one!) (Illustration, courtesy AL-KO.)

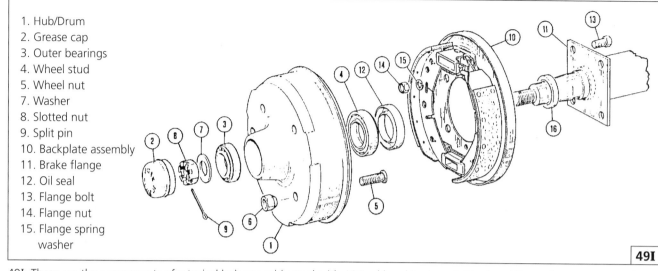

1. Hub/Drum
2. Grease cap
3. Outer bearings
4. Wheel stud
5. Wheel nut
7. Washer
8. Slotted nut
9. Split pin
10. Backplate assembly
11. Brake flange
12. Oil seal
13. Flange bolt
14. Flange nut
15. Flange spring
   washer

49I

49I. These are the components of a typical hub assembly used with AP Lockheed 'automatic' brakes. (Illustration, courtesy Peak Trailers)

IMPORTANT NOTE: Different types of hub have different tightening torque requirements. Check with your caravan's handbook, the original manufacturer or your local caravan dealership for details. Incorrect adjustment will result in excessive wear and bearing damage. We recommend having a trained mechanic check your work before taking the caravan on the road.

Repeat the procedure on the other side of the caravan.

☐ Job 50. Adjust suspension.

B&B-TYPE CHASSIS ONLY

With older caravans built on B&B-type of chassis and running gear, the suspension system is of the coil and hydraulic damper type and it is necessary to periodically adjust the suspension unit. This should be done when the caravan is fully laden to its maximum authorised weight.

Working on one side at a time, jack up the caravan as described earlier and remove the wheel.

50A. Locate the nut at the top of the coil spring and slacken it off by one turn. This nut can often become extremely tight and it may be useful to apply a product such as Castrolease releasing fluid to help loosen the nut. Refit the wheel, lower the caravan back to ground level and load the caravan up to its fully maximum authorised weight.

50B. Chock the caravan's wheels, lower the corner steadies and place axle stands under the axle. Then, from underneath the caravan adjust the bolt at the bottom of the swinging arm until it is parallel with the main axle member.

Come out from under the caravan, jack it up and remove the wheel. Retighten the nut at the top of the coil spring and replace the caravan's wheel.

Repeat the procedure on the other side of the caravan.

RUBBER SUSPENSION

As described earlier, the rubber suspension axle that is the standard fitting on AL-KO and Knott chassis is a maintenance free set-up. In particular DO NOT oil the rubber - oil destroys rubber!

☐ Job 51. Replace gas regulator and hose.

SPECIALIST SERVICE. The regulator and hose that connects the gas bottle to the gas appliances in a caravan should be replaced every 12 months. Use only original equipment spares available from most caravan dealerships.

50A

50B

Job 52. Service gas system.

SPECIALIST SERVICE. While servicing most areas of a caravan are within the abilities of a competent DIY enthusiast, one that should undoubtedly be left to a qualified expert is the gas system. It is strongly advisable to have the gas system checked over by a qualified expert at your local caravan dealership every 12 months.

While this work is being done, if you are in the slightest doubt about any other servicing or maintenance work that you may have carried out on the caravan, ask the experts to check it as a safeguard. It's far better to spend out a few pounds to make sure that everything in the caravan is working efficiently and, more importantly, safely, than have it go wrong at a later date possibly causing greater damage that may well cost a great deal of money to put right.

Job 53. Check seams for leaks.

Check all the seams minutely for cracking and replace sealant where necessary. If the sealant along the exterior seams of a caravan appears to be cracked or flaking, it's essential to reseal those seams. Although this is a pretty simple job, don't be put off if the first few attempts turn out untidy, because the sealant is messy to use and has a tendency to be on the sticky side. Just have plenty of rags available to clean it off and try again.

INSIDE INFORMATION: Before starting, find out which solvent will be needed to clean off the sealer. Try white spirit first, then methylated spirit. If cellulose thinners is needed, use a different sealer, because there is the risk that you will wipe paint off your caravan as you wipe off the excess sealer.

IMPORTANT INFORMATION: This is a job that should only be carried out under cover and preferably after several fine days to dry things out. The last thing that you want is to for rain to get in as you're cleaning the old sealant out of the seam. If you find moisture trapped in the seam, dry it out thoroughly with a hair dryer on a cool setting before starting work. DON'T use the hairdryer too hot or dwell too long in one place because you could blister the paint.

53A. Scrape out the old sealant that has become loose, taking care not to scratch the caravan's paintwork.

FACT FILE: LEAKING SEAMS

"Leaking seams" are two words word that send fear through the heart of any caravanner! Nothing makes a caravan deteriorate faster than moisture getting in through the outer panels and, because of the unavoidable flexing of a caravan's body as it is being towed and used, leaks are inevitable sooner or later. There is, however, no reason why you shouldn't be able to keep your caravan well sealed and cared for, through regular maintenance. It is therefore important to keep a regular check on external body seams.

When choosing which sealant to use, go for the non-hardening, silicone, exterior type. Non-silicone types dry out, crack and are a waste of time, although they are much less expensive. There are a number of different makes on the market and your local caravan accessory shop should be able to supply you with a product specifically for caravans. Whichever type you try do be careful to pick a colour that matches the caravan's body colour.

IMPORTANT NOTE: Make sure you use a sealant recommended by the caravan manufacturer. Not all chemical compositions suit all construction types.

53B. Clean off the surface immediately around the seam with white spirit and a clean cloth.

53C. Place masking tape down either side of the seam to stop any excess sealant sticking to the caravan.

53A

53B

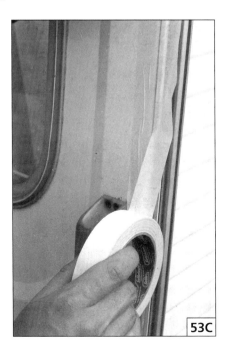
53C

53D. Using the correct sort of sealing gun, carefully and smoothly apply the sealant down the length of the seam.

INSIDE INFORMATION: When you cut the end off the applicator nozzle, cut off as little as you can reasonably get away with. The further down the tapering nozzle you cut, the larger the hole - and the more that sealer will go everywhere! A small hole will also make it easier to inject the sealer deeper into the seam.

Familiarise yourself with the working of the gun before you start. As soon as you finish a 'run', take the pressure off by pressing the release lever on the gun, otherwise sealer will continue to emerge for some time. Do no more than about a meter (one yard) at a time.

53E. Using a spatula, carefully smooth down the sealant. To help give a smooth finish it can help to wet the sealant by dipping the end of the spatula in water.

53F. Remove the masking tape and clean off any excess sealant with white spirit. Although this type of sealant will not harden completely, it should be left for a while to set slightly.

(Photographs courtesy of Caravan Plus/Peter Greenhalf)

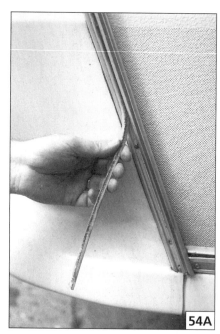

Job 54. Check awning rail seal.

The awning rail is another common area on a caravan which is prone to letting in damp if left untreated. The process of resealing the awning rail is basically very similar to the exterior seams, although there is a little more involved.

54A. Very carefully prise out the plastic insert that often runs along the length of the middle of the awning rail.

54B. Remove the screws, nails or staples that hold the awning rail into place.

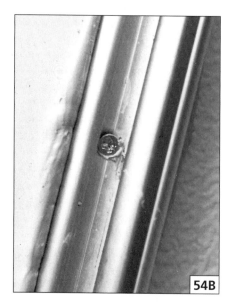

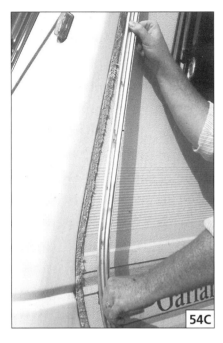

54C. Carefully, lift the awning rail away from the caravan, taking care not to bend it.

INSIDE INFORMATION: You'll find it easier if you have an assistant help you at this stage.

54D. Check the area where the rail was placed for signs of damp. Clean these marks off with hot water and soap.

54E. Using a piece of plastic so as not to damage the surface, clean off the old sealing mastic from the caravan and the awning rail.

54F. Apply some new non-setting, silicone sealant to the side of the caravan where you'll replace the awning rail.

54G. Put the cleaned awning rail back into position and use new screws, nails or staples to fix it in place.

54H. Clean off the excess sealant that might have squeezed out with some white spirit on a rag. Then re-insert the plastic strip.

(Photographs courtesy of Caravan Plus/Peter Greenhalf)

54F

Job 55. Polish windows.

A majority of caravan windows are made from acrylic and are prone to picking up an awful lot of road dirt and minor scratches. For washing the windows down use warm water, a mild detergent and a soft cloth. DO NOT use a sponge on dirty windows. Once the dirt has been removed, dry the windows off with a chamois leather.

54G

As for dealing with small scratches on acrylic windows, a small amount of a cutting compound, such as T-cut, on a soft cloth will help. It won't actually get rid of deep scratches, but it will remove slight clouding and probably improve the clarity of the 'glass'. Removing tar from acrylic windows is a matter of getting hold of a propriety Tar Remover from one of the larger car accessory shops. DO NOT use petrol or other chemicals as these can damage the windows and can cause a fire hazard.

Job 56. Check window seals.

While you're at it, take a good, close look at the rubber seals that run around the windows. When they're a few years old and the sun has been on them for a while, they can begin to crack and perish. Replacements can be purchased from most larger caravan accessory shops and it's simply a matter of removing the old seals and fitting the new ones back in their place.

*INSIDE INFORMATION: i) rubber seals can be the very devil to ease into place when they are dry. Brush on a mild solution of washing up liquid in water, and the job will become far easier! ii) See if you can borrow or hire the special tool from your caravan dealer: it's **much** easier!*

54H

Job 57. Check bodywork.

If the bodywork on your caravan begins to get a bit dull and mucky, the best treatment is to get hold of a bucket, some warm water, a dash of car shampoo, a sponge and give the van a thorough wash-down. The odd spot of polishing with a good quality car wax should help maintain the caravan's sheen.

If the bodywork has succumbed to stains, tough marks or perhaps road tar DO NOT be tempted to use any type of abrasive cleaner. Instead use a soft cloth dampened with some white spirit to clean some of the marks and stains off.

If the paintwork has become scratched or badly faded then there are two options to consider. The first option is to cover the affected area with stickers or reflectors. This is a simple solution and takes very little effort or application time. Cost is also low with stickers and reflectors widely available from most car and caravan accessory shops.

The second option is to respray the affected area. However, while some of the larger caravan manufacturers do occasionally supply touch-up paints through dealerships, older caravans may prove a more difficult problem. One solution is to make do with as close a colour as you can get through a car accessory shop.

INSIDE INFORMATION: Car paint factors regularly mix paint to match car bodywork. Find your local paint factor in Yellow Pages and ask if someone can call in to see you next time they are in your area. Ask them to bring their 'paint chips' - colour cards - with them and they will be able to find the regular, car manufacturer's colour nearest to that of your caravan. Better still, if you can remove the top half of your caravan door for a few hours, remove it and take it to a local body repair shop with their own mixing scheme and have them mix up some paint to match your caravan's colour.

When it comes to covering up actual damage to a caravan's bodywork, the pursuit can prove more demanding, depending on where it is on the body. Dents of up to six inches long on smooth areas of the aluminium wall can generally be filled with the type of body filler available through car accessory shops. This, however, is a very much more complicated job on ribbed aluminium panels. For dents up to about four inches it is possible to include a rough copy of the ribbing without it showing through too much by gently scoring the body filler before it dries, but you'll never get it to look exactly the same unless you are skilled. If the appearance matters to you, make this a SPECIALIST SERVICE item. For larger dents unfortunately, either on smooth or ribbed aluminium panels, it will be necessary to have the panel replaced by an authorised caravan dealer.

When it comes to the plastic panels on a caravan, such as the main front and rear sections, the picture is a lot more straightforward. If the problem is a small crack then it can be filled by using a flexible plastic sealant available from car accessory shops. Unfortunately, anything any larger really requires the panel being replaced by a dealer. Otherwise there's a serious threat of rain getting into the cracks and then into the main internal structure of the 'van.

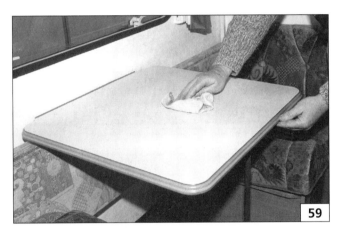

Job 58. Clean upholstery.

Cleaning the upholstery in your caravan is very much the same as the upholstery at home, although obviously on a much smaller scale. One problem that you might encounter is that the seat covers aren't always detachable. In this case there are a number of upholstery cleaners similar to those available for cleaning the interior of cars, suitable for use with the upholstery *in situ*.

If the upholstery is covered with cotton print outers, then it is often necessary to have these dry cleaned. If in doubt, consult your dealer or local dry cleaner.

59

As for the carpets in caravans, any proprietary carpet cleaner should do the job, along with regular attention from a vacuum cleaner. Some modern and continental caravans are now fitted with removable carpets allowing them to be taken out of the caravan and given a more thorough cleaning.

Job 59. Clean interior surfaces.

59. For light marks and smears on general surfaces, the walls or the roof lining use a damp cloth and a mild general purpose cleaner. For plastic or aluminium surfaces make sure that only a very small amount of non-abrasive cleaner is used with tepid water an a soft cloth.

Job 60. Lubricate hinges and catches.

60. While cleaning the furniture, apply a small amount of light oil to the hinges and catches on any doors, drawers and lockers and check that all are working satisfactorily. Nylon catches do break and replacements are generally available.

60

SERVICING & MAINTENANCE

PREPARING FOR STORAGE AT END OF SEASON

☐ Job 61. Check insurance policy!

Make sure that any insurance cover you might have on your caravan covers it when it's left unattended for a long period of time and whether any specific anti-theft measures are compulsory on your policy.

☐ Job 62. Prepare storage area.

62

INSIDE INFORMATION: Do not store your caravan under trees. Not only is there the added risk of storm damage, the resin from some types of tree can cause permanent damage to paintwork.

62. There are a number of options for storing your caravan over the winter:

i) Keep it at home on your driveway. This is a common enough solution and as long as your driveway is wide enough, you should have no problem. However, before you do this, check with your local council (and in your house deeds) to see if they allow caravans to be stored on driveways. Some require that you apply for planning permission first.

ii) Store it at a local site or farm. Often larger sites and farms will put areas aside for storing caravans and this is certainly one way of keeping your van well out of the way. However, there are problems. Caravans are often stored close together which can be disastrous in cases of fire. Security is extremely difficult. It can also be rather expensive!

iii) Specialist storage facilities. Although relatively uncommon, there is a growing number of specialist caravan storage facilities, some of which even offer undercover storage. These are certainly safer than some farms but will undoubtedly cost more and places may be restricted.

To find your local farm, site or specialist caravan storage, consult Yellow Pages or give either The Caravan Club or The Camping and Caravanning Club a call. Alternatively, ask at your local caravan dealership.

Whichever storage option you go for, there are a number of jobs to carry out on your caravan before it can be safely stored away. These will ensure that the caravan will last the winter unaffected by any adverse weather and need only a minimal amount of preparation before being ready for use when the new season comes along.

☐ Job 63. Drain water system.

Just as in your home, if water is allowed to freeze in the pipes of a caravan, the pipes can crack and, when the frozen water thaws, there'll be a flood in your caravan. Therefore it's necessary to drain the caravan's water system.

First, disconnect the water supply and the caravan's battery. Then open all the taps. This should allow any water in the system to drain out. Make sure there are no sagging pipe runs in which water may have gathered.

63. In addition, don't forget the water heater tank. The most common of these is the Carver Cascade type of water heater. Draining this is a simple matter of locating the drainage screw next to the vent, removing it and allowing the tank to drain. This might well take an hour. Once it's finished draining, replace the plug. (Illustration, courtesy Carver)

63

Ensure that you cover up all the water inlets and taps to stop insects crawling in and blocking up the pipes.

☐ Job 64. Remove water filter.

Because the water filter has been busy removing all sorts of impurities from the water, it could be a good breeding ground for bugs over the winter months. Take it out, throw it away at the end of the summer and fit a new one at the start of next season. (See Job 4.)

☐ Job 65. Drain toilet.

Don't forget that the toilet also needs draining and that includes both the waste and water tanks.

66

☐ Job 66. Prepare waste system.

66. Leave the plugs in the kitchen sink and washroom basin to stop any smells from water left in the pipes from getting into the caravan.

☐ Job 67. Clean out refrigerator.

You'll no doubt clean the fridge's storage area as part of your domestic chores, but it should certainly be done before a caravan is to be stored over a long period and before it is used again after being brought out of storage. It may also be necessary if there are spillages from food and drink stored in the fridge. Generally all that is needed to clean the fridge out is the use of plain warm water and a clean cloth.

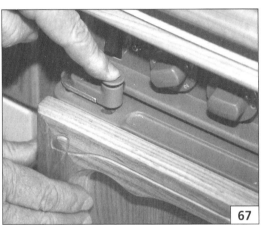

67

INSIDE INFORMATION: If the fridge has a persistent smell, something that can happen if it is left turned off, with the door closed for any period of time, mix a teaspoon of bicarbonate of soda with a cup of warm water and use that to clean out the fridge. This is an excellent way of getting rid of most odours. Once you've washed the fridge out, be sure to dry it well with a clean cloth.

67. Once cleaned out, if you're not planning to use the caravan for some time always make sure that you leave the fridge door in the storage position. This means positioning the retaining pin into the inner of the two holes in the top of the door. In this way air is allowed to circulate through the fridge preventing odours forming and stopping any condensation turning to mould.

68A

☐ Job 68. Prepare curtains and blinds.

68A. Don't leave the flyscreens and blinds in their down position. This can actually put a strain on the roller mechanism and when you go back in the spring to release them, the result might be that they won't roll back into their cassette.

68B. Draw the curtains to prevent creasing and reduce the risk of mould forming.

☐ Job 69. Remove upholstery.

It is possible that the upholstery and cushions in your caravan may become susceptible to any damp that gets into the caravan. So, if you've got the space to store it, remove the upholstery and cushions and store them in the house, somewhere dry.

68B

INSIDE INFORMATION: Putting them in the loft is probably a bad idea. Not only will it be quite damp, you will also run the risk of providing a friendly home for visiting mice, who will probably go on to make a meal of your seating arrangements!

SERVICING & MAINTENANCE

☐ Job 70. Prepare interior.

Leave a simple dehumidifier in the caravan to take out any moisture in the air. If you are fortunate enough to own an electric dehumidifier, let it run inside your caravan for, say, a day a week to keep damp at bay. (You can often hire locally, for the occasional weekend 'drying out' session.) Also, remember to remove any valuables from the caravan and store them somewhere secure.

72

☐ Job 71. Maintain battery.

Remove the caravan's battery so that it's not left to discharge. Over the winter be sure to regularly charge the battery to keep it up to peak condition. Do not store directly placed on a concrete floor.

☐ Job 72. Store gas cylinders.

Remove the caravan's gas cylinders and store them somewhere safe: ALWAYS upright; never on their sides; with the regulator thread cover in place. Store out of doors, well away from heat or anything flammable.

72. While you're at it, cover the gas pipes and regulators to stop any insects getting in.

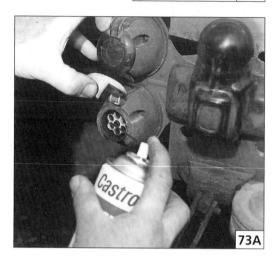

73A

☐ Job 73. Maintain electrical connections.

73A. Apply some water repellent spray to the 12N and 12S plugs and sockets, to stop them corroding. You can then cover the caravan plugs with a plastic bag but be sure to make some holes in the bag to stop the build-up of condensation.

73B. Ensure that the seals on the 12-volt sockets on your car and on the mains socket on the outside of the caravan are sound and that the springs holding the lids closed are working.

73B

☐ Job 74. Maintain tyres.

74A. With the corner steadies down, release the caravan's wheels and fit axle-stand type 'winter wheels' or fit wheelclamps and hitchlocks. If you leave the wheels in place, make sure that you rotate them periodically to keep the bearings lubricated and prevent the tyres from becoming misshapen, otherwise, come next Spring, you'll be towing a caravan with 'square' tyres! (Illustration, courtesy Safe and Secure Products)

74A

74B

74C

75

74B. INSIDE INFORMATION: ArmorAll claim that their aerosol spray-on tyre protector, called Tire Foam, guards against rubber ageing. It certainly brings the tyres up a treat! Clean both sides of the tyre - you spray it on and wipe it off - before putting the tyres 'to bed' or leaving the caravan.

74C. If you remove the wheels, with the chassis supported, tie a plastic bag around the hubs to protect them from the ingress of water.

☐ Job 75. Protect hitch.

75. Grease the hitch and place a cover over the hitch area of the caravan - a bin liner is ideal! - to protect it from the elements and to stop insects crawling inside.

☐ Job 76. Clean paintwork.

Mould may form on the paintwork over the winter months. You can deter it by making sure that the caravan starts the winter clean, using a car wash/wax to give extra protection. If you're feeling extra enthusiastic, you can go over the whole caravan with car wax polish. Don't leave it on unpolished because it's unlikely ever to come off again if you do so!

☐ Job 77. Dry awning.

If the awning is put away damp, it will go mouldy and rotten. Make sure that it is left opened out, perhaps in the spare room with the heating on, until it is thoroughly dry, before packing it away. Now, of course, would be the time to have any repairs or restitching carried out, if necessary.

☐ Job 78. Maintain chassis.

Damp will strike up from beneath, particularly if your caravan is parked outside on anything permeable such as soil or gravel. Also, if the caravan has received any winter usage, prolonged exposure to salt spread on the road will have a damaging effect on a galvanised chassis. Wash the chassis using a hose or pressure washer, taking particular care with corners and crevices and being sure to remove any caked-on mud that can cause a 'poultice' effect when soaked with water and salt. IMPORTANT NOTE: Do not use too high a pressure – don't cause damage with the jet or allow water to penetrate the interior.

EVERY TWO YEARS

80

☐ Job 79. Service mains electrics.

SPECIALIST SERVICE. Every two years, the mains electrical system should be inspected thoroughly by a qualified caravan electrical engineer who is a member of NICEIC or ECA. Ask for a certificate of inspection to be supplied and keep it with this book.

☐ Job 80. Repack hub grease.

80. Because the brakes are in the brake hubs, a binding or overheating brake may cause the hub grease to thin out and require replacement. Do so every two years as a matter of course. If your caravan's wheels have been immersed in water, repack the hubs as soon as possible.

☐ **Job 81. Check exterior lamp seals.**

81A. Over a period of time, lamp seals deteriorate, damp gets in and lighting problems become endemic. Inspect the seals and replace them or carefully apply a smear of apply non-setting silicone sealer to the lamp seals, if new ones are not available.

81B. *INSIDE INFORMATION: 'Jokon' light units don't always have seals but often trap water.*

81C. Drill a small hole in the bottom of each light bulb compartment to let out any water that may gather there.

CHAPTER 6
IMPROVING YOUR CARAVAN

The developing nature of technology and engineering has meant that even the once humble caravan now offers prime potential for being modernised and uprated. This chapter looks at some of the most popular methods of adding to what might otherwise be a basic caravan. This could either be through the installation and fitting of items such as a cassette toilet, water filter or TV aerial, or by simply buying more general accessories like an awning or a generator which don't actually require any real fitment to a caravan.

In most cases there are is a wide variety of models and makes to choose from and it's really a matter of picking the one that most suits your individual needs. However, as a guide, it's advisable to go for the more widely known products that have been available for some time. It's also a good idea to talk to as many other caravanners as possible to find out their experiences of different products as well as checking out product reviews in caravanning magazines. Remember that, as with the caravan itself, there's a good chance that whatever product you buy it's going to have to last you for some time and possibly in some pretty demanding circumstances.

Whenever you're looking to buy a major accessory for your caravan, make sure that you have all the details of the caravan with you, as listed in the *Caravan Data-Base* on page 1 of this book. This is essential so that you can check with the dealership where you're buying the accessory that the model you choose is suitable for your caravan. The last thing that you want is to get a wheelclamp, awning or some other accessory back to your caravan only to find that it doesn't fit.

Checking Electrical Capacity

One of the most important factors to consider before fitting any accessory to a caravan is the electrical power supply that it may require. As explained in *Chapter 3, Using Your Caravan,* a caravan site's mains electricity supply will vary from as little as 4 Amps to as high as 16 Amps. If the demand from any electrical appliances in a caravan exceeds the supply this will result in caravan's electrical circuit breakers automatically cutting out as part of its safety system. It is therefore essential that the power demand of any accessory is known before it is fitted to a caravan.

To calculate whether a site's supply is sufficient to power any number of electrical appliances it is necessary to know that Watts = Volts x Amps. The mains voltage can be taken as a constant 240-volts. If, therefore, a particular site offers a supply of 10 Amps, the maximum combined Wattage of any number of appliances in a caravan that the supply can power is 2400 Watts (10 Amps x 240-volts = 2400 Watts).

The tables in *Chapter 3, PART IV: ON SITE* give an indication of typical current requirements of a number of items of equipment and accessories.

A second important factor to consider when adding anything new to your caravan is its weight. Something like an awning or a generator can weigh in excess of 50kg and this must be taken into account when loading it into a caravan for transportation to a given destination. Something even of the weight of a portable television stored in the wrong place can upset the behaviour of a caravan on the road. So remember to take extra care with loading.

The table in *Chapter 3, PART II: GETTING READY TO GO!* will give you an idea of how much some of the most popular caravanning accessories weigh

Before fitting any equipment to your caravan make sure that you have thoroughly read the fitting instructions and that you have all the necessary tools. There's nothing worse than starting a job only to discover that you're not able to finish it as a result of having the wrong sort of tools or be unable to understand exactly what the instructions mean. If you are in any doubt about how anything works or fits then contact either the manufacturer or your local dealer for advice.

> **SAFETY FIRST!**
> *Before carrying out any work on your caravan be sure to refer to Chapter 1, Safety First! in this book. If you're in any doubt about the work that you're planning to take on, seek expert advice either from the product manufacturer or from your local dealer. It's certainly worth the extra time and cost if it ensures that the job will be carried out successfully.*

IMPROVING YOUR CARAVAN

PART I: FIXTURES

Caravan Toilets

Although it might not immediately seem like the most fascinating of subjects, caravan toilets are often one of the most common accessories to be fitted to a caravan. There are few modern caravans that don't now come with a cassette toilet as standard. However, this has only really been the case since around 1992 and if you own a caravan built before then, there's a good chance that it could be loo-less.

If you're planning to fit a toilet into a caravan, there are two main factors to consider: which type to get and whether it will fit. Of the types available, the most common by far is the Thetford Cassette Porta Potti C4A - a built-in toilet with its own water tank and fitted with a manual flush. Other models include built-in toilets with a flush operated by a 12-volt electric pump while others draw their water supply from a caravan's inboard water supply.

One crucial point to consider before installing a cassette toilet is whether the caravan's washroom is big enough to take it. The Thetford models require a width of 670mm, and this is wider than many washrooms is caravans built before 1988.

If the washroom in your caravan isn't big enough to accept a cassette toilet, there are four alternatives. Firstly, Thetford have also developed an alternative to the standard cassette toilet called the Universal. Although at present it is less common that the standard cassette toilets, this is solely due to its comparative lack of availability and, in time, it will probably become as common as the standard cassette.

The second option is through other manufacturers, such as Fiamma, who supply cassette toilets built to a narrower design. Although similar in many ways to the standard Thetford cassette toilet, the installation for the Fiamma is more complicated than with the Thetford.

The third choice is to go for a free-standing chemical toilet. These require no installation and, as a result, can be transferred from one caravan to another when required. However, they also require servicing, i.e. the waste being emptied and fresh water added, at shorter time intervals than the fully installed cassette variety.

The fourth choice is to buy a toilet tent. This is a separate tent that you can put up close to your caravan to act alongside a free-standing portable toilet, as a remote bathroom. However, these are relatively rare now and as a result are difficult to get hold of.

Fitting a basic Thetford Cassette Porta Potti is certainly one of the more complicated caravan DIY jobs and is certainly best carried out either by a competent fitter or a very experienced DIY enthusiast.

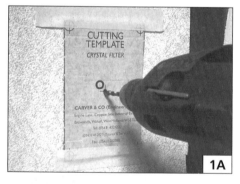

1A

Fitting a Carver Crystal Water Filter

One of the problems with caravanning in different places around the country and with having the water supply standing for some time outside your van is that the water can sometimes develop a less-than-fresh taste. One way to get around this is to fit a water filter.

There are plenty of different types of water filter on the market, from the domestic style jug variety to built-in in-line filters. While the jug variety has the advantage of being usable at home as well as in the caravan, the built-in type can basically just be forgotten about and will work away efficiently until it's time to change the filter.

Of the in-line filters, one of the most popular is the Carver Crystal Filter. Included as standard equipment on many new, high-spec caravans, it's also available in kit form from many caravan accessory outlets and as such makes a good DIY project.

1A. Tape the Carver Crystal filter housing paper template (supplied with the kit) to the inside wall of the caravan where you want the filter to be. It's advisable that this should be as close as possible to the existing water inlet. Drill the pilot hole.

1B

1B. Carefully remove the template and place it on the outside wall of the caravan, using the pilot hole as a guide. Secure the template carefully into position with masking tape.

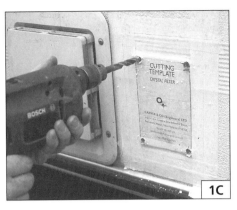

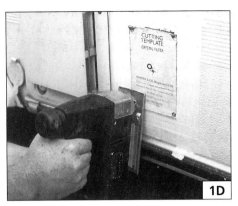

1C. Using an electric hand-drill, drill the four corners marked on the template. Be sure to take your time and make sure that you don't hit any pipes or wires.

INSIDE INFORMATION: Centre punching a caravan outer skin is likely to cause a dent. Insert a new, sharp drill bit of about 3 mm. in size - it's less likely to slip - and drill a pilot hole.

1D. Using a jigsaw, very carefully cut out a hole in the caravan's wall that's the same size as the template. If you're in any doubt about doing this take the caravan to your local dealership where they will probably carry out the work for you.

1E. Connect up the Carver Crystal housing to the caravan's existing water inlet pipe. If necessary, use a new Jubilee clip, but what ever you do, make sure that it's a good seal. However, take care not to overtighten it and damage the hose.

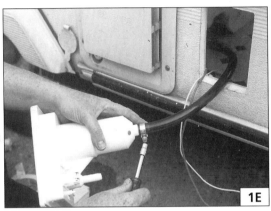

IMPORTANT NOTE!
Before commencing work, ask you caravan dealer where the housing should be situated so that you can be sure to miss the wooden framework of your caravan, as well as wires, pipes, etc.

1F. With the caravan's battery disconnected, reconnect the 12-volt supply from the rear of the old water inlet to the terminals on the new water inlet.

1G. Apply a good quality silicone mastic sealant to the edge of the inlet casing and press it into position. Clean away any excess sealant with white spirit.

1H. Using four self-tapping screws, secure the new inlet into position. Reconnect the battery, plug in the pump and test for leaks.

NOTE: The Carver Crystal Water Filter cartridge will need to be renewed after every 30 days of use. After this time the cartridge loses its effectiveness. When fitting a new water filter it's advisable to smear the filter's 'O' ring with vegetable oil.

Photographs courtesy of Caravan Plus magazine

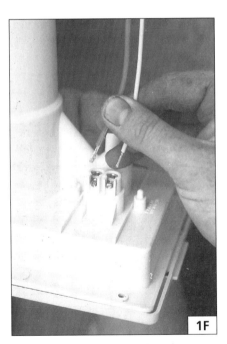

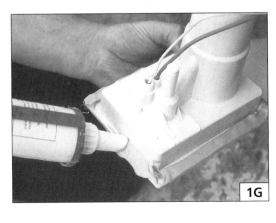

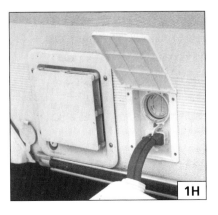

Fitting Blown Air Heating

As caravanning has become an increasingly popular year-round pastime, so the heating systems have become more and more sophisticated. Many of the older and more basic caravans make do with a simple gas heater while the more modern and higher specified models often have the benefit of blown air distribution systems, either with a 1800, 2000 or 3000 series heater through a Junior Blown Air Heating System or a 3000 series heater through a Senior Blown Air Heating System.

Also available is an electric back-up heater, called the Fanmaster, which is an automatically controlled fan designed to distribute warm air through ducts to outlets positioned around the caravan.

Enhancing a basic heater to feature the advantages of blown air is one of the best ways of making sure that you can get the most out of your caravan through being able to use it through the winter months. Easy-to-install kits for the job are available through caravan dealerships.

Fitting a 'Junior' or 'Senior' Blown Air Heating Kit

The process of fitting a Junior or Senior Blown Air Heating kit to a caravan's basic heater follows basically the same procedure. The only differences are that the Junior kit uses a less powerful fan and is therefore only suitable for smaller caravans with up to two blown air outlets, while the Senior kit uses a more powerful fan and can supply up to six blown air outlets. The Senior fan can also be powered by mains electricity.

2A. At the rear of the existing heater casing you will find a pre-cut hole, plus some pre-drilled holes for screws. Remove the pre-cut section.

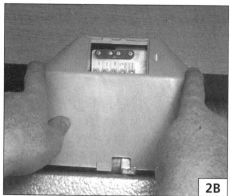

2B. In the kit you'll find a 12-volt fan unit and some screws. With the Senior kit, use the pre-drilled holes and attach the fan unit to the heater casing. With the Junior kit, however, the fan can be connected to, for instance, the inside wall of the wardrobe and joined to the back of the heater by a length of piping.

2C. The warm air is directed by the fan around the caravan through lengths of ducting. When you've chosen where you want the ducting to go, you will need to cut holes through sections of furniture using a 65mm holesaw.

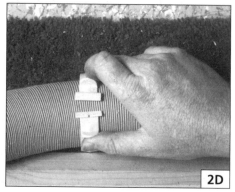

2D. With the route planned and prepared, put the ducting in place and attach it to the wall of the furniture using the clips provided with the kit.

2E. The warm blown air enters the caravan through vents in the base of the furniture. Decide where these vents are to go, use the 65mm holesaw to cut suitable holes and mount the vents in place. Then push the ducting into place.

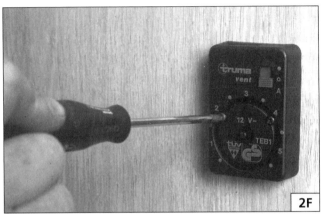

2F. To operate the blown-air system's electric fan, a control unit is supplied with the kit. This is commonly mounted on the side of the wardrobe. Fix it into place, not forgetting to drill a hole at the back for the wiring to reach the fan unit.

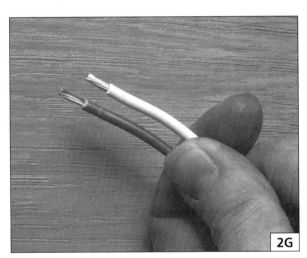

2G. Disconnect the caravan's battery and locate a nearby 12-volt supply to which you can connect the fan's live and negative supply. For safety, fix a 10 Amp fuse in-line.

2H. Back at the fan unit, following the instructions connect the 12-volt live and negative wires. Reconnect the caravan's battery and test the unit.

Photographs courtesy of Caravan Plus magazine.

SAFETY FIRST!
It is essential that any mains electric installation or connections are checked over by a qualified caravan electrician before the system is used.

Fitting an AL-KO Positive Coupling Indicator

It is often said that some of the best ideas are the simple ones and this is certainly the case with the AL-KO Positive Coupling Indicator. This is a device fitted as standard to many caravans from 1993 onwards, that replaces the standard coupling head with a modified version incorporating a button on its top. When the caravan is correctly hitched on to the towing bracket of a car, the button raises slightly to reveal a green band.

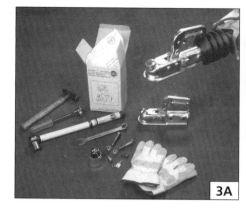

3A. The Positive Coupling Indicator is an excellent way of making sure that your caravan is correctly hitched to your towcar and can be fitted to any caravan equipped with a standard AL-KO hitch. Kits for the purpose can be obtained from larger caravan dealerships.

3B. For safety, ensure that the caravan's handbrake is engaged before starting work. Undo and remove the front coupling head bolt...

3C. ...and use the retaining piece, supplied with the kit, to drift the rear bolt out. This retaining piece ensures that the overrun damper is retained in its correct position.

3D. Remove the coupling head bellows from over the rear flange, if fitted, and lift off the coupling head from the overrun shaft.

3E. Position the replacement Positive Coupling Indicator on to the drawshaft, ensuring that both the fixing holes are aligned.

Fit one of the new bolts supplied with the kit into the front hole and attach the Nyloc nut. Use the other new bolt supplied to drift out the damper retaining piece, and attach the second Nyloc nut.

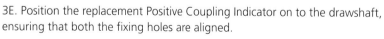

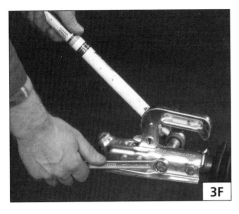

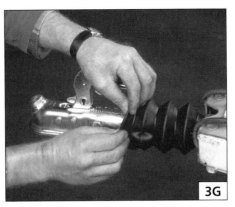

3F. Using a torque wrench, ensure that both fixing nuts and bolts are torqued to the figure specified with whichever model of coupling you are fitting.

3G. Replace the coupling head bellows over the rear flange, if fitted.

Photographs courtesy of AL-KO Kober Ltd.

Fitting Blinds and Flyscreens

One thing that anybody new to caravanning will often find out on their first night away is that caravan curtains can have a vital flaw: when closed, they often leave a gap in the middle that interrupts your privacy and can be far too generous is letting in the early rays of the morning sun when you're trying to have a holiday lie-in.

Another problem is that, when you're away in your caravan during hot weather, and particularly if you're by a river or lake, flies and insects seem to become drawn to the lights in your caravan and the invitation of an open window is simply too much for them to bear.

It's for these reasons that many caravans are fitted with blinds and flyscreens. And for those that aren't, fitting blinds and flyscreens to your caravan is certainly one of the simpler DIY jobs and really one requires only one word of caution. Before getting stuck into the job, make sure that there's enough room around your caravan's windows to fit them. If the top of the window is too close to a roof-locker or overhead shelf, there may not be enough room to attach the cassette that contains the blinds and flyscreens.

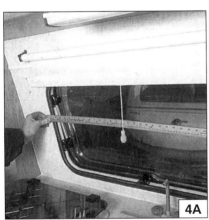

4A. Measure the width and depth of the windows that are going to be equipped with the blinds and flyscreens. Then add an extra 10 mm each side but make sure that a blind unit of this width will actually fit! Use these measurements to make sure that you buy suitable blinds and flyscreens.

4B. Offer up the blind and flyscreen unit, hold it in place above the window and, preferably after using a cordless drill to drill small pilot holes, screw it into place.

4C. Next, position the side guide rails and, depending on the model, either screw or clip these into place. Take care that the guide rails are parallel to the sides of the windows. The guide rails can be cut to length but make sure that they are cut squarely and equally.

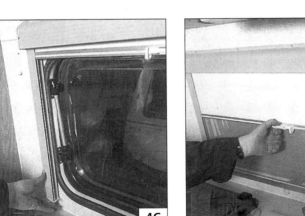

4D. Pull the blind and flyscreen down, first separately and then together, to make sure that they work properly. Then screw the retaining catch into place, if fitted.

Photographs courtesy of Caravan Plus magazine

TV Aerials

When you're away in your caravan there's no reason that you should miss out on you favourite television programme. Caravan TV aerials, and even satellite dish systems, are readily available in a number of different forms and styles. Indeed, many of today's upper range caravans are available with TV aerials as standard equipment.

There are two main types of TV aerials available for caravans, omnidirectional and monodirectional. Then, with each of the two types, comes those that are permanently fixed and those that are removable, although the monodirectional aerial obviously isn't suitable as a permanently fitted option unless you want to have to turn your caravan to face the right direction before tuning in the TV!

Bear in mind that a TV aerial mounted permanently on a caravan's roof can also cause problems with headroom when going under low bridges or boarding a ferry, although the pinnacle at the top of the widely fitted Grade Status omnidirectional aerial is removable to counter this problem.

As for the difference between omnidirectional and monodirectional aerials, it basically comes down to the factors of technology and money. Omnidirectional aerials are generally a permanent attachment to a caravan and will respond to the strongest TV signal coming from any direction without having to 'aim' the aerial to any specific bearing. Unfortunately such attractive benefits mean that omnidirectional aerials are generally more expensive than their mondirectional cousins.

Monodirectional aerials, have to be specifically positioned each time you arrive at a new destination in order to get the best reception. This is simply a matter of trial and error with one person inside the caravan calling out when the TV reception is improving while another person positions the aerial outside. As a tip though, to cut down on the amount of time spent in such pursuits, it's worth simply taking a look at the TV aerials on houses in the area and noting which way they're pointed and copying it.

Sometimes, no matter what type of aerial that's fitted to your caravan or how it's directed, you'll still get a sub-standard picture on your TV. One solution in to have a booster fitted in line. Boosters will help boost a good signal where, perhaps the aerial is a long distance from a transmitter. However, it should be noted that in some circumstances boosters can also increase the strength of electrical noise and interference that can cause problems with a the signal.

INSIDE INFORMATION: One good tip for improving the reception on your caravan's TV is to make the length of the aerial cable as short as possible. Leaving great lengths of aerial cable coiled up often has the effect of detrimentally affecting the quality of reception for your TV.

Fitting a Status TV Aerial

Of the many TV aerials available for caravans, one of the most popular is the Status omnidirectional combined TV and FM radio aerial from Grade that comes with its own booster/power pack. The Status comes in a kit form available from caravan accessory shops, and this includes a majority of the bits and pieces you'll require for fitting it. In addition to the kit, however, you'll need an electric drill, drill bit, some cable clips and some non-drying sealant.

> **SAFETY FIRST!**
> *Whenever working on the roof of a caravan be very careful not to stand or sit on the roof. This may well dent and damage the roof. If you use a ladder to work up high, make sure that it is properly supported and, if possible, have somebody with you to steady it just in case a problem occurs.*

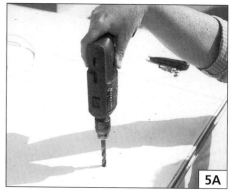

5A

5A. Decide where you want to position the aerial. A recommended place is over the caravan's wardrobe allowing you to drill a guide-hole from the inside and making sure that you're not drilling into any pipes, walls or wires. Then, from the outside, drill through the roof making sure that you leave no sharp edges to cut into the cable.

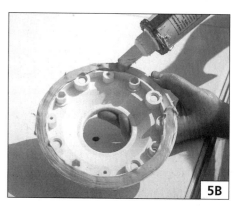

5B

5B. Carefully feed the aerial cable through the hole you've drilled and position the base of the aerial over the hole. For fixing the aerial to a sloping surface the base can be adjusted so that the aerial is level. Then apply plenty of silicone sealant to the bottom of the aerial base to prevent water penetration.

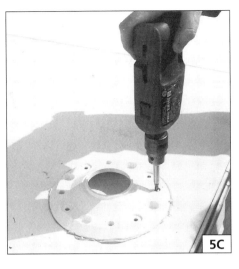

5C. Screw the aerial base into position, allowing any excess sealant to squeeze out on to the caravan's roof. This can be cleaned up with some white spirit on a clean piece of cloth.

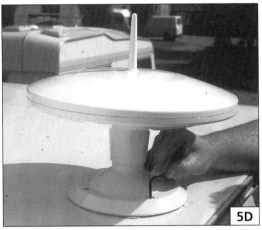

5D. Feed the aerial coaxial making sure that it isn't catching on any sharp edges or becoming coiled up in the aerial base. Place the central area of the aerial into place in the base and lock it into position with the allen key provided with the kit.

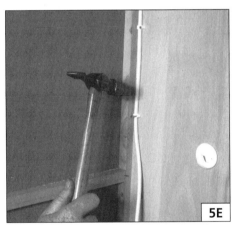

5E. Inside the caravan, find a suitable route for the aerial wiring, through the wardrobe, to wherever you've decided to place the aerial socket. To keep it tidy, try to keep the cable in the corner of the furniture and use cable clips to keep it in place.

5F. Next, decide where you're going to position the aerial's booster unit/power pack. This can either be placed next to wherever you want to put your TV or, if you prefer, it can be hidden away in a roof or bed locker and some extra cable threaded to a remote aerial point. Secure it in place using the two screws supplied.

5G. Then wire the booster/power pack to a 12-volt power supply. Ideally this should be direct connection to the battery or a suitable terminal strip. Do not connect into any other 12-volt power cables as they may carry electrical interference from either an invertor or a transformer.

5H. Plug the coaxial cable into the 'ANT.IN' socket of the booster/power pack. Then run another length of coaxial cable from the caravan TV to either 'TV1.FM' or 'TV2.FM' on the booster/power pack.

Switch on the power pack, turn on the TV and tune in. Check that the gain control is set to normal 'NML'; this may need to be adjusted depending on the strength of local television transmissions.

Photographs courtesy of Caravan Plus magazine.

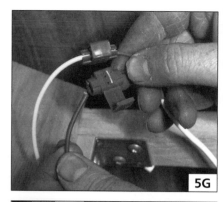

5G

5H

Stabilisers

Stabilisers are sprung devices fitted either on a caravan's hitch or A-frame and are designed to dampen out the swaying motion encountered by caravans in strong winds or when being overtaken by a high-sided vehicle. Before they are fitted is it essential, however, to make sure that the caravan is loaded correctly, in good mechanical order, matched up with a suitable towing vehicle and that both the caravan and towcar's tyres are inflated correctly.

In addition, stabilisers should never be relied upon to improve the towing characteristics of an inherently unstable outfit.

The most common type of stabiliser is the leaf variety fitted from the towcar's towing bracket to the side of the caravan's A-frame. With this sort of stabiliser it is imperative that the adjustable bolt is set to the correct setting. Otherwise the stabiliser will not work correctly.

To adjust and alter the setting of the stabiliser, it is essential that you refer to the manufacturers instructions as each type will have a slightly different method of adjustment.

6A

Fitting a Blade-type Stabiliser

The blade-type of stabiliser is by far the least expensive way of improving the stability of your towing combination. IMPORTANT NOTE: It is strongly recommended that you try towing for the first time without a stabiliser so that you gain a feel for what's involved when the 'tail' (caravan) trys to wag the 'dog' (car). A stabiliser will make the combination far more secure-feeling during normal towing but any instability inherent in the set-up will simply be transferred to a higher and more dangerous speed, so follow the information in *Chapter 2* on preparing your caravan so that it is as stable as possible.

6A. The stabiliser consists of a friction damper bolted to the tow car, either projecting beneath the tow bracket as in this case, or to one side of the tow bracket, and a guide which has to be bolted to the caravan. As you go round a corner, the blade slides through the guide as it turns on the friction damper, but as you're going along the road, the effect of the friction damper is enough to hold the caravan more secure than it otherwise would be. (Illustration, courtesy Tow Sure Products Ltd.)

6B. This type of stabiliser has a bracket bolted between the towball and the tow bracket on the car...

6C. ...and the stabiliser bar slots into the bracket and is held with a thumbscrew while you are travelling along.

6D. When fitting a stabiliser of this type, it is important that the guide is located precisely on the caravan chassis. You will have to remove a fairing, if one if fitted, and cut it so that it fits around the guide bracket. It is also most important to follow the fitting instructions precisely so that the guide is correctly positioned on the caravan's A-frame. (All three illustration, courtesy Bulldog Security Products Ltd.)

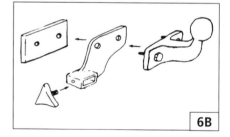

6B

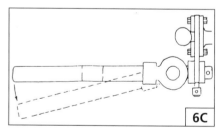

6C

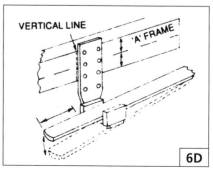

VERTICAL LINE

'A' FRAME

6D

IMPROVING YOUR CARAVAN

AL-KO AKS2000 Stabiliser Fitting Instructions

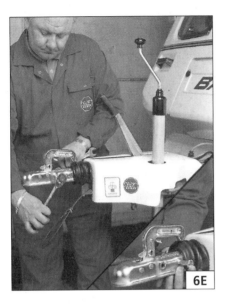
6E

6F

6G

6H

6I

6J

The most common alternative to the leaf type of stabiliser is the hitch mounted type. The most popular of these is the AKS2000 from AL-KO. This actually takes the place of the caravan's standard hitch and fits directly on to the towball when the outfit is on the move.

6E. As a safety precaution, engage the caravan's handbrake. Undo and remove the front coupling head bolt and use the retaining piece supplied with the stabiliser to drift the rear bolt out. This retaining piece ensures that the overrun damper in the hitch remains in the correct position.

6F. Remove the rubber coupling head bellows from over the rear of the coupling head and remove it from the overrun shaft. It's advisable to keep the coupling head in a safe place so, if you change your caravan, you can fit it back to the original caravan allowing the AKS2000 to be fitted to the new caravan.

6G. Measure the diameter of the overrun shaft and, if necessary, fit the spacer(s), as supplied, into the neck of the stabiliser. Position the stabiliser on to the drawshaft, ensuring all the fixing holes are aligned. There should be at least 5mm clearance between the stabiliser handle and the fairing when the handle is in the engaged position.

6H. Fit one of the new bolts supplied with the stabiliser into the front hole and fasten on the nut. Use the other new bolt to drift out the damper retaining piece and bolt the nut into place.

6I. Using a torque wrench, ensure that both fixing bolts are torqued to 86Nm for the bolts marked 8.8 and 120Nm for bolts marked 10.9.

6J. Replace the coupling head bellows over the rear flange or rear coupling head bolt. The stabiliser is now ready for use. IMPORTANT NOTE: Read the handbook supplied before using any stabiliser.

Photographs courtesy of AL-KO Kober Ltd.

PART II: ACCESSORIES

Of course, not all improvements to your caravan will require skill with screwdrivers and spanners. Many of the more popular caravanning accessories can simply to bought from a caravan dealer and used effectively with only the minimum of effort. Mind you, perhaps the first time that you try to put an awning up or start a generator, you might just curse these words. But as the popular saying goes, it's all a matter of practice, practice, practice!

Awnings

An awning is often the first major purchase that a caravanner will buy after getting the caravan itself. It's an ideal way of gaining extra room for your caravan or perhaps providing extra sleeping room for visiting friends or grandchildren.

An awning is basically a tent-type structure that attaches to the side of a caravan. Awnings come in a whole variety of shapes, types, makes and colours. But whichever one you go for it's extremely important to make sure that it's the correct size to fit your caravan.

While most awning manufacturers will have a list of caravans and their awning sizes, there's always the chance that your caravan might not be on their list, particularly if it's an old one. Therefore it's important to know how to measure your caravan to get the correct awning size.

Using either a long piece of string or a tape measure, measure from the ground at the rear, nearside corner, right up around the awning rail down to the ground at the front nearside corner. This distance is the caravan's awning size and is generally referred to in centimetres.

Once you know the awning's size, the next job is to decide which type of awning you want. When it comes to size you can go for anything from a simple porch awning to a large marquee-type model. While the porch awning only really acts as a storage area for muddy boots and wet clothes, the larger awnings extend to sizes capable of seating up to 20 people in comfort.

Remember that the larger the awning you choose, the heavier it will be and the more space you'll take up on site. A site warden will not be at all happy if your awning is so big that it spills on to the neighbouring pitch and you may well have to pay extra for the pleasure of having an awning attached to your caravan.

Types of Awnings

There's more to choosing an awning than a little variety in shape and a choice between brown and green. Choosing the right type of awning for you and your caravan is essential. Differences in material and frame types will affect the awnings price, weight and durability, and, in turn, the success of your holiday.

Frames

The frame inside an awning is as important as the skeleton inside a body. Without it you'll be left with a great floppy heap that's good for nothing. In all, there are three types of frame to choose from: IXL glass fibre, aluminium and steel and each have their own bonuses and failures.

IXL glass fibre has the advantage of being lightweight and strong. It's also impervious to rust and, if treated correctly, should last a long time. However, such qualities don't come cheap and the unfortunate downturn is that IXL frames are generally the most expensive of the different types of frame.

Aluminium is the lightest frame material of the lot, a worthwhile benefit to consider when it comes to loading your caravan. It's also a good sight cheaper. However, just when it all sounded so perfect, it's not quite as strong as IXL glass.

Of the three, steel frames are the cheapest, as well as being the strongest. Unfortunately, such benefits are accompanied by the let-down that steel is also the heaviest of the trio.

Material

As with frames, there are three types of material that awnings are commonly made from. This is probably the area that, more than any other, will help you decide which type of awning you will buy as it, in turn, largely effects the awnings price and durability.

Cotton is the material that has been used longer than any other in the production of awnings, and today it's also the cheapest. In addition it can also breath, which helps to cut down on the amount of condensation that can build up inside. Unfortunately, cotton is also the heaviest of the fabrics and, if left damp for a long period, it can rot. It also has the habit of fading as it gets old.

Another popular material is acrylic fabric. There are a number of different types on the market, varying to a large degree in weight. However, what the different types do have in common is a tendency to last longer than cotton, as well as holding their colour over long periods.

On the down side for acrylic awnings, if stored away when they're damp they are liable to go mouldy. In addition the fabric can't breath, allowing a build up of condensation inside the erected awning.

Airtex is the least common of the awning materials and has the main advantage of the having the most 'breathable' qualities. It's also slightly more expensive than cotton but cheaper than acrylic.

Erecting an Awning

7A. The basic process of erecting an awning will vary little from model to model. However, it is strongly recommended that you read the instructions for erecting whichever awning you decide to go for as the process can vary from make to make. Like most things it's best first attempted slowly and on a still day; windy conditions can make erecting an awning extremely difficult! Having somebody to help out, and a small step to assist you in reaching the top of the caravan will also be extremely useful.

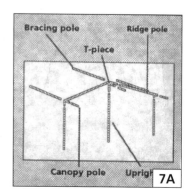

7B. Start off by laying the awning frame out in front of the caravan in roughly the same position as the poles will be when you put them together.

7C. Take the awning out of its storage bag and place it towards the rear on the side that has the awning rail or on the door-side if both sides have an awning rail.

7D. Find the point on the awning rail, generally about head height, where there's an opening large enough to start threading the awning through.

Thread the awning right along the awning rail until it gets to the other end. This is where the step comes in, to help you reach the highest parts of the awning rail.

7E. Once you've got the awning right through, position it so that it hangs squarely on the caravan; no more one side than the other.

7F. Unzip all the awning's doors and windows.

7G. Inside the awning, connect the ridge pole to the T-pieces and put them into position inside the fabric, using the guide pins and eye-holes as guides.

Put the ridge poles into position and adjust them so that they're taut.

Put the centre-upright pole into position and then connect up the central bracing pole. Repeat this procedure with the side-upright and bracing poles and adjust them all so that they're as taut as possible.

7H

7H. Outside, zip up the doors and windows and hammer the corner pegs into position. With the awning looking neat and square, hammer the rest of the pegs into position.

7I. Fix any additional canopy frame poles into place...

7I

7J. ...and then go back inside and lay out the awning groundsheet and any 'extras' such as window blinds.

Photographs courtesy of Caravan Plus magazine.

IMPORTANT NOTE: The most common mistake when putting up an awning for the first time is putting it up inside out. So take a good look at what you're doing before you start!

7J

Awning Care

Like anything else, you must be careful to look after your awning. If the awning gets dirty, don't use detergents to clean it as this will cause it to lose its waterproof quality. Instead, either use plain warm water or wait for it to dry and use a stiff brush.

7K. If an awning does lose its water proof quality, then you'll need to reproof it. There are a number of reproofing products available from most caravan accessory shops. All you have to do is simply spray them on to the affected area and leave them to dry.

If you reproof your awning when it is dirty, the reproofer will actually seal the dirt into the fabric. Therefore it's advisable to spray the affected area from the inside.

7K

When it's time to put the awning away, take care not to store it wet, else it will go mouldy and rot. Instead, roll it up and take it home, and then spread it out somewhere dry, like a garage, so that it can dry out thoroughly.

Pup Tents

An alternative to awnings are pup tents. These are small frame or dome tents that you can erect near you caravan without actually attaching them to it. These are particularly popular with older children who want some extra space and can be trusted to sleep on their own.

Fitting an Awning Light

Most caravans have a 12-volt awning light fitted above the entrance door on the out-side of the caravan. This has two purposes. First, it acts as a guide to help you find the way back to your caravan at night on a dark site. Second, it provides some illumination for the inside of an awning if it is attached to the side of your caravan.

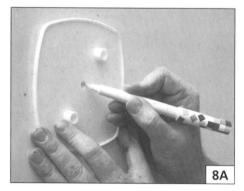
8A

For caravans that aren't equipped with an awning light, fitting one to your caravan is a pretty basic procedure, although obviously the method will alter slightly from type to another. The model shown here is by Britax.

First disconnect the caravan's 12-volt battery

8A. Position the awning light on the side of the caravan where you want to fix it. Make sure that it's not going to get in the way of the door opening and closing. Using the back plate of the light as a guide, mark the shape of the light on the wall and drill an 8mm hole towards the middle.

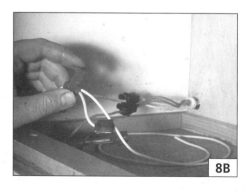
8B

8B. Feed the awning light's 12-volt wires through the hole and attach them to a suitable 12-volt power source. Don't forget to include a 5 Amp fuse in-line.

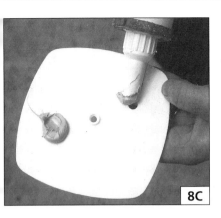

8C

8C. Apply some non-drying silicone mastic sealant to the back of the awning light.

8D. Push the awning light's back plate firmly into position on the caravan wall, feed the wires through the hole in the wall and through the back plate, and screw it into place.

8E. Fit the light unit to the backplate. Connect up the wiring with the white live wire to the switch and the green earth wire to the bulb holder. Reconnect the caravan's battery.

Levelling Devices

Making sure that your caravan is level on site is essential to ensure optimum comfort and in order to make sure that the fridge works effectively. To help with this task, there are a number of levelling devices available on the caravan accessory market.

Items such as the Lock'n'Level and the Rise & Clamp take the dual role of wheelclamp and levelling device. After clamping them on to the wheel of your caravan, they use an inbuilt jacking system to raise the caravan off the ground on one side until it becomes level. Once raised, the caravan's corner steadies can be lowered to stabilise it.

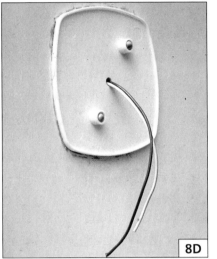

8D

Also available are heavy gripping blocks onto which a caravan can be towed or pushed in order to raise one side of the caravan. As a cheap alternative to such products you can simply use sections of wood piled in such a way as to steadily raise the caravan. However, care should be taken that wood used in such a manner is of a sufficient quality to be able to take the weight of a caravan over a prolonged period.

IMPORTANT NOTE: Never use the caravan's corner steadies as jacks to level the caravan as this will cause damage to the chassis.

Towing Mirrors

Hitch a caravan up behind your car and you will soon notice that the car's own wing mirrors are generally useless for seeing behind the caravan. Having a good view of what is going on behind the caravan is obviously vital for on the road safety, particularly when overtaking and reversing. It is therefore essential that extension towing mirrors are fitted. Towing mirrors come in a whole variety of shapes and sizes. Even so, there are basically only two types - door-mounted and wing-mounted.

8E

9A. Door-mounted towing mirrors are either attached directly on to the car's existing mirrors or by clipping on to the door itself. Of the mirror mounted variety, some will obscure the car's existing mirror in order to give a wider rearward view while others will still allow at least a little amount of vision from the standard mirrors.

They are almost all held in place by fixing adjustable rubber straps around the back of the car's own door mirrors and it is essential that these straps are fixed as tightly as possible. The last thing that you want is for the towing mirrors to become disconnected when the outfit is on the move.

As for the door-mounted variety, these often slide in at the top of the door between the side of the window glass and are then steadied at the bottom with a heavy duty elastic strap.

The benefit of the door mounted type of towing mirror is that they can be easily adjusted by the driver from his seat rather than having to rely on somebody else moving the wing-mounted mirrors in order to give the driver a clear rearward vision.

9B. Wing-mounted mirrors, as their name suggests, attach by means of clips and elastic straps to the front wings of the car. Like the door-mounted variety, many are fitted with reflectors on the back so that they are visible to on-coming motorists at night.

9A

9B

IMPROVING YOUR CARAVAN

Spare Wheel Carriers

Surprisingly, relatively few caravans are sold with a spare wheel as standard. Of those that are, the spare wheels are usually stored in one of two places: either in the centre of the front, exterior gas bottle locker or slung underneath on a purpose built cradle.

The problems that can often occur when storing a spare wheel in the front exterior gas bottle locker is that it limits storage space and can help exceed the noseweight limit. A useful alternative therefore, as well as being a common DIY fixture, is to fit an underslung spare wheel carrier.

10A. By far the most common spare wheel carrier is the type manufactured by the caravan chassis running gear specialists, AL-KO. Their spare wheel carrier is designed to work in conjunction with the holes punched into the chassis behind the AL-KO axle. Under no circumstances, however, should extras holes be cut or drilled in a caravan's chassis as this will adversely affect the integral strength of the chassis.

10B. The AL-KO spare wheel carrier is designed with telescopic arms, making putting the carrier in place a simple matter of extending the arms until they fit into the holes and locking them in place with the bolts provided.

10A

Generators

As caravans become more complex and better equipped, so they have also grown increasingly dependent on a 240-volt electricity supply. However, although most commercial sites offer this as a standard facility, there are circumstances where it is not available. This is something often encountered by caravanners who prefer to stay on more remote sites, or who belong to owners clubs which have special permission to rally on private land: Great for staying somewhere a bit different; useless for powering any items that rely on mains electricity.

11. One common answer to the problem is to get hold of a generator. These supply a remote power source that should be adequate to deal with most mains powered caravan equipment. Commonly available from most large caravan accessory outlets, these generators are generally petrol or gas powered, easy to operate and offer caravanners a greater degree of flexibility when choosing their holiday location.

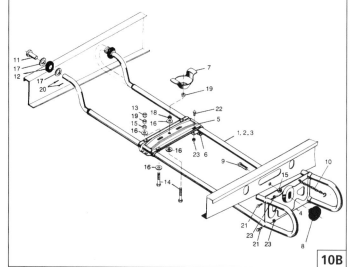

10B

One important thing to consider when deciding which generator to buy is the power output that it delivers. This is measured in Watts and is generally shown by the designation of the generator. For example, the Honda EX650 can deliver up to 650 Watts. However, it is crucial to note that this figure customarily refers to the PEAK power output and can only be delivered for limited amounts of time. The actual power output that the generator will deliver for a majority of the time may well be around 10% lower than the peak figure. This 'working figure' is often shown in the owner's handbook that will come with the generator.

Therefore, when choosing which generator is best suited to your caravan's needs, decide which products will commonly be drawing their power from it, tot up their power requirement and make sure that the generator you buy has a greater working power output than the total.

Once this is done, there are two further important points to consider.

11

First, there's the matter of the Hertz (Hz) rating of the generator's power output. Most British domestic 240-volt electrical products are designed to run at 50Hz. However, some generators feature a switch allowing the output to be increased to a 60Hz rating. This 60Hz output gives a higher, but less steady output; one that could improve the performance of the likes of a lamp or a hairdryer. However, for more sensitive electrical items, such as TVs and tape players, a more conventional 50Hz output may be essential.

When it comes to even more sensitive items, such as computers and word processors, generators of the type commonly used by caravanners may be quite inappropriate because of the fluctuating nature of their power output.

The second point to keep in mind with generators considers the start-up capacity required by some electrical items. Of these, a microwave cooker is a good example. While a microwave cooker may require a power supply of 1000W to work correctly, it may also need an initial start up 'burst' of up to 3000W to get going, a figure far outside of the capacity of most generators suitable for caravans.

All generators designed for the caravan market will have some type of overload system which will cut in if the power demand from the caravan is in excess of the peak output.

The third point to remember, if you want to stay popular, is the question of noise. Take a look at noise, or decibel rating of all the generators you are interested and remember that decibel (dB) rat-

> **SAFETY FIRST!**
> *Whenever using or transporting a petrol operated generator, be sure to take extreme care with the fuel. Be sure to store it in the correct type of container, keep it away from naked flames and children. Similarly take care of petrol fumes and remember that an empty container that has been used for storing petrol is even more highly flammable and explosive than one with petrol inside it.*

ings rise exponentially: a small numerical increase means a huge increase in sound! Also remember that a generator's earthing system may be incompatible with some caravan on-board equipment. If in doubt, get expert advice.

Whenever handling a petrol container, wear protective gloves and take care to keep the petrol out of contact with your skin and eyes. If your eyes do come into contact with petrol, rinse copiously with running water and seek immediate medical attention.

Microwave Cookers

Although examples of a caravan being equipped with a microwave cookers as standard equipment are very rare, such accessories are becoming increasingly popular. As at home, they provide an extra dimension to the caravan's cooking potential by creating a quick way of heating up a meal for the family.

Microwave cookers, however, often require a relatively high mains electricity power supply and, as a result, it is essential that you are aware of the supply available to the caravan and the demand required by the microwave.

Although a microwave cooker may be rated at, for example, 600 Watts, this will be referring to its output and not its required input. In fact, such a cooker may require an input as high as 1100 Watts. It is therefore a common occurrence that microwaves are unsuitable if the mains electricity supply on a site is lower than 8 Amps.

PART III: CARAVAN SECURITY

There's one unfortunate fact about caravans, one that is becoming increasingly difficult to ignore. More and more of them are getting stolen every year. Thefts from storage compounds are generally the most common, but even if you store your caravan right outside your house, there's still a chance that somebody will be interested in helping himself to it.

There are a number of devices on the market to protect your caravan from theft and although the determined thief may have developed ways and means around most of them, that doesn't stop you making it as difficult for them as possible. Generally if a thief can't get away with your caravan within five minutes, he'll give up.

Wheelclamps

12. Caravan wheelclamps come in a whole variety of designs and colours but all do roughly the same job. Whichever one you choose you should make sure that it fits right around the wheel of the caravan and, once fitted, can't be slid off, even with the tyre deflated. Also be sure to check that the lock can't simply be removed by hammering a hole punch into it. It might sound doubtful, but stories of

thieves removing wheelclamps in under 30 seconds are too common to ignore. (Illustration, courtesy Safe and Secure Products.)

Hitchlocks

Hitchlocks, as their name suggests, lock over the hitch of the caravan making them inaccessible to a potential thief's towcar bracket. Hitchlocks should only really be fitted as an additional security measure along with a wheelclamp as alone they can be quite ineffective as thieves have been known to simply put a rope around the hitch, lock and all, tie the other end to their (stolen?) vehicle and use it to tow the caravan off.

If you do fit a hitchlock, make sure that it covers the bolts that attach the hitch to the caravan's A-frame. Otherwise a thief can simply unbolt and remove the locked hitch, fit an unsecured one in its place and make off with the van.

Many caravans are stolen when they've been left unattended for a short while in a layby or at a motorway service-station. In order to protect caravans in such circumstances, certain hitchlocks are designed to lock the caravan on to the car for when the outfit is stationary, making it difficult for the caravan to be removed. However, under no circumstances should such a hitchlock be attached to the outfit when it is on the move.

Tracker Units

One of the most effective methods of countering caravan theft is through tracking units designed to be hidden within the walls and chassis of the caravan. These remain inert until the caravan is stolen. Then, when activated, tracer units are used to discover the whereabouts of the caravan. Unfortunately these units are often quite expensive, (although generally only a fraction of the value of the caravan itself), and only come into their own once the caravan has actually been stolen. It's therefore advisable to use them in conjunction with another more obvious security device, such as a wheelclamp although the retrieval rate of caravan stolen after being fitted with these units is said to be very high.

Intruder Alarms

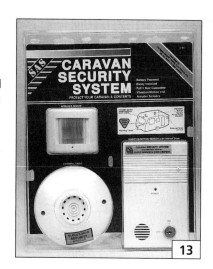

13. Infra-red detectors can be armed to sound an alarm if a heat source, such as a human body is detected nearby. However, these are vulnerable to false alarms caused by sunlight or passing animals.

Movement detectors, meanwhile, will sound their alarm if the caravan is moved, such as when being hitched up. Both type of alarm can be effective if the caravan is stored somewhere where the alarm can be heard by an owner. However, unless the alarm is heard before the thief has a chance to destroy the unit, it may prove ineffective. (Illustration, courtesy Safe and Secure Products.)

Security Posts

Security posts effectively block a caravan's removal from its storage position by being locked into the ground in front of the caravan's storage position. Some are also designed to act in conjunction with a hitchlock, allowing the caravan to be locked on to the top of the security post. However, they are only as strong as the locks that hold them in place so, if you are relying on a security post to protect your caravan, make sure that it's built of high-grade steel and has a high-security lock.

Corner Steady Locks

By locking one or more of the caravan's corner steadies down it obviously makes it difficult to move a caravan. Caution should be taken, however, when relying solely on this form of security as it can be countered by a thief simply sawing the corner steadies off the caravan and replacing them with new ones at a later date.

Caravan Safes

No matter how well you may secure your caravan, the simple truth is that an unattended caravan holds little challenge to the determined thief who's more interested in breaking in to it than making off with it. While the best advice is not to leave anything of any value in an unattended caravan, there is an alternative.

Caravan safes have become more popular over the last few years. Generally big enough to hold a camera, wallet and other smaller valuables, they can be bolted to a caravan's wall or floor and are most effective when hidden inside a bed locker or wardrobe.

Fitting the AL-KO Caravan Safe is a relatively straight-forward procedure and follows the basic procedure of other types on the market.

i) Choose where you want to put the safe and place it roughly in position to check that it fits, can be opened easily and doesn't cover any vents, electrical or gas components.

ii) Take the safe out again and place the mounting plate on the floor. Use the holes as guides to drill four 6.5mm holes, first making very sure that you aren't going to hit any concealed pipes or wires.

iii) Remove the mounting plate and put the safe back into position so that the holes in the bottom of the safe match up with those that you have just drilled.

iv) Outside the caravan, put the mounting plate into position under the caravan and insert the retaining bolts. Lock them into position, making sure that the dome headed bolts are on the outside.

Insurance

14. Unlike cars, it isn't a legal requirement to have a caravan insured. It is, however, a recommended practice. Both The Caravan Club and The Camping and Caravanning Club organise their own insurance schemes, as do the National Caravan Council and several specialist insurance companies. Similarly many insurance companies that deal with car and house coverage will be able to offer a policy for your caravan.

IMPORTANT NOTE: While on the subject of insurance, it is essential that you check that your towcar's insurance covers it for towing a caravan. If not you will be committing a criminal offence when towing a caravan because your towcar's insurance will be invalidated. Check with your insurer and CHECK BEFORE SWITCHING TO A TEMPTINGLY CHEAP CAR INSURANCE POLICY!

APPENDIX 1 RECOMMENDED CASTROL LUBRICANTS

1 Hitch and Towball

Castol LM Grease

2 Jockey Wheel

Castrol Everyman Oil (in a can)

3 Corner Steadies

Castrol LM Grease

4 Hub Bearings

Castrol LM Grease

5 Brake Cable and Rods

Castrol LM Grease (if grease nipple fitted)
Castrol Everyman Oil (on other exposed parts)

6 Brake Mechanism - areas of metal-to-metal contact

Proprietary brand of high melting point brake grease such as Castrol PH Grease - NOT conventional high melting point grease.

7 General

Castrol Flick Easing Oil (aerosol)
Castrol Everyman Oil (in a can)

IMPORTANT NOTE: If your caravan is fitted with a friction head stabiliser, such as the AL-KO AKS2000, DO NOT lubricate either the inside of the hitch or the towcar's towball. (Illustration, courtesy AL-KO Kober Ltd.)

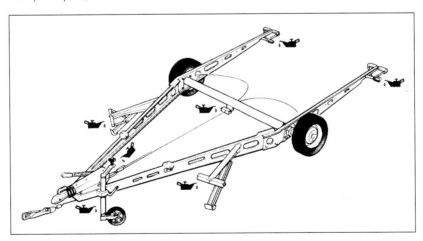

This book is produced in association with Castrol (U.K.) Ltd.

"Castrol are pleased to be associated with this book because it give us the opportunity to make life simpler for those who wish to service their own cars and caravans. Castrol have succeeded in making oil friendlier and kinder to the environment by removing harmful chlorine from our range of engine lubricants which in turn prolongs the life of a car's catalytic convertor (when fitted), by noticeably maintaining the tow car's engine at peak efficiency. In return, we ask you to be kinder to the environment, too ... by taking your used oil to your Local Authority Amenity Oil Bank. It can then be used as a heating fuel. Please do not poison it with thinners, paint, creosote or brake fluid because these render it useless and costly to dispose of."

Castrol (U.K.) Ltd

APPENDIX 2 - TECHNICAL TERMS

12N and 12S leads: the grey and black leads that run from the caravan to the car when on the move. Used to power the caravan's roadlights and selected equipment.

Awning: tent-like constructions of various sizes that fits to side of a caravan to provide extra living space.

Awning rail: a rail along the sides and roof of a caravan used for attaching the awning.

A-frame: the pointed section right at the chassis at the front of the caravan that connects the hitch to the body.

Blown air heating: a system of central heating where a heater's output is channelled through vents to different areas of the caravan.

Butane: a type of gas available in blue gas bottles and commonly used by caravanners.

Cassette toilet: A type of chemical toilet common in most modern caravans where treated waste collects in a removable compartment which can be emptied at specified points on a caravan site.

Corner steadies: metal legs on the underside of each corner of a caravan to make it steady when on site.

CRIS: Caravan Registration and Identification Scheme - a 17 digit number unique to a caravan used to prove ownership.

Electric hook-up: facility on a caravan site which allows a mains electrical supply to be connected up to a suitable caravan.

Ex-works weight: the unladen weight of a caravan, as it leaves the factory. Also known as the 'unladen weight'.

Fairing: a moulded section that covers a caravan's A-frame.

Fanmaster: an accessory to a standard gas caravan heater that provides a blown-air central heating system with the option of an electric heating element.

Gas locker: an exterior locker, usually at the front of a caravan, used for holding gas bottles. Space is often made available for spare wheels and other accessories.

GRP: Glass reinforced plastic. A glass fibre reinforced material used for manufacturing moulded caravan parts.

Hitch: the point at the front end of the A-frame which attaches to a car's towball when the caravan is being towed.

Hitchlock: a security device which locks over a hitch to stop thieves hitching the caravan up.

Kerbweight: The weight of an empty car: see **Chapter 3.** The general rule for outfit matching is to make sure that the laden weight of a caravan does not exceed 85% of the towcar's kerbweight.

Leisure battery: a type of battery, especially suitable for caravans, designed to hold a charge, and discharge completely over a long period.

Load margin: the amount of weight that a caravan can have safely loaded aboard. This is decided by the manufacturer and should never be exceeded. It is the difference between the unladen weight and maximum laden weight.

LPG: Liquid Petroleum Gas, such as propane and butane, both of which are used widely in caravanning.

Maximum laden weight: the weight of a caravan loaded to its maximum allowable margin.

Noseweight: the amount of weight that is exerted downwards on to a car's towball by a caravan's hitch. This can be measured by a noseweight gauge.

Outfit: a car and caravan hitched up together.

Pitch: an area set aside on a caravan site for an outfit to be placed.

Propane: a type of LPG available in red gas bottles and commonly used by caravanners.

Pup tent: A small tent often pitched near the caravan and used as a separate area for children to sleep in.

Regulator: a device to control the flow of gas from a gas bottle to the appliances in a caravan.

Sandwich construction: common form of construction used for caravan walls and floors.

Snaking: an excessive side to side movement caused by an unstable outfit.

Space heater: the basic heater in a caravan.

Stabiliser: a sprung device fitted on either a caravan's hitch or A-frame designed to dampen out the swaying motion encountered by caravans in strong winds or when being overtaken by a high-sided vehicle.

Superpitch: a system where a caravan's water, electric and supplementary supplies can be connected up on a pitch through a single service point.

Towcar: the car or vehicle used for towing a caravan.

Towing bracket: the structure that connects the towcar to the caravan.

Towball: a 50mm ball at the end of the towing bracket that fits up inside the caravan's hitch.

Unladen weight: see 'ex-works weight'.

VIN: Vehicle Identification Number: A unique number etched on to the windows and chassis of every caravan manufactured since 1991.

APPENDIX 3
SPECIALISTS & SUPPLIERS

CARAVAN MANUFACTURERS
ABI Caravans Ltd, Swinemoor Lane, Beverley, North Humberside. HU17 0LJ. Tel: 01482 862976.

Avondale Coachcraft Ltd, Carlyon Road, Atherstone, Warwickshire, CV9 1JE. Tel: 01827 715231.

Bailey Caravans Ltd, South Liberty Lane, Bristol, Avon, BS3 2SS. Tel: 01179 665967.

Bessacarr Caravans Ltd, Rowms Lane, Swinton, Mexborough, South Yorkshire, S64 8AD. Tel: 01709 582438.

Buccaneer Caravans Ltd, The Airfield, Full Sutton, York, North Yorkshire, YO4 1HS. Tel: 01759 72325.

Carlight Trailers Ltd, Church Lane, Sleaford, Lincs, NG34 7DE. Tel: 0529 302120.

Castleton Caravans Ltd, Tinneys Lane, Sherbourne, Dorset, DT9 3EA. Tel: 01935 812539.

Coachman Caravans Ltd, Amsterdam Road, Suttone Fields Industrial Estate, Hull, North Humberside, HU8 0XF. Tel: 01482 839737.

Compass Caravans Ltd, Riverside Industrial Estate, Langley Park, Durham, Co. Durham, DH7 6TY. Tel: 0191 373 0899.

Craftsman Caravan Company Ltd, Annie Reed Road, Beverley, North Humberside, HU17 0LF. Tel: 01482 861563.

Crown Caravans, Delves Lane, Consett, Co.Durham, DH8 7LG. Tel: 01207 503477.

Elddis Caravans (Consett) Ltd, Delves Lane, Consett, Co.Durham, DH8 7LG. Tel: 01207 503477.

Fleetwood Caravans Ltd, Hall Street, Long Melford, Suffolk, CO10 9JP. Tel: 01787 378705.

Gobur Caravans Ltd, Peacock Way, Melton Constable, Norfolk, NR24 2BY. Tel: 01263 860031.

Lunar Caravans Ltd, Sherdley Road, Lostock Hall, Preston, Lancs, PR5 5JF. Tel: 01772 37628.

Sprite Leisure Group Ltd, The Oaks Business Park, Oaks Drive, Newmarket, Suffolk, CB8 7SX. Tel: 01638 663251.

Swift Group Ltd, Dunswell Road, Cottingham, North Humberside, HU16 4JS. Tel: 01482 847332.

Vanroyce, Mamby Road By-Pass, Immingham, South Humberside, DN40 2DW. Tel: 01469 577944.

SUPPLIERS
AL-KO Kober Ltd, Queensway, Royal Leamington Spa, Warwickshire, CV31 3JP. Tel: 01926 452828.

Bulldog Security Products Ltd, Units 2, 3, 4 Streeton Road, Much Wenlock, Shropshire, TF13 6DH. Tel: 01952 728171.

Calor Gas Ltd, Appleton Park, Riding Court Road, Datchet, Slough, SL3 9JG. Tel: 01753 540000.

Camping Gaz (GB) Ltd, 9 Albert Street, Slough, Berks, SL1 2BH. Tel: 01753 691707.

Carver and Co (Engineers) Ltd, Engine Hill, Coppice Side Industrial Estate, Brownhills, Walsall, West Midlands, WS8 7ES. Tel: 01543 452122.

Castrol (UK) Ltd, Burmah House, Pipers Way, Swindon, Wiltshire, SN3 1RE. Tel: 01793 452222.

Electrolux Ltd, Oakley Road, Luton, Bedfordshire, LU4 9QQ. Tel: 01582 494111.

Eurocamp Independent, Princess Street, Knutsford, Cheshire, WA16 6BN. Tel: 01565 625544.

Fiamma UK Sales, Evershed Wells and Hind, 10 Newhall Street, Birmingham, B3 3LX. Tel: 0121 233 2001.

Gunson Ltd, Coppen Road, Dagenham, Essex, RM8 1NU. Tel: 0181 984 8855.

Indespension, Head Office, Belmont Road, Bolton, Lancs. BL1 7AG. Telephone free on 0800 720 720 for your nearest stockist.

Kamasa Tools, Saxon Industries, Lower Everland Road, Hungerford, Berkshire, RG17 0DX.

Safe and Secure Products, Chestnut House, Chesley Hill, Wick, Nr Bristol. BS15 5NE. Tel: 0117 937 4737

SP Tyres UK Ltd, Fort Dunlop, Birmingham, B24 9QT. Tel: 0121 384 444.

Thetford Ltd, Unit 6, Centrovell Estate, Caldwell Road, Nuneaton, Warks, CV11 4UD. Tel: 01203 341941.

Tow Sure Products Ltd, 151-183 Holme Lane, Hillsborough, Sheffield, S6 4JP. Tel: 01742 341656

Tyreservices Great Britain (Tyron Safety Wheels), P.O. Box 82, Church Lane, Wolverhampton, WV2 4BU. Tel: 01902 28311.

CLUBS AND ORGANISATIONS
The Camping and Caravanning Club Ltd, Greenfields House, Westwood Way, Coventry, CV4 8JH. Tel: 01203 694995.

The Caravan Club, East Grinstead House, East Grinstead, West Sussex, RH19 1UA. Tel: 01342 326944.

The National Caravan Council, Catherine House, Victoria Road, Aldershot, Hants, GU11 1SS. Tel: 01252 318251.

MAGAZINES
Caravan Plus, Warners Group Holdings, The Maltings, West Street, Bourne, Lincs, PE10 0PH. Tel: 01778 393313

Caravan Life, Suite 2, 1st Floor, Northburgh House, Northburgh Street, Clerkenwell, London, EC1V 0AY. Tel: 0171 490 8141.

Caravan Magazine, Link House, Dingwall Avenue, Croydon, Surrey, CR9 2TA. Tel: 0181 686 2599.

Practical Caravan, Haymarket Magazines Ltd, 38-42 Hampton Road, Teddington, Middlesex, TW11 0JE. Tel: 0181 943 5733.

APPENDIX 4 - SERVICE HISTORY

This chapter helps you keep track of all the servicing work and day to day requirements that are necessary when owning and using a caravan. However, the jobs listed here should only be refered as a checklist. It is important that you refer to Chapter 5, Servicing and Maintenance for full details of how to carry out each job listed here and for essential safety information, all of which is essential when you come to carry out this work.

Wherever possible, the jobs listed in this section have been placed in a logical order to help you make progress on your caravan. You'll see space at each service interval for you to write down the date for each area of work that is carried out. This could be extremely useful for future reference and to help build-up a service history of your caravan.

PREPARING FOR THE START OF THE SEASON

Job 1. Check interior for damp.
Job 2. Prepare refrigerator.
Job 3. Check water system.
Job 4. Change water filter.
Job 5. Clean paintwork.
Job 6. Check interior lights.
Job 7. Check awning.
Job 8. Check 12 volt connectors.
Job 9. Check towcar wiring.
Job 10. Check towbracket mountings.
Job 11. Check rear suspension.
Job 12. Check car tyre pressures.
Job 13. Check headlamp alignment.
Job 14. Check indicator warning.
Job 15. Check towing mirrors.

PREPARING FOR STORAGE AT END OF SEASON

Job 61. Check insurance policy!
Job 62. Prepare storage area.
Job 63. Drain water system.
Job 64. Remove water filter.
Job 65. Drain toilet.
Job 66. Prepare waste system.
Job 67. Clean out refrigerator.
Job 68. Prepare curtains and blinds.
Job 69. Remove upholstery.
Job 70. Prepare interior.
Job 71. Maintain battery.
Job 72. Store gas system.
Job 73. Maintain electrical connections.
Job 74. Maintain tyres.
Job 75. Protect hitch.
Job 76. Clean paintwork.
Job 77. Dry awning.
Job 78. Maintain chassis.

YEAR ONE

EVERY WEEK, OR BEFORE EVERY LONG JOURNEY

Job 16. Check caravan tyre pressures.
Job 17. Check caravan tyres condition.
Job 18. Check caravan tyres' tread depth.
Job 19. Check wheel rims.
Job 20. Check wheelnuts for tightness.
Job 21. Check exterior lights.
Job 22. Check break-away cable.
Job 23. Check caravan battery.
Job 24. Check mains electricity system.
Job 25. Check fridge vents.
Job 26. Check heater flue.
Job 27. Clean out cassette toilet.
Job 28. Clean out water system.
Job 29. Adjust water pressure.
Job 30. Replacing a microswitch.
Job 31. Clean drainage system.

TWICE A SEASON, OR EVERY THREE MONTHS

First carry out the following jobs.

☐ Job 16. Check caravan tyre pressures.
☐ Job 17. Check caravan tyres condition.
☐ Job 18. Check caravan tyres' tread depth.
☐ Job 19. Check wheel rims.
☐ Job 20. Check wheelnuts for tightness.
☐ Job 21. Check exterior lights.
☐ Job 22. Check break-away cable.
☐ Job 23. Check caravan battery.
☐ Job 24. Check mains electricity system.
☐ Job 25. Check fridge vents.
☐ Job 26. Check heater flue.
☐ Job 27. Clean out cassette toilet.
☐ Job 28. Clean out water system.
☐ Job 29. Adjust water pressure.
☐ Job 30. Replacing a microswitch.
☐ Job 31. Clean drainage system.

☐ Job 32. Lubricate over-run.

☐ Job 33. Lubricate jockey wheel.

☐ Job 34. Lubricate corner steadies.

☐ Job 35. Lubricate braking system external parts.

☐ Job 36. Check and lubricate car towball.

☐ Job 37. Lubricate caravan coupling head.

☐ Job 38. Lubricate external hinges and locks.

ONCE A SEASON, OR EVERY THREE THOUSAND MILES, IF SOONER

First carry out the following jobs.

☐ Job 16. Check caravan tyre pressures.

☐ Job 17. Check caravan tyres condition.

☐ Job 18. Check caravan tyres' tread depth.

☐ Job 19. Check wheel rims.

☐ Job 20. Check wheelnuts for tightness.

☐ Job 21. Check exterior lights.

☐ Job 22. Check break-away cable.

☐ Job 23. Check caravan battery.

☐ Job 24. Check mains electricity system.

☐ Job 25. Check fridge vents.

☐ Job 26. Check heater flue.

☐ Job 27. Clean out cassette toilet.

☐ Job 28. Clean out water system.

☐ Job 29. Adjust water pressure.

☐ Job 30. Replacing a microswitch.

☐ Job 31. Clean drainage system.

☐ Job 32. Lubricate over-run.

☐ Job 33. Lubricate jockey wheel.

☐ Job 34. Lubricate corner steadies.

☐ Job 35. Lubricate braking system external parts.

☐ Job 36. Check and lubricate car towball.

☐ Job 37. Lubricate caravan coupling head.

☐ Job 38. Lubricate external hinges and locks.

☐ Job 39. Adjust brakes at the wheel.

☐ Job 40. Adjust handbrake and over-run.

☐ Job 41. Replacing a Bowden cable, when necessary.

☐ Job 42. (PART I). Replace AP Lockheed brake shoes (when necessary).

☐ Job 42. (PART II). Replace AL-KO brake shoes, when necessary.

☐ Job 42. (PART III). Replace Knott brake shoes only.

☐ Job 43. Check for chassis damage.

☐ Job 44. Check chassis corrosion.

☐ Job 45. Check suspension springs.

☐ Job 46. Check hydraulic shock absorbers.

EVERY 12 MONTHS, OR AT THE END OF EVERY SEASON

First carry out the following jobs.

☐ Job 16. Check caravan tyre pressures.

☐ Job 17. Check caravan tyres condition.

☐ Job 18. Check caravan tyres' tread depth.

☐ Job 19. Check wheel rims.

☐ Job 20. Check wheelnuts for tightness.

☐ Job 21. Check exterior lights.

☐ Job 22. Check break-away cable.

☐ Job 23. Check caravan battery.

☐ Job 24. Check mains electricity system.

☐ Job 25. Check fridge vents.

☐ Job 26. Check heater flue.

☐ Job 27. Clean out cassette toilet.

☐ Job 28. Clean out water system.

☐ Job 29. Adjust water pressure.

☐ Job 30. Replacing a microswitch.

☐ Job 31. Clean drainage system.

☐ Job 32. Lubricate over-run.

☐ Job 33. Lubricate jockey wheel.

☐ Job 34. Lubricate corner steadies.

☐ Job 35. Lubricate braking system external parts.

☐ Job 36. Check and lubricate car towball.

☐ Job 37. Lubricate caravan coupling head.

☐ Job 38. Lubricate external hinges and locks.

☐ Job 39. Adjust brakes at the wheel.

☐ Job 40. Adjust handbrake and over-run.

☐ Job 41. Replacing a Bowden cable, when necessary.

☐ Job 42. (PART I). Replace AP Lockheed brake shoes (when necessary).

☐ Job 42. (PART II). Replace AL-KO brake shoes, when necessary.

☐ Job 42. (PART III). Replace Knott brake shoes only.

☐ Job 43. Check for chassis damage.

☐ Job 44. Check chassis corrosion.

☐ Job 45. Check suspension springs.

☐ Job 46. Check hydraulic shock absorbers.

☐ Job 47. Check stabiliser.

☐ Job 48. Check wheel hub for wear.

☐ Job 49. Replace wheel bearing.

☐ Job 50. Adjust suspension.

☐ Job 51. Replace gas regulator and hose.

☐ Job 52. Service gas system.

☐ Job 53. Check seams for leaks.

☐ Job 54. Check awning rail seal.

☐ Job 55. Polish windows.

☐ Job 56. Check window seals.

☐ Job 57. Check bodywork.

☐ Job 58. Clean upholstery.

☐ Job 59. Clean interior surfaces.

☐ Job 60. Lubricate hinges and catches.

SERVICE HISTORY

YEAR TWO

EVERY WEEK, OR BEFORE EVERY LONG JOURNEY

Job 16. Check caravan tyre pressures.

Job 17. Check caravan tyres condition.

Job 18. Check caravan tyres' tread depth.

Job 19. Check wheel rims.

Job 20. Check wheelnuts for tightness.

Job 21. Check exterior lights.

Job 22. Check break-away cable.

Job 23. Check caravan battery.

Job 24. Check mains electricity system.

Job 25. Check fridge vents.

Job 26. Check heater flue.

Job 27. Clean out cassette toilet.

Job 28. Clean out water system.

Job 29. Adjust water pressure.

Job 30. Replacing a microswitch.

Job 31. Clean drainage system.

TWICE A SEASON, OR EVERY THREE MONTHS

First carry out the following jobs.

☐ Job 16. Check caravan tyre pressures.

☐ Job 17. Check caravan tyres condition.

☐ Job 18. Check caravan tyres' tread depth.

☐ Job 19. Check wheel rims.

☐ Job 20. Check wheelnuts for tightness.

☐ Job 21. Check exterior lights.

☐ Job 22. Check break-away cable.

☐ Job 23. Check caravan battery.

☐ Job 24. Check mains electricity system.

☐ Job 25. Check fridge vents.

☐ Job 26. Check heater flue.

☐ Job 27. Clean out cassette toilet.

☐ Job 28. Clean out water system.

☐ Job 29. Adjust water pressure.

☐ Job 30. Replacing a microswitch.

☐ Job 31. Clean drainage system.

☐ Job 32. Lubricate over-run.

☐ Job 33. Lubricate jockey wheel.

☐ Job 34. Lubricate corner steadies.

☐ Job 35. Lubricate braking system external parts.

☐ Job 36. Check and lubricate car towball.

☐ Job 37. Lubricate caravan coupling head.

☐ Job 38. Lubricate external hinges and locks.

ONCE A SEASON, OR EVERY THREE THOUSAND MILES, IF SOONER

First carry out the following jobs.

☐ Job 16. Check caravan tyre pressures.

☐ Job 17. Check caravan tyres condition.

☐ Job 18. Check caravan tyres' tread depth.

☐ Job 19. Check wheel rims.

☐ Job 20. Check wheelnuts for tightness.

☐ Job 21. Check exterior lights.

☐ Job 22. Check break-away cable.

☐ Job 23. Check caravan battery.

☐ Job 24. Check mains electricity system.

☐ Job 25. Check fridge vents.

☐ Job 26. Check heater flue.

☐ Job 27. Clean out cassette toilet.

☐ Job 28. Clean out water system.

☐ Job 29. Adjust water pressure.

☐ Job 30. Replacing a microswitch.

☐ Job 31. Clean drainage system.

☐ Job 32. Lubricate over-run.

☐ Job 33. Lubricate jockey wheel.

☐ Job 34. Lubricate corner steadies.

☐ Job 35. Lubricate braking system external parts.

☐ Job 36. Check and lubricate car towball.

☐ Job 37. Lubricate caravan coupling head.

☐ Job 38. Lubricate external hinges and locks.

☐ Job 39. Adjust brakes at the wheel.

☐ Job 40. Adjust handbrake and over-run.

☐ Job 41. Replacing a Bowden cable, when necessary.

☐ Job 42. (PART I). Replace AP Lockheed brake shoes (when necessary).

☐ Job 42. (PART II). Replace AL-KO brake shoes, when necessary.

☐ Job 42. (PART III). Replace Knott brake shoes only.

☐ Job 43. Check for chassis damage.

☐ Job 44. Check chassis corrosion.

☐ Job 45. Check suspension springs.

☐ Job 46. Check hydraulic shock absorbers.

EVERY 12 MONTHS, OR AT THE END OF EVERY SEASON

First carry out the following jobs.

☐ Job 16. Check caravan tyre pressures.

☐ Job 17. Check caravan tyres condition.

☐ Job 18. Check caravan tyres' tread depth.

☐ Job 19. Check wheel rims.

☐ Job 20. Check wheelnuts for tightness.

☐ Job 21. Check exterior lights.

☐ Job 22. Check break-away cable.

☐ Job 23. Check caravan battery.

☐ Job 24. Check mains electricity system.

☐ Job 25. Check fridge vents.

☐ Job 26. Check heater flue.

☐ Job 27. Clean out cassette toilet.

☐ Job 28. Clean out water system.

☐ Job 29. Adjust water pressure.

☐ Job 30. Replacing a microswitch.

☐ Job 31. Clean drainage system.

☐ Job 32. Lubricate over-run.

☐ Job 33. Lubricate jockey wheel.

☐ Job 34. Lubricate corner steadies.

☐ Job 35. Lubricate braking system external parts.

☐ Job 36. Check and lubricate car towball.

☐ Job 37. Lubricate caravan coupling head.

☐ Job 38. Lubricate external hinges and locks.

☐ Job 39. Adjust brakes at the wheel.

☐ Job 40. Adjust handbrake and over-run.

☐ Job 41. Replacing a Bowden cable, when necessary.

☐ Job 42. (PART I). Replace AP Lockheed brake shoes (when necessary).

☐ Job 42. (PART II). Replace AL-KO brake shoes, when necessary.

☐ Job 42. (PART III). Replace Knott brake shoes only.

☐ Job 43. Check for chassis damage.

☐ Job 44. Check chassis corrosion.

☐ Job 45. Check suspension springs.

☐ Job 46. Check hydraulic shock absorbers.

☐ Job 47. Check stabiliser.

☐ Job 48. Check wheel hub for wear.

☐ Job 49. Replace wheel bearing.

☐ Job 50. Adjust suspension.

☐ Job 51. Replace gas regulator and hose.

☐ Job 52. Service gas system.

☐ Job 53. Check seams for leaks.

☐ Job 54. Check awning rail seal.

☐ Job 55. Polish windows.

☐ Job 56. Check window seals.

☐ Job 57. Check bodywork.

☐ Job 58. Clean upholstery.

☐ Job 59. Clean interior surfaces.

☐ Job 60. Lubricate hinges and catches.

EXTRA JOBS FOR THIS YEAR

☐ Job 79. Service mains electrics.

☐ Job 80. Repack hub grease.

☐ Job 81. Check exterior lamp seals.

YEAR THREE

EVERY WEEK, OR BEFORE EVERY LONG JOURNEY

Job 16. Check caravan tyre pressures.
Job 17. Check caravan tyres condition.
Job 18. Check caravan tyres' tread depth.
Job 19. Check wheel rims.
Job 20. Check wheelnuts for tightness.
Job 21. Check exterior lights.
Job 22. Check break-away cable.
Job 23. Check caravan battery.
Job 24. Check mains electricity system.
Job 25. Check fridge vents.
Job 26. Check heater flue.
Job 27. Clean out cassette toilet.
Job 28. Clean out water system.
Job 29. Adjust water pressure.
Job 30. Replacing a microswitch.
Job 31. Clean drainage system.

TWICE A SEASON, OR EVERY THREE MONTHS

First carry out the following jobs.

☐ Job 16. Check caravan tyre pressures.

☐ Job 17. Check caravan tyres condition.

☐ Job 18. Check caravan tyres' tread depth.

☐ Job 19. Check wheel rims.

☐ Job 20. Check wheelnuts for tightness.

☐ Job 21. Check exterior lights.

☐ Job 22. Check break-away cable.

☐ Job 23. Check caravan battery.

☐ Job 24. Check mains electricity system.

☐ Job 25. Check fridge vents.

☐ Job 26. Check heater flue.

☐ Job 27. Clean out cassette toilet.

☐ Job 28. Clean out water system.

☐ Job 29. Adjust water pressure.

☐ Job 30. Replacing a microswitch.

☐ Job 31. Clean drainage system.

☐ Job 32. Lubricate over-run.

☐ Job 33. Lubricate jockey wheel.

☐ Job 34. Lubricate corner steadies.

☐ Job 35. Lubricate braking system external parts.

☐ Job 36. Check and lubricate car towball.

☐ Job 37. Lubricate caravan coupling head.

☐ Job 38. Lubricate external hinges and locks.

ONCE A SEASON, OR EVERY THREE THOUSAND MILES, IF SOONER

First carry out the following jobs.

☐ Job 16. Check caravan tyre pressures.

☐ Job 17. Check caravan tyres condition.

☐ Job 18. Check caravan tyres' tread depth.

☐ Job 19. Check wheel rims.

☐ Job 20. Check wheelnuts for tightness.

☐ Job 21. Check exterior lights.

☐ Job 22. Check break-away cable.

☐ Job 23. Check caravan battery.

☐ Job 24. Check mains electricity system.

☐ Job 25. Check fridge vents.

☐ Job 26. Check heater flue.

☐ Job 27. Clean out cassette toilet.

☐ Job 28. Clean out water system.

☐ Job 29. Adjust water pressure.

☐ Job 30. Replacing a microswitch.

☐ Job 31. Clean drainage system.

☐ Job 32. Lubricate over-run.

☐ Job 33. Lubricate jockey wheel.

☐ Job 34. Lubricate corner steadies.

☐ Job 35. Lubricate braking system external parts.

☐ Job 36. Check and lubricate car towball.

☐ Job 37. Lubricate caravan coupling head.

☐ Job 38. Lubricate external hinges and locks.

☐ Job 39. Adjust brakes at the wheel.

☐ Job 40. Adjust handbrake and over-run.

☐ Job 41. Replacing a Bowden cable, when necessary.

☐ Job 42. (PART I). Replace AP Lockheed brake shoes (when necessary).

☐ Job 42. (PART II). Replace AL-KO brake shoes, when necessary.

☐ Job 42. (PART III). Replace Knott brake shoes only.

☐ Job 43. Check for chassis damage.

☐ Job 44. Check chassis corrosion.

☐ Job 45. Check suspension springs.

☐ Job 46. Check hydraulic shock absorbers.

EVERY 12 MONTHS, OR AT THE END OF EVERY SEASON

First carry out the following jobs.

☐ Job 16. Check caravan tyre pressures.

☐ Job 17. Check caravan tyres condition.

☐ Job 18. Check caravan tyres' tread depth.

☐ Job 19. Check wheel rims.

☐ Job 20. Check wheelnuts for tightness.

☐ Job 21. Check exterior lights.

☐ Job 22. Check break-away cable.

☐ Job 23. Check caravan battery.

☐ Job 24. Check mains electricity system.

☐ Job 25. Check fridge vents.

☐ Job 26. Check heater flue.

☐ Job 27. Clean out cassette toilet.

☐ Job 28. Clean out water system.

☐ Job 29. Adjust water pressure.

☐ Job 30. Replacing a microswitch.

☐ Job 31. Clean drainage system.

☐ Job 32. Lubricate over-run.

☐ Job 33. Lubricate jockey wheel.

☐ Job 34. Lubricate corner steadies.

☐ Job 35. Lubricate braking system external parts.

☐ Job 36. Check and lubricate car towball.

☐ Job 37. Lubricate caravan coupling head.

☐ Job 38. Lubricate external hinges and locks.

☐ Job 39. Adjust brakes at the wheel.

☐ Job 40. Adjust handbrake and over-run.

☐ Job 41. Replacing a Bowden cable, when necessary.

☐ Job 42. (PART I). Replace AP Lockheed brake shoes (when necessary).

☐ Job 42. (PART II). Replace AL-KO brake shoes, when necessary.

☐ Job 42. (PART III). Replace Knott brake shoes only.

☐ Job 43. Check for chassis damage.

☐ Job 44. Check chassis corrosion.

☐ Job 45. Check suspension springs.

☐ Job 46. Check hydraulic shock absorbers.

☐ Job 47. Check stabiliser.

☐ Job 48. Check wheel hub for wear.

☐ Job 49. Replace wheel bearing.

☐ Job 50. Adjust suspension.

☐ Job 51. Replace gas regulator and hose.

☐ Job 52. Service gas system.

☐ Job 53. Check seams for leaks.

☐ Job 54. Check awning rail seal.

☐ Job 55. Polish windows.

☐ Job 56. Check window seals.

☐ Job 57. Check bodywork.

☐ Job 58. Clean upholstery.

☐ Job 59. Clean interior surfaces.

☐ Job 60. Lubricate hinges and catches.

YEAR FOUR

EVERY WEEK, OR BEFORE EVERY LONG JOURNEY

Job 16. Check caravan tyre pressures.

Job 17. Check caravan tyres condition.

Job 18. Check caravan tyres' tread depth.

Job 19. Check wheel rims.

Job 20. Check wheelnuts for tightness.

Job 21. Check exterior lights.

Job 22. Check break-away cable.

Job 23. Check caravan battery.

Job 24. Check mains electricity system.

Job 25. Check fridge vents.

Job 26. Check heater flue.

Job 27. Clean out cassette toilet.

Job 28. Clean out water system.

Job 29. Adjust water pressure.

Job 30. Replacing a microswitch.

Job 31. Clean drainage system.

TWICE A SEASON, OR EVERY THREE MONTHS

First carry out the following jobs.

☐ Job 16. Check caravan tyre pressures.

☐ Job 17. Check caravan tyres condition.

☐ Job 18. Check caravan tyres' tread depth.

☐ Job 19. Check wheel rims.

☐ Job 20. Check wheelnuts for tightness.

☐ Job 21. Check exterior lights.

☐ Job 22. Check break-away cable.

☐ Job 23. Check caravan battery.

☐ Job 24. Check mains electricity system.

☐ Job 25. Check fridge vents.

☐ Job 26. Check heater flue.

☐ Job 27. Clean out cassette toilet.

☐ Job 28. Clean out water system.

☐ Job 29. Adjust water pressure.

☐ Job 30. Replacing a microswitch.

☐ Job 31. Clean drainage system.

- [ ] Job 32. Lubricate over-run.
- [ ] Job 33. Lubricate jockey wheel.
- [ ] Job 34. Lubricate corner steadies.
- [ ] Job 35. Lubricate braking system external parts.
- [ ] Job 36. Check and lubricate car towball.
- [ ] Job 37. Lubricate caravan coupling head.
- [ ] Job 38. Lubricate external hinges and locks.

ONCE A SEASON, OR EVERY THREE THOUSAND MILES, IF SOONER

First carry out the following jobs.

- [ ] Job 16. Check caravan tyre pressures.
- [ ] Job 17. Check caravan tyres condition.
- [ ] Job 18. Check caravan tyres' tread depth.
- [ ] Job 19. Check wheel rims.
- [ ] Job 20. Check wheelnuts for tightness.
- [ ] Job 21. Check exterior lights.
- [ ] Job 22. Check break-away cable.
- [ ] Job 23. Check caravan battery.
- [ ] Job 24. Check mains electricity system.
- [ ] Job 25. Check fridge vents.
- [ ] Job 26. Check heater flue.
- [ ] Job 27. Clean out cassette toilet.
- [ ] Job 28. Clean out water system.
- [ ] Job 29. Adjust water pressure.
- [ ] Job 30. Replacing a microswitch.
- [ ] Job 31. Clean drainage system.
- [ ] Job 32. Lubricate over-run.
- [ ] Job 33. Lubricate jockey wheel.
- [ ] Job 34. Lubricate corner steadies.
- [ ] Job 35. Lubricate braking system external parts.
- [ ] Job 36. Check and lubricate car towball.
- [ ] Job 37. Lubricate caravan coupling head.
- [ ] Job 38. Lubricate external hinges and locks.

- [ ] Job 39. Adjust brakes at the wheel.
- [ ] Job 40. Adjust handbrake and over-run.
- [ ] Job 41. Replacing a Bowden cable, when necessary.

- [ ] Job 42. (PART I). Replace AP Lockheed brake shoes (when necessary).
- [ ] Job 42. (PART II). Replace AL-KO brake shoes, when necessary.
- [ ] Job 42. (PART III). Replace Knott brake shoes only.
- [ ] Job 43. Check for chassis damage.
- [ ] Job 44. Check chassis corrosion.
- [ ] Job 45. Check suspension springs.
- [ ] Job 46. Check hydraulic shock absorbers.

EVERY 12 MONTHS, OR AT THE END OF EVERY SEASON

First carry out the following jobs.

- [ ] Job 16. Check caravan tyre pressures.
- [ ] Job 17. Check caravan tyres condition.
- [ ] Job 18. Check caravan tyres' tread depth.
- [ ] Job 19. Check wheel rims.
- [ ] Job 20. Check wheelnuts for tightness.
- [ ] Job 21. Check exterior lights.
- [ ] Job 22. Check break-away cable.
- [ ] Job 23. Check caravan battery.
- [ ] Job 24. Check mains electricity system.
- [ ] Job 25. Check fridge vents.
- [ ] Job 26. Check heater flue.
- [ ] Job 27. Clean out cassette toilet.
- [ ] Job 28. Clean out water system.
- [ ] Job 29. Adjust water pressure.
- [ ] Job 30. Replacing a microswitch.
- [ ] Job 31. Clean drainage system.
- [ ] Job 32. Lubricate over-run.
- [ ] Job 33. Lubricate jockey wheel.
- [ ] Job 34. Lubricate corner steadies.
- [ ] Job 35. Lubricate braking system external parts.
- [ ] Job 36. Check and lubricate car towball.
- [ ] Job 37. Lubricate caravan coupling head.
- [ ] Job 38. Lubricate external hinges and locks.
- [ ] Job 39. Adjust brakes at the wheel.
- [ ] Job 40. Adjust handbrake and over-run.
- [ ] Job 41. Replacing a Bowden cable, when necessary.

- [ ] Job 42. (PART I). Replace AP Lockheed brake shoes (when necessary).
- [ ] Job 42. (PART II). Replace AL-KO brake shoes, when necessary.
- [ ] Job 42. (PART III). Replace Knott brake shoes only.
- [ ] Job 43. Check for chassis damage.
- [ ] Job 44. Check chassis corrosion.
- [ ] Job 45. Check suspension springs.
- [ ] Job 46. Check hydraulic shock absorbers.

- [ ] Job 47. Check stabiliser.
- [ ] Job 48. Check wheel hub for wear.
- [ ] Job 49. Replace wheel bearing.
- [ ] Job 50. Adjust suspension.
- [ ] Job 51. Replace gas regulator and hose.
- [ ] Job 52. Service gas system.
- [ ] Job 53. Check seams for leaks.
- [ ] Job 54. Check awning rail seal.
- [ ] Job 55. Polish windows.
- [ ] Job 56. Check window seals.
- [ ] Job 57. Check bodywork.
- [ ] Job 58. Clean upholstery.
- [ ] Job 59. Clean interior surfaces.
- [ ] Job 60. Lubricate hinges and catches.

EXTRA JOBS FOR THIS YEAR

- [ ] Job 79. Service mains electrics.
- [ ] Job 80. Repack hub grease.
- [ ] Job 81. Check exterior lamp seals.

APPENDIX 5
WHAT YOUR VEHICLE CAN TOW

Arriving at a capacity for caravans is not as straightforward as you might think. The towing capacities quoted by vehicle manufacturers are largely a measure of the vehicle's ability to hill start with that load attached. However, for modern vehicles with their relatively high power to weight ratios the safe handling of the combination is likely to constrain pulling capacity long before engine power.

Many factors affect the handling of a combination: on the vehicle, wheelbase, wheel track, centre of gravity and springing: on the trailer, length, width centre of gravity and suspension.

Vulnerability to cross winds and motorway side draught further complicates behaviour.

However, as a general rule, the major handling factor is the relative weight of the towing vehicle and the load.

The National Caravan Council recommends that trailer gross weight should not exceed 85% of the kerb weight of the vehicle, and we agree. Under exceptional circumstances with a carefully loaded trailer an experienced tow person may feel happy towing at 100%, but this should be an absolute upper limit for private use. Four wheel drives will tow carefully designed and loaded trailers at over 100% acceptably.

In the tables below we use the 85% figure for domestic cars but for 4 wheel drives we quote manufacturers figures.

Actual performance at these weights will vary from vehicle to vehicle and trailer to trailer. If you are choosing a combination for regular towing further advice can be gathered from friends, specialist magazines and caravan/trailer manufacturers.

MANUFACTURER & MODEL	TOWCAR KERB WEIGHT Kg	MAXM CARAVAN BKD. Kg	NOSE WEIGHT Kg
ALFA ROMEO			
155 1.8 Twin Spark	1205	1025	50
155 2.0 Twin Spark/Lusso	1215	1030	50
155 2.5 V6	1290	1095	50
155 Cloverleaf 4	1390	1180	50
164 2.0i Twin Spark/Lusso	1200	1020	50
164 3.0i 24v Super	1295	1100	50
164 24v Cloverleaf	1425	1210	50
AUDI			
80	1185	1005	50
80 TD	1270	1080	50
80 TDi	1270	1080	50
80 2.0E	1230	1045	50
80 16V	1270	1080	50
80 2.6E	1430	1215	50
80 2.8E Quattro	1425	1210	50
Coupe 16V	1190	1010	50
Coupe 2.6E	1305	1110	50
Coupe 2.8E Quattro	1320	1120	50
100 2.0E	1325	1125	50
100 2.6E	1400	1190	50
100 2.8E Quattro	1500	1275	75
100 TDi	1320	1120	50
100 TDi 6.Sp	1420	1205	50
100 2.0E Est.	1375	1145	50
100 2.8E Est.	1450	1230	50
100 TDi/6.Sp Est.	1470	1250	50
100 2.8E Quattro Est.	1550	1315	75
V8	1710	1450	75
BMW			
316i	1125	955	50
318i	1140	970	50
318iS Coupe	1240	1055	50
320i/SE	1270	1080	50
320i Coupe	1315	1120	50
325i/SE	1295	1100	50
325i Coupe	1330	1130	50
316i Touring	1165	990	50
318i Touring	1200	1020	50
325i Touring	1270	1080	50
518i/SE	1330	1130	50

MANUFACTURER & MODEL	TOWCAR KERB WEIGHT Kg	MAXM CARAVAN BKD. Kg	NOSE WEIGHT Kg
520I/SE	1440	1225	50
525i/SE/Sport	1475	1250	50
525ix/SE	1570	1335	50
535i/SE/Sport	1525	1295	50
520i/SE Touring	1530	1300	50
525i/SE Touring	1575	1340	50
525ix/SE Touring	1650	1400	50
730i/SE	1600	1360	50
730i V8	1700	1445	50
740i Auto	1790	1520	50
740iL Auto	1830	1555	50
CITROEN			
AX 14D Echo 3dr.	720	610	50
AX 14D Echo 5dr/TZD	735	625	50
AX 14 TZX	785	670	50
AX GT 3dr.	790	670	50
AX GTi	790	670	50
ZX Reflex/Avantage/Aura	950	810	75
ZX 1.6i Aura	995	845	75
ZX 1.9D Reflex/Avan/Aura	1020	870	75
ZX Funo	1005	855	75
ZX 1.9TD Avan/Aura/Volc	1100	935	75
ZX 2.0 Volcane	1050	890	75
ZX 1.9i Volcane Auto	1055	895	75
ZX 16V	1150	980	75
BX 16 TXi	965	820	70
BX 17 TGD	985	835	70
BX 19 TXD	985	835	70
BX TXD Turbo	985	835	70
BX TZD Turbo	1070	910	70
BX 19 GTi	1020	865	70
BX 16 TXi Est.	1000	850	70
BX 19 TXD Est.	1030	875	70
BX TZD Turbo Est.	1075	915	70
XM 2.0i/Si/SEi	1310	1110	100
XM 2.0i/Si/SEi Turbo	1400	1190	100
XM Turbo D/SD/SED	1375	1165	100
XM V6 3.0SEi	1420	1205	100
XM V6 24V	1470	1250	100
XM 2.0i/Si Est.	1380	1170	100
XM 2.0i/Si Turbo Est.	1500	1275	100
XM Turbo SD Est.	1450	1230	100
XM V6 3.0SEi Est.	1500	1275	100

MANUFACTURER & MODEL	TOWCAR KERB WEIGHT Kg	MAXM CARAVAN BKD. Kg	NOSE WEIGHT Kg
DAIHATSU			
Charade 1.3 CXi	815	690	50
Charade 1.3 GXi	805	685	50
Applause 1.6 GXi/GLXi	930	790	50
Sportrak 1.6 STi	1100	2400	50
Sportrak 1.6 ELi/ELXi	1170	2400	50
Fourtrak 2.2 GX	1475	3500	50
Fourtrak 2.8 DL	1485	3500	50
Fourtrak 2.8 TDL/TDX	1485	3500	50
FIAT			
Uno 1.4ie S	840	710	50
Tipo 1.4 Formula/S	945	800	70
Tipo 1.6 S/SX	970	825	75
Tipo 1.9 TD SX	1105	940	80
Tipo 2.0ie 16V	1175	995	80
Tempra 1.6 S/SX	1030	875	70
Tempra 2.0ie SX	1150	980	70
Tempra 1.9 Tds	1150	975	70
Tempra 1.6 S Stat Wag	1095	930	70
Tempra 2.0ie SX Stat Wag	1250	1060	70
Tempra 1.9 Tds Stat Wag	1220	1040	70
FORD			
Fiesta 1.3 LX 3dr.	830	705	50
Fiesta 1.3 LX 5dr.	850	720	50
Fiesta 1.3 Ghia 5dr.	860	730	50
Fiesta 1.8 LD 3dr.	875	745	50
Fiesta 1.8 LD 5dr.	895	760	50
Fiesta XR2i	965	820	50
Escort 1.3 3dr.	990	840	50
Escort 1.3 5dr.	1010	860	50
Escort 1.4 L/LX/Ghia	1080	920	50
Escort 1.6i L/LX 16V	1100	935	50
Escort 1.6i Ghia 16V	1140	970	50
Escort 1.8i LX 16V 3dr.	1050	890	50
Escort 1.8i LX 16V 5dr.	1070	910	50
Escort 1.8i Ghia 16V 5dr.	1090	925	50
Escort 1.8D 3dr.	1010	860	50
Escort 1.8D L/LX 5dr.	1025	870	50
Escort XR3i 16V	1080	920	50
Escort XR3i Cabriolet	1145	975	50
Escort 1.3 Est.	1045	890	50
Escort 1.4 Est.	1085	920	50
Escort 1.4 L Est.	1095	930	50
Escort 1.4 LX Est.	1035	880	50
Escort 1.4 Ghia Est.	1130	960	50
Escort 1.6i L/LX 16V Est.	1135	965	50
Escort 1.6i Ghia 16V Est.	1175	1000	50
Escort 1.8i LX 16V Est.	1140	970	50
Escort 1.8i Ghia 16V Est.	1175	1000	50
Escort 1.8D Est.	1140	970	50
Escort 1.8D L Est.	1150	980	50
Escort 1.8D LX Est.	1155	980	50
Orion 1.4 LX/Ghia	1010	855	50
Orion 1.6 LX 16V	1105	940	50
Orion 1.6 Ghia 16V	1145	975	50
Orion 1.8D L	1100	935	50
Orion 1.8D LX	1060	900	50
Orion 1.8 LX 16V	1070	910	50
Orion 1.8 Ghia 16V	1090	925	50
Orion 1.8 Ghia Si 16V	1105	940	50
Mondeo 1.6/LX/GLX	1070	910	50
Mondeo 1.8 LX	1075	915	50
Mondeo 1.8 GLX	1095	930	50
Mondeo 2.0 GLX	1140	970	50
Mondeo 2.0 Si	1155	980	50
Mondeo 2.0 Ghia	1190	1010	50
Mondeo 2.0 Si 4 x 4	1245	1055	50
Maverick 2.4i SWB	1620	2800	100
Maverick 2.7 TD SWB	1730	2800	100
Maverick 2.4i LWB	1750	2800	100
Maverick 2.7 TD LWB	1850	2800	100
Granada 1.8i LX	1260	1070	75
Granada 2.0i GLX	1270	1080	75
Granada 2.0i Ghia	1280	1085	75
Granada 2.9i GLX Auto	1335	1135	75

MANUFACTURER & MODEL	TOWCAR KERB WEIGHT Kg	MAXM CARAVAN BKD. Kg	NOSE WEIGHT Kg
Granada 2.9i Ghia Auto	1350	1150	75
Scorpio 2.0i Auto	1305	1110	75
Scorpio 24V Auto	1425	1210	75
Granada 2.0i LX/GLX Est.	1320	1120	75
Granada 2.0i Ghia Est.	1340	1140	75
Granada 2.9i GLX Auto Est.	1390	1180	75
Granada 2.9i Gh Auto Est.	1415	1205	75
Scorpio 2.0i Auto Est.	1365	1160	75
Scorpio 2.9i Auto Est.	1455	1235	75
HONDA			
Civic 1.5 LSi 3dr.	950	805	50
Civic 1.5 LSi 4dr.	995	845	50
Civic 1.5 VEi	935	795	50
Civic 1.6 ESi	1000	850	50
Civic 1.6 VTi 3dr.	1075	910	50
Civic 1.6 VTi 4dr.	1115	945	50
Concerto 1.5i	1035	880	50
Concerto 1.6i	1075	910	50
Concerto 1.6i-16/SE	1090	925	50
Accord 2.0/2.0i	1225	1040	50
Accord 2.2i 4WS	1325	1125	50
Accord Aerodeck/SE	1400	1190	50
Accord Coupe	1760	1200	50
Legend	1575	1335	50
Legend Coupe	1565	1330	50
Prelude 2.0	1235	1050	75
Prelude 2.3	1270	1080	75
HYUNDAI			
X2 1.3 Sonnet/LS 3dr/4dr.	910	770	50
X2 1.3 LS 5dr.	925	785	50
X2 1.5 GSi 3dr.	910	770	50
X2 1.5 GSi 4dr/5dr.	925	785	50
Lantra 1.6 GLSi	1095	930	50
Lantra 1.8 Cdi	1155	980	50
Lantra 2.0 Cdi 16V	1250	1065	50
Coupe MVi	1040	885	50
Coupe MVTi	1040	885	50
ISUZU			
Trooper SWB 3.2 V6	1795	3000	120
Trooper LWB 3.2 V6	1880	3000	120
Trooper SWB 3.1 TD	1900	3000	120
Trooper LWB 3.1 TD	1985	3000	120
JAGUAR			
XJ6 3.2 Sovereign	1795	1495	50
XJ6 4.0 Sovereign/Daimler	1820	1495	50
XJS 4.0 Coupe	1705	1450	50
XJS V12 Coupe	1820	1860	50
XJ12/Daimler Double 6	1985	1685	50
JEEP			
Cherokee 2.5 Sport	1450	3300	90
Cherokee 4.0 Limited	1505	3300	90
Wrangler 2.5	1390	2500	80
Wrangler 4.0	1455	2500	80
KIA			
Pride 1.3 LX 3dr.	755	640	50
Pride 1.3 LX 5dr.	770	655	50
LADA			
Riva 1500 E/L	1025	870	45
Riva 1500 L Est.	1015	860	45
Samara 1300 E/L 3dr/5dr.	900	765	45
Samara 1300 L 4dr.	915	780	45
Samara 1500 GL 3dr/5dr.	900	765	45
Samara 1500 GL 4dr.	915	780	45
Niva 4WD	1149	1574	45

WHAT YOUR VEHICLE CAN TOW

LANCIA

MANUFACTURER & MODEL	TOWCAR KERB WEIGHT Kg	MAXM CARAVAN BKD. Kg	NOSE WEIGHT Kg
Dedra 1.6ie	1055	895	75
Dedra 1.8ie	1140	970	75
Dedra 2.0ie	1160	985	75
Thema 2.0 16V/LE	1300	1105	75
Thema 2.0 Turbo 16V LS	1330	1130	75

LAND ROVER

MANUFACTURER & MODEL	KERB	CARAVAN	NOSE
Defender 90 2.5 Tdi	1790	4000	75
Defender 110 2.5 Tdi	2050	4000	75
Discovery Mpi 3dr.	1890	2750	75
Discovery Mpi/S 5dr.	1925	2750	75
Discovery V8i 3dr.	1920	4000	75
Discovery 200 Tdi 3dr.	2005	4000	75
Discovery 200 Tdi 5dr.	1990	4000	75
Discovery 200 Tdi S 5dr.	2050	4000	75
Range Rover Vogue TDi	2050	4000	75
Range Rover Vogue EFi	1955	4000	75
Range Rover Vogue SE	2000	4000	75
Range Rover Vogue LSE	2150	4000	75

MAHINDRA

MANUFACTURER & MODEL	KERB	CARAVAN	NOSE
340 Classic/Sport	1285	1500	100
540 Classic/Sport	1335	1500	100
MM 740	1395	1500	100

MAZDA

MANUFACTURER & MODEL	KERB	CARAVAN	NOSE
121 GLX	830	700	50
323 1.3i LX 3dr.	945	800	50
323 1.6i GLX 4dr.	985	835	50
323F 1.6i GLX	1000	850	50
323F 1.8i GT	1080	915	50
323 1.6i GLX Est.	1025	870	50
626 1.8i GLX 4dr.	1145	970	50
626 1.8i GLX 5dr.	1180	1000	50
626 2.0i GLX 4dr.	1180	1000	50
626 2.0i GLX 4dr. Auto	1210	1025	50
626 2.0i GLX 5dr.	1280	1085	50
626 2.0i GLX 5dr. Auto	1250	1060	50
626 2.5i GT 5dr.	1280	1065	50
626 2.5i GT 5dr. Auto	1315	1115	50
MX-3.1 6i Auto	1075	910	50
MX-3 1.8	1130	960	50
MX-5	990	695	50
MX-6	1195	1015	50
MX-6 Auto	1225	1040	50
Xedos 6 2.0i V6	1195	1015	50
Xedos 6 2.0i V6 Auto	1230	1045	50

MERCEDES

MANUFACTURER & MODEL	KERB	CARAVAN	NOSE
190 D	1175	995	75
190 D 2.5	1230	1045	75
190 E 1.8	1155	980	75
190 E	1165	990	75
190 E 2.6	1270	1080	75
200 E 4V	1360	1155	75
220E	1370	1165	75
220 CE	1385	1175	75
250 D	1385	1175	75
280 E	1490	1265	75
320 E/CE	1490	1265	75
300 D	1435	1220	75
500 E	1695	1440	75
300 TD Est.	1560	1325	75
200 TE 4V Est.	1470	1250	75
220 TE Est.	1480	1260	75
280 TE Est.	1590	1350	75

MANUFACTURER & MODEL	TOWCAR KERB WEIGHT Kg.	MAXM CARAVAN BKD. Kg	NOSE WEIGHT Kg
320 TE Est.	1590	1350	75
G-Wagen 300 GES 2dr.	2080	2620	75
G-Wagen 300 GEL 4dr.	2220	2950	75
G-Wagen 300 GDS 2dr.	2085	2620	75
G-Wagen 300 GDL 4dr.	2225	2950	75

MITSUBISHI

MANUFACTURER & MODEL	KERB	CARAVAN	NOSE
Colt 1300 GLi 12V	910	775	75
Colt 1600 GLXi 16V	945	805	75
Colt 1600 GLXi 16V Auto	965	805	75
Colt 1800 GTi 16V	995	845	75
Lancer 1600 GLXi 16V	1050	890	75
Lancer 1800 GTi 16V	1120	950	75
Galant 1.8 GLSi 16V	1180	1005	75
Galant 1.8 GLSi 16V Auto	1200	1020	75
Galant 2.0 GLSi 16V	1230	1045	75
Galant 2.0 GLSi 16V Auto	1250	1060	75
Galant 2.0 V6 24V	1330	1130	75
Galant 2.0 V6 24V Auto	1350	1145	75
Galant 1.8 GLSi 16V 5dr.	1220	1035	75
Gal. 2.0 GLSi 16V Auto 5dr.	1240	1055	75
Galant 2.0 GLSi 16V 5dr.	1270	1080	75
Gal. 2.0 GLSi 16V Auto 5dr.	1290	1095	75
Galant 2.0 V6 24V 5dr.	1370	1165	75
Gal. 2.5 V6 24V 4WD/4WS	1540	1310	75
Space Runner 1800-16V	1180	1000	75
Space Wagon 2000-16V	1295	1100	75
Sigma	1560	1325	75
Sigma Est.	1540	1310	75
Shogun TD 3dr.	1750	2800	75
Shogun TD 5dr.	1945	3300	75
Shogun V6 3dr.	1735	2800	75
Shogun V6 5dr.	1915	3300	75

NISSAN

MANUFACTURER & MODEL	KERB	CARAVAN	NOSE
Sunny 1.4 L/LX 3dr.	1005	855	75
Sunny 1.4 L/LX 4dr.	1015	860	75
Sunny 1.4 L/LX 5dr.	1020	865	75
Sunny 1.6 LX 4dr/5dr.	1055	895	75
Sunny 1.6 SLX 4dr.	1040	885	75
Sunny 1.6 SLX 5dr.	1070	910	75
Sunny 1.6 SR	1025	870	75
Sunny 2.0 DL/DLX 4dr.	1090	925	75
Sunny 2.0 DL/DLX 5dr.	1115	950	75
Sunny 2.0 GTi	1125	955	75
Sunny 1.6 L Est.	1055	895	75
100 NX	940	800	75
Primera 1.6L	1065	905	75
Prim. 1.6L 5dr/SLX 4dr.	1085	920	75
Primera 1.6 LX	1075	910	75
Primera 1.6LX 5dr.	1095	930	75
Primera 1.6DLX 5dr.	1105	940	75
Primera 2.0 DLX	1155	980	75
Primera 2.0 DLX 5dr.	1175	995	75
Primera 2.0 LX	1150	975	75
Primera 2.0i LX Auto	1175	995	75
Primera 2.0i LX 5dr.	1170	995	75
Prim. 2.0i LX 5dr. Auto	1195	1015	75
Primera 2.0 DSLX	1165	990	75
Primera 2.0 DSLX Auto	1175	995	75
Primera 2.0 DSLX 5dr.	1185	1005	75
Prim. 2.0 DSLX 5dr Auto	1195	1015	75
Primera 2.0i SLX	1160	985	75
Primera 2.0i SLX Auto	1185	1005	75
Primera 2.0i SLX 5dr.	1180	1000	75
Prim. 2.0i SLX 5dr. Auto	1205	1025	75
Primera 2.0i SGX	1165	990	75
Primera 2.0i SGX Auto	1190	1010	75
Primera 2.0i SGX 5dr.	1185	1005	75
Prim. 2.0i SGX 5dr. Auto	1210	1025	75

MANUFACTURER & MODEL	TOWCAR KERB WEIGHT Kg	MAXM CARAVAN BKD. Kg	NOSE WEIGHT Kg
NISSAN Cont'd			
Primera 2.0e GT	1190	1010	75
Primera 2.0e GT 5dr.	1210	1025	75
Primera 1.6 LX Est.	1155	980	75
Primera 1.6 SLX Est.	1175	995	75
Primera 2.0i LX Est.	1190	1010	75
Prim. 2.0i LX Est. Auto	1210	1025	75
Primera 2.0i SLX Est.	1215	1030	75
Prim. 2.0i SLX Est. Auto	1235	1050	75
200 SX	1200	1020	75
200 SX Auto	1220	1035	75
Serena 1.6 LX	1385	1180	75
Serena 2.0 SLX	1485	1200	75
Serena 2.0 SGX	1500	1200	75
Serena 2.0D LX	1465	1200	75
Serena 2.0D SLX	1490	1200	75
Maxima V6/S	1380	1175	75
Maxima SE	1385	1180	75
Patrol GR SLX Dsl. 3dr.	2070	3500	100
Patr. GR SLX/SGX Pet.5dr.	2115	3500	100
Patr. GR SGX Diesel 5dr.	2230	3500	100
Terranno	1730	2800	100

PEUGEOT

MANUFACTURER & MODEL	KERB	CARAVAN	NOSE
106 XT 1.4i	815	690	50
106 XSi 1.4i	855	495	50
205 XR 1.4i	845	715	50
205 XL Auto 1.6	845	715	50
205 GR 1.4i	840	710	50
205 Auto 1.6	875	740	50
205 Style D/XLD/GLD/GRD	875	740	50
205 XRDT/GRDT	925	785	50
205 GTi 1.9	880	745	50
205 CJ 1.4i Cabriolet	900	765	50
205 CTi 1.9 Cabriolet	935	795	50
306 1.4 XN/XL/XR	890	755	60
306 1.6 XL/XR/XT	910	770	60
306 1.8 XT	950	805	60
405 Style/GL 1.4i	1030	875	60
405 Style GL/GR 1.6i	1075	915	60
405 GL/GR 1.8i	1095	930	60
405 Style/GLD/GRD 1.9	1120	950	60
405 GLD/GRD/STD Turb 1.9	1150	980	60
405 GR/SR/ST 2.0i	1140	970	60
405 Mi16	1180	1005	60
405 Style/GL 1.6i Est.	1085	920	80
405 Sty/D/GLD/GRD 1.9 Est	1165	990	80
405 GL/GR 1.8i Est.	1140	970	80
405 GLD/GRD/STD T. Est.	1210	1030	80
405 GR/ST 2.0i Est.	1170	995	80
605 2.0 SLi/SRi/SVi	1325	1125	80
605 3.0 SV	1415	1200	80
605 3.0 SVE	1460	1240	80
605 SVE 24	1460	1240	80
605 SRDT/SLD/SVDT	1430	1215	80

PROTON

MANUFACTURER & MODEL	KERB	CARAVAN	NOSE
1.3 GE/GL/GLS	950	810	75
1.5 GL/GLS	980	835	75
1.5 SE	990	840	75

RENAULT

MANUFACTURER & MODEL	KERB	CARAVAN	NOSE
Clio 1.4 RN	830	650	50
Clio 1.4 RT 3dr.	845	715	50
Clio 1.4 RT 5dr.	855	725	50
Clio 1.4 S	840	715	50
Clio 1.9 RL/RN	900	765	50
Clio 1.8 RT	865	735	50
Clio 16V	980	795	50
Clio Baccara 1.4 Auto	895	750	50
19 RL 1.4 3dr.	945	805	50

MANUFACTURER & MODEL	TOWCAR KERB WEIGHT Kg	MAXM CARAVAN BKD. Kg	NOSE WEIGHT Kg
19 RL/RN/RT 1.4 4/5dr.	960	815	50
19 RL/RN 1.9D	1030	875	50
19 RT 1.8	1045	890	50
19 1.8 Cabriolet	1125	955	50
19 RN/RT 1.9 TD	1080	920	50
19 16V 1.8	1125	955	50
19 Cabriolet 16V	1190	1000	50
21 TS Prima/GTS	990	840	50
21 GTX	1085	920	50
21 GTD	1040	880	50
21 2L Turbo	1190	1010	50
21 Savanna TS/GTS	1035	880	50
21 Savanna GTX	1155	980	50
21 Savanna GTD	1145	975	50
Safrane RT 2.0	1395	1185	-
Safrane RXE V6	1495	1270	-
Espace 2.0 RN/RT/RXE	1320	1120	75
Espace 2.9 RT/RXE	1390	1180	75

ROVER

MANUFACTURER & MODEL	KERB	CARAVAN	NOSE
Metro 1.4 S 3dr.	825	700	55
Metro 1.4 S 5dr.	840	715	55
Metro 1.4 L 3dr.	840	715	55
Metro 1.4 L/SL 5dr.	855	725	55
Metro 1.4 GS	865	735	55
Metro 1.4 LD 3dr.	840	460	55
Metro 1.4 LD 5dr.	855	460	55
Metro 1.4 SD 3dr.	845	460	55
Metro 1.4 SD 5dr.	860	460	55
Metro GTa 16V cat 3dr.	860	730	55
Metro GTa 16V cat 5dr.	875	745	55
Metro GTi 16V cat	880	750	55
Maestro Clubman 2.0D/DLX	1090	925	45
Maestro 1.3 Clubman	945	805	45
Montego 2.0D Clubman Est.	1210	1030	45
Montego 2.0D Country Est.	1240	1055	45
Montego 2.0 LXi/SLXi Est.	1185	1010	45
Mont. 2.0 DLX/DSLX Est.	1220	1035	45
Montego 2.0 Country Est.	1195	1015	45
214 Si 16V 3dr.	1020	865	50
214 Si 16V 5dr.	1030	875	50
214 SLi 16V	1050	890	50
214 GSi 16V	1065	905	50
214 Cabriolet	1075	915	50
216 GTi 16V 3dr.	1095	930	50
216 SLi	1065	905	50
216 GSi	1075	915	50
216 GTi 16V 5dr.	1120	950	50
216 Coupe	1075	915	50
216 Cabriolet 16V	1135	965	50
218 SD	1145	975	50
218 SLD Turbo	1185	1000	50
220 GTi 16V	1195	1000	50
220 Coupe	1155	980	50
220 Turbo Coupe	1185	1005	50
220 GTi Turbo	1210	1000	50
414 Si/SLi 16V	1025	870	50
416 Si/SLi/GSi 16V	1075	915	50
418 SLD	1145	975	50
418 SLD Turbo	1160	985	50
418 GSD Turbo	1170	995	50
420 SLi 16V	1165	990	50
420 GSi/Exec 16V	1175	1000	50
420 GSi Sport	1185	1000	50
420 GSi Sport Turbo	1220	1000	50
620i	1255	1065	50
620Si	1270	1080	50
620 SLi/GSi	1310	1115	50
623i S	1320	1120	50
623 GSi	1370	1165	50
820i 4dr.	1335	1135	70
820i 5dr.	1365	1160	70
820 Si 4dr.	1350	1150	70
820 Si 5dr.	1380	1175	70
820 SLi 4dr.	1385	1180	70
820 SLi 5dr.	1415	1205	70

TOWING INFORMATION FROM INDESPENSION TRAILERS

APPENDIX FIVE

WHAT YOUR VEHICLE CAN TOW

ROVER Cont'd

MANUFACTURER & MODEL	TOWCAR KERB WEIGHT Kg	MAXM CARAVAN BKD. Kg	NOSE WEIGHT Kg
825 D 4dr.	1440	1225	70
825 D 5dr.	1470	1250	70
825 SD 4dr.	1450	1235	70
825 SD 5dr.	1480	1260	70
825 SLD 4dr.	1485	1025	70
825 SLD 5dr.	1515	1025	70
827 Si 4dr.	1390	1180	70
827 Si 5dr.	1420	1205	70
827 SLi 4dr.	1425	1210	70
827 SLi 5dr.	1455	1235	70
Vitesse	1500	1275	70
Sterling 4dr.	1460	1240	70
Sterling 5dr.	1500	1275	70
800 Coupe	1440	1225	70

SAAB

MANUFACTURER & MODEL	TOWCAR KERB WEIGHT Kg	MAXM CARAVAN BKD. Kg	NOSE WEIGHT Kg
900i/SE	1285	1090	90
900i Convertible	1310	1110	90
900SE/Aero LPT	1285	1090	90
900S Convertible LPT	1330	1130	90
900 Turbo S	1285	1090	90
900 Convertible S	1310	1115	90
9000 2.0i CS/CSE	1305	1110	90
9000 2.0i LPT CS/CSE	1425	1210	90
9000 2.3i CSE	1325	1125	90
9000 2.3T CS/CSE	1370	1165	90
9000 2.0i CD/CDE	1425	1210	90
9000 2.0i LPT CD/CDE	1425	1210	90
9000 2.3i CDE	1445	1225	90
9000 2.3T CD/CDE/Griffin	1465	1245	90

SEAT

MANUFACTURER & MODEL	TOWCAR KERB WEIGHT Kg	MAXM CARAVAN BKD. Kg	NOSE WEIGHT Kg
Ibiza 1.5 SXi	915	775	70
Ibiza 1.7D SL/SLX 3dr.	950	805	70
Ibiza 1.7D SL/SLX 5dr.	970	825	70
Ibiza 1.7i Sportline	915	775	70
Toledo 1.6i CL	985	835	70
Toledo 1.8 GLi/GLXi	1015	860	70
Toledo 1.8 16V GTi	1055	895	70
Toledo 2.0 GTi	1030	875	70
Toledo 1.9 D CL	1030	875	70
Toledo 1.9 TD GLX	1120	950	70

SKODA

MANUFACTURER & MODEL	TOWCAR KERB WEIGHT Kg	MAXM CARAVAN BKD. Kg	NOSE WEIGHT Kg
Favorit LXi/Plus	875	745	50
Favorit GLXi	895	750	50
Favorit LXi Est.	920	750	50
Favorit GLXi Est.	930	750	50

SUBARU

MANUFACTURER & MODEL	TOWCAR KERB WEIGHT Kg	MAXM CARAVAN BKD. Kg	NOSE WEIGHT Kg
Legacy 2.0i GL 4WD	1275	1080	70
Legacy 2.0 Turbo 4WD	1375	1000	70
Legacy 2.2 GX 4WD	1280	1085	70
Legacy 2.0i GL 4WD Est.	1345	1140	70
Leg. 2.0 Turbo 4WD Est.	1425	1000	70
Legacy 2.2 GX 4WD Est.	1375	1165	70
SVX	1610	1200	75

SUZUKI

MANUFACTURER & MODEL	TOWCAR KERB WEIGHT Kg	MAXM CARAVAN BKD. Kg	NOSE WEIGHT Kg
Swift 1.3 GS	775	660	50
Swift 1.3 GLX	805	685	50
Swift 1.3 GTi	835	710	50
Samurai Sport Soft Top	930	1000	50
Samurai LWB Est.	970	1000	50
Vitara Est. Soft Top	1010	1000	50
Vitara JLX SE Est. S/T	1075	1000	50
Vitara JLX Est. 5Dr.	1190	1500	50

TOYOTA

MANUFACTURER & MODEL	TOWCAR KERB WEIGHT Kg	MAXM CARAVAN BKD. Kg	NOSE WEIGHT Kg
Starlet 1.3 GLi	840	715	75
Corolla 1.3 XLi 3dr.	995	845	75
Corolla 1.3 XLi 5dr.	1000	850	75
Corolla 1.3 GLi 3dr.	1000	850	75
Corolla 1.3 GLi 4dr.	990	840	75
Corolla 1.3 GLi 5dr.	1030	875	75
Corolla 1.3 GLi Est.	1015	865	75
Corolla 1.6 GLi 4dr.	1020	865	75
Corolla 1.6 GLi/Exec 5dr.	1060	900	75
Corolla 1.8 GXi 3dr.	1070	910	75
Carina E 1.6 XLi 4dr.	1175	1000	75
Carina E 1.6 XLi 5dr.	1180	1005	75
Carina E 1.6 GLi 4dr/5dr.	1190	1010	75
Carina E 2.0 XLD 4dr.	1250	1060	75
Carina E 2.0 XLD 5dr.	1270	1080	75
Carina E 2.0 GLi 4dr.	1225	1040	75
Carina E 2.0 GLi 5dr.	1245	1060	75
Carina E 2.0 Exec 4dr.	1250	1060	75
Carina E 2.0 Exec 5dr.	1270	1080	75
Carina E 2.0 GTi 4dr.	1280	1090	75
Carina E 2.0 GTi 5dr.	1300	1105	75
Camry GLi	1395	1185	75
Camry V6 GX	1510	1280	75
Camry GLi Est.	1415	1205	75
Camry V6 GX Est.	1565	1330	75
Celica GT	1260	1070	75
Celica GT-Four	1520	1200	75
Supra 3.0i	1540	1310	75
Supra Turbo	1600	1360	75
Landcruiser II	1800	3500	120
Landcruiser VX	2410	3500	150
Previa	1800	1530	75

VAUXHALL

MANUFACTURER & MODEL	TOWCAR KERB WEIGHT Kg	MAXM CARAVAN BKD. Kg	NOSE WEIGHT Kg
Corsa 1.4i LS 3dr.	850	720	75
Corsa 1.4i LS 5dr.	875	740	75
Corsa 1.4i Flair 3dr.	865	735	75
Corsa 1.4i SRi	875	740	75
Corsa 1.4i GLS	905	770	75
Corsa 1.5D Merit 3dr.	890	755	75
Corsa 1.5D Merit 5dr.	915	780	75
Corsa 1.5TD LS 3dr.	905	770	75
Corsa 1.5TD LS/GLS 5dr.	930	790	75
Corsa 1.6i GSi 16V	960	815	75
Astra 1.4i Merit 3dr.	930	790	75
Astra 1.4i Merit 5dr.	950	805	75
Astra 1.4i Merit 4dr.	960	815	75
Astra 1.4i L/LS 4dr.	980	835	75
Astra 1.4i L/LS 3dr.	950	805	75
Astra 1.4i L/LS 5dr.	965	820	75
Astra 1.4i LS 4dr.	990	840	75
Astra 1.4i LS 3dr.	955	810	75
Astra 1.4i LS 5dr.	975	825	75
Astra 1.4i GLS	1015	860	75
Astra 1.4i Si 4dr.	1010	860	75
Astra 1.4i Si 3dr.	975	825	75
Astra 1.4i Si 5dr.	995	845	75
Astra 1.4i CD 4dr.	1030	875	75
Astra 1.4i CD 5dr./	1020	865	75
Astra 1.6i GLS 4dr.	1035	880	75
Astra 1.6i GLS 5dr.	1020	865	75
Astra 1.6i Si 4dr.	1030	875	75
Astra 1.6i Si 3dr.	995	845	75
Astra 1.6i Si 5dr.	1015	875	75
Astra 1.6i CD 4dr.	1040	885	75

VAUXHALL Cont'd

MANUFACTURER & MODEL	TOWCAR KERB WEIGHT Kg	MAXM CARAVAN BKD. Kg	NOSE WEIGHT Kg
Astra 1.6i CD 5dr.	1030	875	75
Astra 1.7D Merit 3dr.	1005	845	75
Astra 1.7D Merit 5dr.	1025	845	75
Astra 1.7D LS 4dr.	1055	850	75
Astra 1.7D LS 5dr.	1040	845	75
Astra 1.7D GLS 4dr.	1080	850	75
Astra 1.7D GLS 5dr.	1065	845	75
Astra 1.7TD LS 4dr.	1115	950	75
Astra 1.7TD LS 5dr.	1040	845	75
Astra 1.7TD GLS 4dr.	1140	970	75
Astra 1.7TD GLS 5dr.	1130	960	75
Astra 2.0i SRi 4dr.	1090	925	75
Astra 2.0i SRi 3dr.	1060	900	75
Astra 2.0i SRi 5dr.	1075	910	75
Astra 2.0i CD 4dr.	1120	950	75
Astra 2.0i CD 5dr.	1110	940	75
Astra 2.0i GSi 16V	1130	960	75
Astra 1.6i Convertible	1000	850	75
Astra 2.0i Convertible	1050	890	75
Astra 1.4i Merit Est.	995	795	75
Astra 1.4i Merit Est.	1005	855	75
Astra 1.4i L Est.	1010	795	75
Astra 1.4i LS Est.	1020	865	75
Astra 1.4i GLS Est.	1070	910	75
Astra 1.6i Si Est.	1055	895	75
Astra 1.6i GLS Est.	1075	910	75
Astra 1.7D Merit Est.	1070	795	75
Astra 1.7D LS Est.	1085	795	75
Astra 1.7D GLS Est.	1120	795	75
Astra 1.7TD LS Est.	1150	980	75
Astra 1.7TD GLS Est.	1175	1000	75
Astra 2.0i SRi Est.	1125	795	75
Cavalier 1.6i Envoy 4dr.	1090	925	75
Cavalier 1.6i Envoy 5dr.	1105	940	75
Cavlier 1.6i LS 4dr.	1105	940	75
Cavalier 1.6i LS 5dr.	1125	955	75
Cavalier 1.6i GLS 4dr.	1120	950	75
Cavalier 1.6i GLS 5dr.	1140	970	75
Cavalier 1.7 DLS 4dr.	1145	850	75
Cavalier 1.7 DLS 5dr.	1160	850	75
Cavalier 1.7 LS TD 4dr.	1185	965	75
Cavalier 1.7 LS TD 5dr.	1200	1000	75
Cavalier 1.7 GLS TD 4dr.	1195	1000	75
Cavalier 1.7 GLS TD 5dr.	1215	1000	75
Cavalier 1.7 CD TD 4dr.	1215	1000	75
Cavalier 1.7 CD TD 5dr.	1235	1000	75
Cavalier 1.8i LS 4dr.	1125	955	75
Cavalier 1.8i LS 5dr.	1140	970	75
Cavalier 1.8i GLS 4dr.	1135	965	75
Cavalier 1.8i GLS 5dr.	1155	980	75
Cavalier 2.0i LS 4dr.	1160	985	75
Cavalier 2.0i LS 5dr.	1175	990	75
Cavalier 2.0i 4WD 4dr.	1300	1105	75
Cavalier 2.0i GLS 4dr.	1170	995	75
Cavalier 2.0i GLS 5dr.	1190	1010	75
Cavalier 2.0 SRi/CD 4dr.	1190	1010	75
Cavalier 2.0 SRi/CD 5dr.	1205	1025	75
Cavalier 2.0 SRi 16V 4dr.	1225	1040	75
Cavalier 2.0 SRi 16V 5dr.	1240	1055	75
Cavalier 2.0i Dip 4dr.	1220	1035	75
Cavalier 2.0i Dip 5dr.	1250	1060	75
Cavalier Turbo 4 x 4	1225	1040	75
Calibra 2.0i	1195	1015	75
Calibra 2.0i 16V	1215	1035	75
Calibra Turbo 4 x 4	1370	1165	75
Carlton 2.0i Plaza	1295	1100	75
Carlton 2.0i L	1225	1040	75
Carlton 2.0i GL	1310	1115	75
Carlton 2.0i CD/CDX	1315	1115	75
Carlton 2.0i Diplomat	1340	1140	75
Carlton 2.3 L TD	1395	1185	75
Carlton 2.3 GL TD	1410	1195	75
Carlton 2.3 CD TD	1420	1205	75
Carlton 2.6i CDX	1410	1195	75
Carlton 2.6i Diplomat	1435	1220	75
Carlton 3.0 GSi 24V	1435	1220	75
Carlton 2.0i Club/L Est.	1275	1080	75
Carlton 2.0i Plaza Est.	1330	1130	75
Carlton 2.0i GL Est.	1355	1150	75
Carlton CD/Diam/CDX Est.	1360	1155	75
Carlton 2.3 L TD Est.	1435	1100	75
Carlton 2.3 GL TD Est.	1460	1150	75
Carlton 2.3 CD TD Est.	1475	1150	75
Carlton 2.6i CDX Est.	1455	1235	75
Senator 2.6i CD	1400	1190	75
Senator 3.0i CD 24V	1540	1310	75
Frontera 2.0i Sport	1560	2000	75
Frontera 2.4i 5dr.	1720	2000	75
Frontera 2.3 TD	1785	2000	75
Monterey	1795	3000	120

VOLVO

MANUFACTURER & MODEL	TOWCAR KERB WEIGHT Kg	MAXM CARAVAN BKD. Kg	NOSE WEIGHT Kg
440 1.6 Li	1025	870	75
440 Li/Si/SE	1020	865	75
440 SE/GLT 2.0i	1055	895	75
440 Turbo	1090	925	75
460 Li/Si/SE	1020	865	75
460 SE/GLE/CD 2.0i	1055	895	75
480 S	1045	890	75
480 ES 2.0i	1055	895	75
480 Turbo	1090	925	75
240 Torslanda/SE Est.	1430	1215	75
240 SE 2.3 Est.	1430	1215	75
850 SE/GLT 2.0	1455	1235	75
850 GLT 2.5	1480	1255	75
850 SE/GLT 2.0 Est.	1455	1235	75
850 GLT 2.5 Est.	1460	1240	75
940 S/SE	1460	1240	75
940 S/SE/GLE 2.3	1460	1240	75
940 S/SE/Went/GLE Turbo	1495	1270	75
940 SE/GLE TD	1530	1300	75
940 2.3 Turbo	1500	1275	75
940 S/SE Est.	1460	1240	75
940 S/SE/GLE 2.3 Est.	1460	1240	75
940 S/SE/Went/GLE Tur.Est.	1495	1270	75
940 SE/GLE TD Est.	1530	1300	75
940 2.3 Turbo Est.	1500	1275	75
960 24V	1570	1335	75
960 24V Est.	1525	1295	75

VW

MANUFACTURER & MODEL	TOWCAR KERB WEIGHT Kg	MAXM CARAVAN BKD. Kg	NOSE WEIGHT Kg
Polo 1.3 CL/Genesis	775	650	50
Polo Coupe 1.3 CL/Genesis	780	650	50
Polo Coupe 1.3 GT	780	650	50
Polo G40 1.3	830	650	50
Golf 1.4 CL 3dr.	960	795	50
Golf 1.4 CL 5dr.	985	795	50
Golf 1.8 CL	1030	875	50
Golf 1.9 CL/GL TD	1080	920	50
Golf GTi 3dr.	1035	880	50
Golf GTi 5dr.	1060	900	50
Golf VR6 3dr.	1155	980	50
Golf VR6 5dr.	1180	1005	50
Golf GTi Sportline/Rivage	965	820	50
Vento 1.8 CL/GL	1075	915	50
Vento 1.9 CLD/GLD	1105	940	50
Vento 2.0 GL	1085	920	50

VW Cont'd

MANUFACTURER & MODEL	TOWCAR KERB WEIGHT Kg	MAXM CARAVAN BKD. Kg	NOSE WEIGHT Kg
Vento 2.8 VR6	1210	1030	50
Passat L	1125	955	85
Passat L TD	1150	975	85
Passat CL/GL	1155	980	85
Passat CL/GL TD	1225	1040	85
Passat GL 16V	1210	1030	85
Passat VR6	1300	1105	85
Passat L Est.	1150	975	85
Passat L TD Est.	1215	1000	85
Passat CL/GL Est.	1180	1000	85
Passat CL/GL TD Est.	1250	1060	85
Passat GL 16V Est.	1235	1050	85
Passat VR6 Est.	1325	1125	85
Corrado 16V	1095	930	50
Corrado VR6	1210	1030	50
Caravelle 2.0 GL/CL	1485	1260	100
Caravelle 2.4 GLD/CLD	1565	1330	100
Caravelle 2.5 GL	1565	1330	100

YUGO

MANUFACTURER & MODEL	TOWCAR KERB WEIGHT Kg	MAXM CARAVAN BKD. Kg	NOSE WEIGHT Kg
Sana 1.4/LS/GL	910	770	-

TOWING INFORMATION FROM INDESPENSION TRAILERS

APPENDIX 6 - WHAT TO TAKE

However good your memory may be, you would be hard pushed to remember all of the thousand and one things you'll need to take on a caravanning holiday. And the act of trying to remember it all can take some of the pleasure away from going on a trip - and that's where the following list comes in. Use the list shown below, adding your own personal requirements in the spaces provided under each category and we guarantee - you'll still forget something! But at least the following lists will help you to ensure that you've got 99% of what you will need and the rest, you can always do without or purchase when you get there. You're going on holiday after all!

FORWARD PLANNING

- [ ] Cancel milk and papers.
- [ ] Check household insurance policy is up to date.
- [ ] Disconnect TV aerial from set and electrical equipment.
- [ ] Inform neighbours, relatives, Neighbourhood Watch, Police (if interested).
- [ ] Lock house, doors/windows and shed. Leave key with neighbour?
- [ ] Turn off gas/water/electricity. (N.B. Freezer, central heating froststat and alarm need power!)
- [ ] . . . .
- [ ] . . . .
- [ ] . . . .

PAPERWORK

- [ ] Bank and Credit Cards.
- [ ] Cash, cheques and foreign currency.
- [ ] Cheque Books/Travellers Cheques.
- [ ] Club Membership Cards.
- [ ] Contact telephone numbers.
- [ ] Driving Licence.
- [ ] Green card and card documents if touring abroad.
- [ ] Insurance Certificate.
- [ ] Log Books.
- [ ] Maps and guides.
- [ ] Pens/paper/stamps etc.
- [ ] . . . .
- [ ] . . . .

CAR

- [ ] First Aid Kit.
- [ ] Foot pump.
- [ ] Fuel can.
- [ ] Overseas requirements, eg. spare bulbs, snow chains, fire extinguisher, according to country.
- [ ] Stabiliser.
- [ ] Temporary windscreen.
- [ ] Towball cover.
- [ ] Towing mirrors.
- [ ] Tow rope.
- [ ] Tyre pressure gauge.
- [ ] Warning triangle.
- [ ] . . . .
- [ ] . . . .

CARAVAN

- [ ] 12v Battery.
- [ ] 240v mains lead and adaptor.
- [ ] Awning and fittings.
- [ ] Chemical fluid/sachets.
- [ ] Chemical toilet.
- [ ] Corner steady brace.
- [ ] Corner steady pads.
- [ ] Extension lead 12v.
- [ ] Fire blanket.
- [ ] Fire extinguisher.
- [ ] First Aid Kit.
- [ ] Fresh water container(s).

- [ ] Fresh water hoses.
- [ ] Gas cylinders and spanner.
- [ ] Gas hose - spare.
- [ ] Gas mantles - spare.
- [ ] Groundsheet.
- [ ] Hitch lock.
- [ ] Insect screens.
- [ ] Lamps.
- [ ] Levelling blocks.
- [ ] Mains polarity tester.
- [ ] Nose weight indicator.
- [ ] Spare fuses/bulbs.
- [ ] Spirit level.
- [ ] Step.
- [ ] Submersible pump.
- [ ] Toilet tent.
- [ ] Waste water container(s).
- [ ] Waster water hoses.
- [ ] Wheel chocks.
- [ ] Wheel lock.
- [ ] . . . .
- [ ] . . . .
- [ ] . . . .

TOOLS & EQUIPMENT

- [ ] Jack - Car and Caravan.
- [ ] Spare keys - Car and Caravan.
- [ ] Spare wheel/tyre - Car and Caravan.
- [ ] Tools - Car and Caravan.

WHAT TO TAKE

- [ ] Wheelbrace - Car and Caravan.
- [ ] Torch and batteries.
- [ ] . . . .
- [ ] . . . .

HOUSEHOLD

- [ ] Adhesive tape.
- [ ] Air freshener.
- [ ] Aluminium foil.
- [ ] Ant killer/powder.
- [ ] Ashtrays.
- [ ] Barbecue/accessories.
- [ ] Beach 'gear'.
- [ ] Biscuit tin.
- [ ] Bread bin.
- [ ] Breadboard/knife.
- [ ] Broom.
- [ ] Butter dish.
- [ ] Can/bottle opener.
- [ ] Cheese grater.
- [ ] Cleaning cloths.
- [ ] Clock.
- [ ] Clothes brush.
- [ ] Clothes line/rack/pegs.
- [ ] Coat hangers.
- [ ] Colander.
- [ ] Coolbox/freezer packs.
- [ ] Corkscrew.
- [ ] Crockery.
- [ ] Cruet.
- [ ] Cutlery.
- [ ] Drinks.
- [ ] Dusters.
- [ ] Dustpan and brush.
- [ ] Egg Cups.
- [ ] Fish slice.
- [ ] Folding chair.
- [ ] Folding table.
- [ ] Food.
- [ ] Glasses/tumblers.
- [ ] Grill pan.
- [ ] Insect spray.
- [ ] Kettle.

- [ ] Kitchen knives/tools.
- [ ] Kitchen rolls.
- [ ] Matches/lighter.
- [ ] Measuring jug.
- [ ] Mixing bowl.
- [ ] Mop and bucket.
- [ ] Needles/thread.
- [ ] Polythene bags/food wrap.
- [ ] Rubbish bags.
- [ ] Saucepans.
- [ ] Scissors.
- [ ] Seal top containers.
- [ ] Shoe cleaning kit.
- [ ] Shopping bags.
- [ ] Sieve.
- [ ] Soap powder.
- [ ] String.
- [ ] Sunlounger.
- [ ] Table cloths.
- [ ] Tablemats.
- [ ] Tea/coffee pot.
- [ ] Tea strainer.
- [ ] Tissues.
- [ ] Toilet paper.
- [ ] Towels.
- [ ] Tray(s).
- [ ] Vacuum flask.
- [ ] Washing-up bowl/scourer.
- [ ] Washing-up liquid.
- [ ] Whisk.
- [ ] . . . .
- [ ] . . . .
- [ ] . . . .
- [ ] . . . .
- [ ] . . . .

BEDDING

- [ ] Air bed pump.
- [ ] Blankets.
- [ ] Camp bed(s) - awning.
- [ ] Hot water bottles.
- [ ] Pillows/cases.
- [ ] Sheets/liners.

- [ ] Sleeping bags/duvets.
- [ ] . . . .
- [ ] . . . .
- [ ] . . . .

PERSONAL

- [ ] Clothing.
- [ ] Flannel.
- [ ] Footwear.
- [ ] Hairbrush/comb.
- [ ] Handcleanser (Swarfega).
- [ ] Insect repellent.
- [ ] Make-up etc.
- [ ] Medicines etc.
- [ ] Nail scissors.
- [ ] Rainwear.
- [ ] Shaving kit/mirror.
- [ ] Soap/soapbox.
- [ ] Sun glasses.
- [ ] Sun hats.
- [ ] Suntan oil.
- [ ] Swimwear.
- [ ] Toilet bag.
- [ ] Toothbrush/paste.
- [ ] Umbrella.
- [ ] Wellington boots.
- [ ] . . . .
- [ ] . . . .

RECREATION

- [ ] Binoculars.
- [ ] Books.
- [ ] Camera/films.
- [ ] Games.
- [ ] Playing cards.
- [ ] Radio/cassette player and tapes.
- [ ] Toys.
- [ ] Travel games for journey.
- [ ] TV/aerial.
- [ ] Video camera/tapes.
- [ ] . . . .
- [ ] . . . .